MOHANJI

THE POWER OF PURITY

ESSENTIAL ESSAYS & ANSWERS

About Spiritual Paths and Liberation

Teachings of Mohanji: His communions, essays, correspondences and transcribed satsang Q & A's (up until 2010).

Compiled by Marina Wolny

Gurulight

Cover design:
Mohana Hanumatananda

First edition published by Author house 2011
Fourth edition published by GuruLight 2017

Email: info@gurulight.com
Web: www.gurulight.com

ISBN: 978-81-933091-7-9

Gurulight

This book is surrendered
To the Great Masters of every path
who guided people through time;
To all the Masters who exist on earth and in other realms;
To all the wisdom and knowledge
that flows from them like an eternal river
which is consistently nourishing the seekers of each generation;
To the known and unknown Masters of
the past, present and future, in all the planes of existence
and the grand tradition that flows through
hundreds of Spiritual Gurus forever . . .

It is YOU who must make the effort
The Master only points the way
—Buddha

CONTENTS

PREFACE

COMMUNIONS WITH THE Higher Masters happened to me in the path of my spiritual journey as a seeker. I have been speaking, writing and answering questions on these subjects since many years. However all these expressions were lying scattered. Marina Wolny, with great conviction and determination, collected and organized them to compile this book for sharing with the world. Even though all the communications have been spontaneous, extempore, contextual, or in reply to someone's personal question, the answers can be considered as universal.

I feel that understanding of the following three questions will help you to connect better with the contents in the book:

Who am I?
Where do I come from?
And why was this book compiled?

In the highest sense, I am a piece of the Parabrahma, just another soul like you. You and I are the same. We are one. In relation to you, whoever you think I am, I am that. Every being has various roles. So it depends on how you see me, perceive me, feel me, understand me—that makes me who I am, in relation to you. We have various roles to play in one lifetime. We mean different entities to different people. We are not any one thing. We are a mixture of everything. Yet, we are nothing also. In the night, when you sleep, all these dualities vanish and you become one with the sleep, one with the perfect nothingness of deep sleep. When you wake up, the conscious mind brings forth all the relationships that could make your existence in the world. So you are, always in relation to something else.

I come from the same place where you have come from. We are children of one Father. You may call him the way you like, Father, Allah or Parabrahma. All the embodied beings came from Him and go back to Him. All of us have our roles to play here and then we will leave. If you look at the whole show as a witness, you will see the divine hand in everything; the hand of the Father. I hope I did not confuse you. What you perceive me to be, I am that. Do not get stuck with this image of me. I could leave it any day. The energy will remain. It will even grow, as it need not live within the parameters of a limited body. To exist in a body is like existing in a cage. I always feel for the animals and birds that are caged. Our soul is just like that. The body is a cage. Just like the animal or bird being used to a cage, we are used to our body. Just like the animals or birds explore possibilities within the parameters of their cage, we explore various experiences using the body. The fact remains that we are essentially caged. We have the choice of liberation. Liberation is reduced dependency on all aspects of body, mind and intellect. That's the advantage that human beings have. We can achieve enlightenment in one lifetime. But, we have to walk the path till the end. We have to keep walking. Nobody else can do it for us. This is individualistic.

This book has been compiled to aid you to find your SELF and help you to stay with your own soul. Please do not be fooled by the illusions outside your window.

I wish you great spiritual evolution in this life.

God Bless You

Love and love alone

M

ACKNOWLEDGEMENTS

MARINA WOLNY WAS inspired to present all the expressions which have been happening through me over the years in a book for sharing with a wider audience. My sincere appreciation and thanks goes to Marina whose perseverance and dedication, actually made this compilation possible.

I would like to thank those who communicated the questions that provoked the answers that are presented in this book. The contexts are relatively new, but the wisdom behind these words are eternal. I do not own the wisdom or the words. They all are just happening through me. We are all transitory beings. We can own nothing on earth, on a permanent basis. Yet, I would like to thank all those who were connected with me and clarified many questions with me time and again. If you had not asked anything, this book would not have happened. The mission is to help increase the awareness of the generations, to cultivate selflessness and purity in thoughts, words and actions. The giant pillars of the mission are Faith and Purity.

I would like to thank my wife Devi Mohan who has been taking care of various aspects of my life, including the mission, meditations, satsangs and everything else. How can I thank her enough?

Sincere thanks to the Global Management Team. With inherent purity, and perfect awareness of the path and the mission, their dedication and silent thoughts, words and actions have tremendously helped to evolve the mission. They continue to serve and lead selflessly. I would also like to thank all the Shaktipat/ energy transfer initiates, who are serving the world unassumingly, silently and effectively. By conducting meditations and empowering people, they have helped in the unburdening of their heavy baggage of samskaras or inherent impressions. Their selflessness and dedication is moving the wheels of our mission. They are invaluable.

I appreciate and thank the contribution of Mrs. Shanthy Vaidya for her artwork portraying Navanath gurus and Ms. Caroline Moscato for her careful proofreading of the manuscript.

I thank my parents Dr. P. K. Namboothiri and Mrs. Sreedevi, my brother Manoj and my Grandfather Late T. Sankaran Namboothiripad, who had been a pillar of strength for me during my formation times. I gratefully acknowledge their contribution in my existence on earth.

A special thanks to my uncle Prof. T.M Sankaran and Aunt Mrs. Thankamani Sankaran for fostering me as parents during a part of my student days. My sincere thanks and gratitude to my uncles Sri.T.M Narayanan and Sri.T.M Anujan and their families for their sincere love and support in my life. I express my deepest gratitude to Mata Devi Vanamali, who always guided unconditionally.

My deepest respects and humble prostrations at the feet of Sri.Sri.Sri. Vittalananda Saraswati Maharaj (Vittal Babaji) whose suggestions and changes are incorporated in this book. My humble prostrations at the feet of Baba Ganeshananda Giri Maharaj, Vasudevan Swami of Vajreswari, Devi Amma, Lamperi Babaji, and last but not least, Avadhoota Nadananda who stood by me and supported me through time without fail.

My late daughter Ammu (Sreedevi Mohan) had been my greatest teacher. She walked the earth for barely five years. But the wisdom that she showered on all of us cannot be measured in terms of anything. My heartfelt gratitude to Ammu too, considering her to be elder to me, because she left her body ahead of me. My gratitude and thanks to Ammu's mother and my ex-wife Saritha too.

This is the fourth reprint. This book has reached many people across the world. This book is also translated into a few languages. This book has inspired many people to walk the path of pathlessness, which gives me a lot of satisfaction. Many people have come forward in many countries over the years to spread the message of liberation . My sincere thanks to all of you, who have helped us spread the message of liberation in your region and beyond.

My sincere thanks to the GuruLight publication team too. Once again, I would like to thank all those who assisted our publications so selflessly. Conviction brings forth purpose. Purpose inspires courage and timeliness. Hence, conviction is all you need, in what you do. Thank You.

I sincerely thank all the people who ever came into my life and will come in the future. All those who helped me understand and experience various realities of our existence on earth, one way or the other. All those who walked with me from time to time, those who gave me food, money, job, shelter or clothes, those who believed in me, those who loved me, cared for me, hated me, supported me, cheated me, thanked me, criticized me, judged me, scandalized me, understood me, misunderstood me . . . .I thank everyone. My life comprises of everyone. I have no enemies. I love all and I serve all. Last but not least, I would like to thank the grand tradition of Lord Dakshinamoorthy, Lord Krishna as Guruvayoorappan, Great Siddhas, Great Nagas, Guru Dattatreya and the Dattatreya Tradition, Akkalkot Maharaj, Shirdi Sai Baba, Sathya Sai Baba, Navnath Sadhus, Mahaavtar Babaji and the Gurus of the Kriyayoga Tradition, Bhagawan Nithyananda, Ramana Maharshi, Lord Jesus and all the Great and Self-less Masters who ever walked on earth and will ever walk on earth. I humbly surrender all that I did and will ever do, at their lotus feet. Great Masters continue their work, with or without their physical body. They continue to work through many. I surrender myself fully, completely and with full faith at the feetless feet of the Supreme God, Parabrahma. The Supreme Father, who manifests through every being, through time and space, eternally. I do not exist. Only HE exists.

Finally, thanks to all those who found this book, and found this book helpful in understanding certain aspects of their existence. Thank You for your presence. May you attain the highest liberation in this life.

Remain Blessed.

Yours
Mohanji

A NOTE FOR THE READERS

Mohanji is in a state of expanded consciousness connected to the Divine when essays or blogs are written through him. This is also true during the meditations and satsangs when he answers questions from spiritual seekers. In order to retain the original context and spirit behind his delivery, certain language errors pertaining to grammar or punctuations have purposefully NOT been corrected during the transcribing, compiling and editing process. This is a note to invite the reader to focus on the essence of the texts and subtle messages found between the lines.

—M. Wolny

SIGNS OF THE TIMES

A Sharing

WHILE TRAVELLING, WAITING at airports or cooling the heels at hotel rooms, televisions were pouring in stories of woe and nothing else. Man made problems. Unrest. Calamities. Destruction of lives and properties. It saddens me to think that people are just wreaking havoc senselessly. Sign of the times? There is nothing to justify violence.

We are essentially existing in turbulent times. There have been turbulent times in the past, too. But then there was no media to instantly bring it to your eyes. Now it's instant. You can see people dying in the streets and feel nothing about it. Constant feeding of violence to our eyes and to our mind, makes both of these faculties insensitive. We will not care for anything anymore. We have become indifferent to other people's sorrows.

Collective consciousness is very powerful. When groups of people live in fear and suppression, there are bound to be calamities. When the fear factor overwhelms, death and destruction takes place. We bring such realities onto ourselves. Consistent positive actions, words and reassurances could slowly change the mindset of people. We are not used to accepting positive things without questioning and doubting. We are used to accepting and storing negative emotions effortlessly. We even crave for it. We even develop a sadistic outlook in that context.

I am not suggesting anything, as one man can do nothing

against the collective consciousness of masses. One thing we can do. We can choose to be positive, despite the negativities around us. How? By cleansing our insides consistently, deliberately. By trashing all negative thoughts as unwanted enemies to our own peace. By removing anger, hatred and all kinds of negative thoughts, deliberately. By forgiving and giving. By ensuring that we do at least one positive action every day. By touching someone, even unknown to us at this time, and making that person feel loved and cared. By reaching out and helping the helpless. Maybe we could provoke a movement of positiveness. Destruction is very easy. All it takes is sheer madness. Creation is very difficult. Destruction also paves way to new creations. While we do not endorse destruction, let us maintain the above optimism that there is room for creation here. All I am suggesting is: please reach out and assist a poor person in your neighbourhood. Please listen and do something about someone else's plight. Let us not consider others as outside of ourselves. They all are extension of ourselves. All are part of ourselves. We exist in comparison with others. This means relativity. Relationships. Build bridges. We cannot help negativity. Negativity automatically grows. It needs no fertilizers. It breeds by itself. Positiveness needs to be cultivated, nurtured and well groomed. We should always express our own culture. This is the culture of LOVE. Non-violence. Let's express that.

While I am praying for all those who suffered, I sincerely hope that at the end of all these calamities, peace will prevail. Peace must prevail. There is no other choice. Violence is barbaric. Such acts do not have longevity. They come and go. They disrupt calm and affect many lives, while they happen. Nature does the cleansing act, consistently. But, the impression of a barbaric act always remains at the location. It gets written in the subconscious of nature. It stays. The same is with acts of compassion.

I wish all of those who are hearing this, happiness and courage. Please do not lose heart. Be brave and take people to wisdom and love. We can only love. Love more. Do something positive every day, consistently. Do not be shaken by barbaric acts of selfish people, those people without higher awareness.

Uncertainties

Q: Wars are affecting the world. Why do we have to go through these uncertainties?

M: Greed provokes wars. Wars create uncertainties. Plato has said: "Only the dead actually saw the end of the war." Greed is increasing. The problem is man's lack of understanding or awareness. This is a very small life that we are involved in. A very short life. All you need is love. There is no need for hatred and suffering. But, we create them. And then, we complain. When the mind is shrunk because of hatred and negativities, man acts without thinking. This means emotional acts, emotional outbursts, emotional driving, emotional eating, everything emotional.

The intellect goes for a walk or takes vacation. When intellect is not available, emotions play havoc and life becomes miserable. People sometimes try to drown their emotions in intoxication too. We have seen that around us.

Wars begin at home. An unsettled mind unsettles the society. Collective unsettlement creates calamities. Continuous calamities lead to wars. So, the birth of the war happens in the mind. Then it takes shape in the outside world.

We have to watch our thoughts, words and action. Sadistic thoughts must be replaced with higher awareness of our existence. We must demonstrate the acts of kindness consistently. We must educate children to do charity and help freely, unconditionally. Kindness, charity, compassion etc. must be cultivated. We must think and act consciously and never emotionally.

One person cannot change the society. Yet, one person can set an example. So, the nature of society should not be an excuse for our lack of efforts in doing good. Society has never really understood great thinkers during their time. Society also tends to eliminate what they cannot understand. This never deterred a great thinker, ever. They always went ahead with their mission and died peacefully. The kingdom of heaven has always been within themselves. So, one man can definitely set examples.

The bottom line is, your soul is pure. Stay with your soul. All contamination is external as far as the soul is concerned. Keep it external and keep destroying waste. Life will flower.

Q: You had said that man's greed is the root cause of all the problems of the world. You also said that ruining the planet earth will ruin life on earth too. Are you talking about global warming? Do you think there will be another ice age or flood?

M: I think we discussed this over a private mail. Maybe I did not clarify the point enough. Flood and devastation are possible, not ice age. The ice caps are melting and the deluge could devastate countries.

When earth happened, the energy sources required for peaceful habitation also happened. They are the Sun and Wind. Water and Fire also are energy sources. According to me, the oil within the earth is like the fluid that assists the movements of the joints of our body. Minus those fluids, the earth will crack. Thus, we have made many cracks on earth. We have released all the poisons, which were earlier trapped inside the earth, into the sky. We have also brought forth non-recyclable materials out of the bowels of the earth. When the guts are spilled, death is imminent. It could be today or tomorrow.

Imbalances in earth's ecosystem will create all kinds of problems, floods, global warming, earthquakes, tsunamis, so on and so forth. Also some deadly viruses which remained frozen in the polar ice are getting liberated with the warming. We have no idea what kind of devastation that can create.

Look at it from every angle. Nature provides for existence of all its beings. There is perfect synchronicity. Sun does not take holidays. Rain does not create more water than nature needs, until we change the cycle of nature. When cleansing is required, floods are created. Lightning also burns poisonous gases in the sky. The ozone layers protect life from toxic radiation. We have been provided with everything. We have also been provided with superior intellect to understand life and its nature, as well as to understand nature too.

We have also destroyed forests and our fellow beings, that had equal rights over earth, like us, and we have polluted the water of the world with immature handling of wastes. Now, we are trying to recycle and survive. Is this lack of vision, greed or indifference?

When profits become the priority, life—including thoughts, words and action—gets compromised. Actions become insensitive. People do not care anymore. Wars take place. Destruction happens. Earth has faced many such occurrences of devastation because of private agendas in the past. It's experiencing the same in the present too.

If we use solar energy and wind or water energy, this is harmonious with nature. There are no poisons released into the skies. We cannot ignore the actions of the present and look at the future. Today's actions are tomorrow's reality. The result of today's action happens tomorrow. If we create a better today, we could look at a better tomorrow.

The Shift

The changes are accented due to the impending shift. It is not only changes in the realms of physical earth, but also the emotional, spiritual as well as economic earth. Insensitiveness, greed, barbarism, cruelty, sadism and all such negative aspects of our existence must pave the way to unconditional love. This is the shift. This is a shift of consciousness.

Sometimes, we need a very hard push to wake up. We all are in the slumber of unconscious existence. Most of our activities pertaining to our body, mind and intellect are controlled by our subconscious. Our conscious mind is a renegade. It wanders all the time. It aids the senses, at the same time it does not stay with one sense all the time. You can only use one sense at a time effectively. There is no such thing as multitasking. It means only an increase in speed of action or lesser attention per action, thought or word. We can fully consciously engage only in one action at a time, with the firm presence of mind. The more we do it, the more we will exist in the present. The more we hand over the subconscious controlled activities to the conscious mind, the more we stay out of habits. The lesser the unconscious activity, the more we will be in the present. The more we are in the present, the more we evolve into the being level.

So, it's not the activities such as meditation or pranayam per se that equip you to handle the shift. It is the consciousness achieved through these methods that helps. Nobody knows the depth of the 2012 shift as yet. There are many speculations. Trash all that. Get into the being level. Reduce unconscious actions. Do everything with awareness. You will shift into the being level. This shift will take you through 'the shift'. There will be lesser anxieties and fears, which stem out of the oscillating mind. When you develop equanimity, there is no tragedy. It does not matter what happens outside, we will be firmly established on the platform of universal love. We will be operating on an objective basis. No expectations, no frustrations. This is what will help in the shift.

Increase in the quantity of water due to global warming and water borne diseases, could wreak catastrophe and submerge some islands of the world. The increase in the frequency or the possibility of polar shifts could jeopardise our entire communication system, electricity and technology. We could feel quite helpless. The kind of helplessness that a war-affected generation might have felt, minus the hope for improvement in the future.

So, being-ness is the key. Staying objective is the way.

Relativity

Q: Why is there so much negativity in the world?

M: Negativity is primarily in the minds of men. We only see its external expressions in the world outside. There are only dualities in the world. Dualities are essentially expressions of relativity. Relativity expresses itself as duality. If there is no high, there is no low. If there is no tall, there is no short. If there is no white, there is no black. So on and so forth. So, dualities define our relative existence. Positiveness and negativeness are interdependent. One cannot exist without the other. They coexist.

Our existence is also relative. We are taller than . . . , we are richer than . . . , we are more intelligent than . . . , we are better than . . . etc. There is always something relative to compare with. This is expressed and defined more clearly in relationships. In relationship to the daughter, he is the father. In relationship with that woman, he is her husband etc. Relationships are also expressions of relativity. Relationships have come out of relativity. So, if we understand relativity and relationships along with the dualities that make it tangible, we will understand the basic fabric of our terrestrial existence.

Dualities are neither good nor bad. Relativity is neither good nor bad. Everything just is. There is no comparison because the absence of one is the relative absence of the other.

What we call good and bad is essentially the judgment of our conscious mind. When we sleep, this faculty of judging something is absent. So, in reality, everything is only an experience. The experiencer, using the tools that he possesses, such as body, mind, intellect, senses, ego etc. experiences some thought, word or action, and decides based on his conditioning, whether the experience was excellent, good, bad or ugly. The experienced, the experience and in a certain way, the experiencer have nothing to do with it. Everything is momentary and relative. This judgment or impression of an event gets registered in our subconscious mind. This data is stored in our hard drive.

And similar situations get judged in similar ways, even if they are drastically different. Mind refuses to accept changes. This creates fears and uncertainties. Thus the subconscious mind churns out one's realities.

Familiarity also breeds monotony. Man craves for changes.

Thus, results are a plenty. Billions of expressions are possible in relationships. The choices in creating thoughts, words, actions and events are many.

So, positive and negative are part of our existence. We call the shots. When we stay objective and neutral (as a witness) nothing will affect us. We will look at everything as maya, illusion or the play of God. It's a grand opera. There have to be heroes and villains. The beautiful and the ugly. The actors may not be aware of the depth of their own character or the character of others.

Those who watch the show can only make judgments based on what they perceive or their individual level of understanding. Even that could be untrue because each person operates from their level of awareness.

So, relativity is the key. Unity is the solution. Being one with the Father or Parabrahma will dissolve dualities and relativities. This state is Sat-Chit-Ananda, eternal bliss state. That's where our soul started the journey. That's where our soul will eventually end its journey, once it's done with the eternal birth and death cycle. Hence, paying heed to the soul is essential. For this, we must go beyond our role play. We must stay with the only truth which is of permanent nature, our soul. Everything else is temporary and relative. Just float through impermanence, unaffected and be with your soul. And keep remembering that relativity is the biggest gift that God gave himself. Relativity gave Him the executional power in creation and billions of options to play with.

We also have the power—but duality conceals it. Non-understanding masks it. When we shift to the being level through spiritual practices, we express it and experience it. We become one with the creator and assume all His powers. The whole duality within us dissolves and transforms into unconditional love, universal love. An unselfish existence. We see only ourselves in every being. We will never harm any being through our thoughts, words or action.

Hence the real and only worthwhile journey is into ourselves—OUR SELVES. There is nowhere else to go.

The Present Time

Present time is turbulent. The best way to go through this time is to keep a very low profile. Just watch. No reactions. Performing through the intellect. No confrontations. Some people are waiting for an opportunity to explode. Be in the present. You cannot escape. You have to go through it. You have to experience it. That is why situations are created to give you experiences and for you to learn to respond. If you see the whole universe, you see calamities in every aspect. There are upheavals at financial, political and family levels.

This is the time of changes. All states and statuses are changing. Situations are changing. If you try to fast-forward now, it's not going to help. It will only create trouble. Even at the unit level, family level, there will be a lot of pressure and chaos. There will be frictions and fights in the family. The world outside will also be the same way, even at political and country level. It's a shake-up to collapse the weak. It is inevitable. With this shake up, things will change for the better. The weak will collapse. Those who can't survive will perish. Those who can survive will be of higher consciousness. Those who cannot survive will be of lower consciousness. They will be more future oriented and will be materialistic. Those who live in the present, future will be brighter for them. If you cannot live in the present, future is going to be very dark for you. So, the more you expect from the future, the more troubles you will have. You have to tackle the present with the intellect, with buddhi. Be aware of the time and relax. The wheels of change and upheaval will reflect some time.

Q: If someone finds himself/herself in a high position/ profile, then what can be done?

M: Whether it is at the top of the family, an organisation or a country, all people have their minds in agitation right now. Just watch how things are evolving. Do not react. Just respond. In this type of situation, if you think you can hold the rein, it's bound to slip out of your hands. So just watch.

Use intellect (buddhi) and not emotion because using emotion will be bad for you and also for others. Everyone's mind is like a battlefield—one spark is enough to ignite. At whatever level you are—junior or senior, in a unit as well as in public, at all levels, just watch, observe and move carefully. Understand that people are creating problems for you because they are insecure. It is not because they want to create a problem for you. Insecurities are at the highest level for everyone now because of the upheavals in energy levels in the world. So people would not know what to do. When they are imbalanced within, the imbalance will manifest outside as well. Wait, watch, observe, respond. The more you react the more calamities will happen. There is a saying: "In the feast of ego, everybody goes home hungry." So that is what will be happening. More egos will come, more egoists will come up, and more will be dissatisfied.

Q: And how NOT to react?

M: Ok. If you are using your intellect more than your emotion, then it automatically becomes a response. If you are reacting then understand that it is the 'emotion' which is working. Intellect is blocked and hence unavailable. When you are using your 'response' power it is basically your 'intellect' which is in command, 'emotions' are not in command. Observe yourself responding and reacting. Go to your spine *more*. Practice the 360 Degrees meditation (see appendix).

If senses are pushing you to react, it indicates that emotions are in command. When emotions are in command, the catastrophic reaction happens. It will happen at micro and macro level. Be very careful. You have to survive. Not that if you go somewhere else things will be better. NO. This is happening everywhere.
Read newspapers and you will know. How many people are dying every day. How many calamities are happening?

Consciousness shift is clearly visible now. Those of the higher consciousness will survive. And how do you operate in higher consciousness? Start using 'intellect' more than 'emotion'. You will get all sorts of questions coming up. Just drop them. There is no other way. Just understand that if you are getting questions then it is your 'ego' that is working. You cannot do anything with the ego. The more you use the ego, the more calamities will be happening.

Message is thus: you have perfection; you have strength, rely on that. Keep the connection of the Masters; all those eternal Masters with whom you have been connected and keep surrendering everything to them. They are definitely available and they are protecting. Sometimes self-reliance is not possible, especially in such situations, so then rely on the Masters, rely on God. Faith should not be conditional (e.g. "If this happens to me then I have faith in you, if this doesn't happen then my faith will be shaken.").

Our mind works only conditionally. "If you have money I love you, if you don't 'thank you very much'." That is how the human mind works. No, it should be unconditional. Once we look at the whole picture, higher awareness will automatically act. Before things happen we will know—that is the whole story. Everything is temporary, situation to situation. Use your intellect. Buddhi is the stick you should walk with. Emotions must only be watched. When you are emotional, you should know that it is not essential. For instance, when you are angry, do not get involved in the anger. Whenever you want to cry, just cry because that is a sort of cleansing. You need not cry in front of all. Go to one place, be with yourself and when there are too many clouds, let it rain off. If you want to get angry, get angry—BUT then watch yourself getting angry. Do not get involved with the anger. So the impact will not be there and the corresponding emotions will not get stored in your personal hard drive.

Q: Can we completely restrict our emotions though?

M: Yes. Only through observation can you do that. Letting go of emotion is more of a 'theory' to most people. How do you do that? By watching yourself getting emotional and accepting those emotions as part of yourself. Because we usually say we are emotional in a positive way, but it is not so. You are emotional in the negative aspect too. We can be this and we can be that. Both are fine and are part of you. Watch that. In this way, you will lose the attachment to them. So whether it is a good emotion or a bad emotion you will not be attached to it. It will not bother you. Otherwise you will become an 'egoist' at some point of time if not all points of time. If the emotions hurt you, should you just let go? Yes. But let go does not mean theoretically. Letting go actually means by blessing or by forgiving or by being detached from the emotions deep within. Understand that this is a part of our existence. Give importance to the situation to decipher the learning and then thank and forget. Some people stay on with the situation. Emotions are to be taken as emotions, because, even though they are temporary, they are a part of you. There is nothing bad about it because it is your constitution.

There is good and bad in everybody. No one is complete and perfect. Duality is part of our existence, it is like day-night or sleeping-wakeful state. Emotions are part of duality. Everyone has a unique constitution with a bright side and a dark side. But only the bright side is shown. That does not mean there is no dark side. It is hidden. People like to present themselves properly. But true acceptance will be acceptance of your bright side as well as your dark side. You watch both of them and how it all works. Be the witness of your emotions, always. This will minimize the impact. Impact happens only if you are involved. The ego is hurt if someone scolds you or abuses or curses— emotions are bursting and we develop a feeling of revenge against that person. So the thoughts, words and actions become ugly and disproportionate. It will become a problem for you. But if you watch and accept them, then you are very balanced. Nothing touches you.

Life

Time has given tremendous insecurity and anxiety to many people. Some worry about lapse of time or the nearing of their death. Some worry about unfulfilled desires which they have accumulated while living this life. Some fear about debts. Some fear about the lives of their own children, ignoring the basic fact that they are also individual karmic beings and you can do nothing about their prarabdha or baggage. Some fear about people. Some fear about the unknown. Thus, all people fear about something. Fear also attracts such incidents in our life. Just like love attracts, fear also attracts. Kindly note how animals and birds are not bound by time!!!

Long life is not important. 'Life' in our life is very important. The amount of energy and 'life' while living is very important. 'Life-less' days are burdens. A life without energy and 'life' is mere existence. There is no power in it. Most people are handling this life without 'life'. It is like the dead—living, filled with lethargy and negativity. On the other side, some are pressured for pleasure and they exhaust themselves not knowing what they are seeking and where to find it. They keep running for nothing. So it is the 'life' in our life which is more important than a long life that drags on for nothing. Death is only a transition, a stock taking of karmas before we take another life.

Clinging on to this body is useless, unless there are karmas to tackle and things to be accomplished. That agenda our conscious mind cannot understand.

A fulfilling life is one lived with benevolence. If a person has been able to express love and compassion to fellow beings all through his/her life, it has been a life well lived. If someone led a life without any concern for the poor and needy, especially if that life was filled with anxiety and fear about oneself, it is definitely a life ill spent. So wake up, buckle up. Get on to the nearest mountain and roar out your liberation. Express your liberation through selfless actions. Take on command. Please do not be a backdrop or a doormat. Be your own leader first and then be a leader in the external world. One who cannot lead himself well, cannot lead others. One who has vested interests will falter today or tomorrow. Not feeling is no virtue. Lack of benevolent action leaves us basic, unrefined. Beware.

I wish You Great Health, Supreme Bliss, Grace of the Masters and the Lord Almighty, Ability to express love, kindness and compassion, Ability to be satisfied with whatever is available and be grateful about it, Ability to make others feel happy and grateful—I wish you everything that can be justifiably and legitimately possessed, as a temporary custodian. I wish You Peace, Joy and Happiness forever.

God Bless You, Always . . . May you be successful in all your selfless efforts.

KARMA

Karmic Road Map

Q: I have been reading various books about Karma. I find this topic very intriguing. I liked the answers that you gave in the past about Karma. I thought your answers are straight forward, believable and clear. I would appreciate if you could give me an example as to how karma works and how, sometimes, one's actions become incomprehensible to society. You had mentioned that society discards and even executes those who do not comply with the beaten tracks of existence.

M: I wish I could explain karma in simple terms. Karma is complex. There are trillions of permutations and combinations possible in karma. An action plus emotion gets stored in our data bank. This forms the root of karma. Action could be at thought level or word level too. So in all three levels of our existence, karma is created. I will tell you a story, how powerful karma is and how it works.

The Story . . .

One man loved a woman deeply. He was a student then. She was a student too. Both were not earning and hence their respective parents effectively blocked their love affair. Of course, there was also caste or colour difference. Whatever the problem was, the result was that they could not marry. The man became a school teacher and before he could re-approach the girl's parents for her hand in marriage, she was diagnosed with blood cancer and she soon left her body. This man loved her so deeply that he never got married in his life ever again. She also loved him, but could not spend her life with him. They both deeply regretted their separation.

Many years went by. The man is now 54. A student in his class started loving him deeply. She was a teenager and he was 54. She could not understand why, she loved him so deeply nor could he comprehend. He tried his best to stay away from the girl, but she would not leave him. He could not recognize the soul of his past lover nor could she. It was a different life.

This time, he was already suffering from lung cancer, due to his systematic abuse of his body, as he was bottling the anger and frustration of losing his old lover. He could never get over his devastation of losing his lover. He got addicted to smoking and alcohol.

His teenage female student still loved him. Soon, the teacher retired and was quite bedridden. His student would visit him, against his will. He usually did not have sufficient money to treat himself. She would even sell her ornaments and buy him medicines. Many times, he asked her why she was sacrificing so much for an old man. She did not have any direct answer, but she was determined. Soon her parents came to know about her frequent visits to her teacher's house and even found out that her jewels were missing. She was questioned and she told the truth. Her father became extremely furious and threw her out of the house. He considered it as a shame and insult for the whole family, that his daughter loved a man who is older than himself. He feared that this act of his daughter would give him and his family terrible shame and defamation. He feared that the society would excommunicate him and his family.

She had nowhere to go. She went to the house of her teacher.

Stayed there against his will. He was in physical agony as well as mental agony. She dropped her studies halfway through, because she had no money, and worked part time in a fabric shop and earned their daily bread. The doctors told her that he would possibly die in a couple of months.

She asked him to marry her and he refused. He tried his very best to bring her to her senses. She requested him to at least give her a baby. He denied that also. She relentlessly pressurized him and finally, he agreed, despite his ill health.

She became pregnant with his child. She managed to take care of her sick lover and her pregnancy for a few months until he died. He left his house and property in her name. She delivered a healthy boy child. She was still in her very early 20s. Later, she sold the property and house, and now lives in an ashram off Bangalore, India. The owner of the ashram adopted both the mother and child. The child is quite evolved. The mother completed her karmic agenda and reached the spiritual path soon afterwards. This is one example of how karma works.

The society and her parents could never understand her actions. They condemned her as crazy. Even she did not know why she was doing what she did. The karmic push made her do it. This is the power of karma. The master who adopted her and her child knew her path and supported it, when she had completed her karmic agenda with her teacher and lover of a past life. She regretted leaving him in her past life so much, that in this life, that was her key agenda and all other things just became secondary.

Trust this gives clarity to your thought. Often a real life story explains things better than many theories.

Q: I understand that situations in a person's life happen due to one's karma and that circumstances are based on the Lord's Grace. Is this a correct statement? If not could you elaborate on this?

M: Karma can be broadly divided into two. The set of karmas (prarabdha) that provoked you to take this gross body (this birth or this life) and all the experiences that you are experiencing now. The new set of karmas (aagamya) that you are acquiring while you live the old set of karma. It becomes a mixture as we live on. Sometimes we cannot differentiate between the brought forward and the recently acquired. As I mentioned earlier, it is the emotion that attaches an incident to your subconscious, which eventually becomes your agenda or karma.

Grace of Gurus or God oils the chain of your bicycle. You have to ride it. Oiling the chain makes the journey smoother. When you are on the edge of nirvana, sometimes a Master will take away the remnants of your samskaras and even karmas and sometimes will help your liberation too. Otherwise no Master takes anyone's karmas. He only guides people on how to stay liberated. Staying liberated reduces karmas.

Events happen according to the agenda and sequence that is set before you took the journey. The karmic road map is strictly followed. Everything falls within that. If a family does not have the karmic agenda to experience parenthood, they will never have children. If you have the eligibility to become a millionaire, you will become one and nobody can stop you. Thus goes the pre-plan.

Remembrance of Things Past

What I am writing here is about two lives of one soul. This is just to show how traits were brought forward and experienced, without conscious awareness. I have received many questions about transit of karma over lives. I hope this will give you a clear insight. As I had mentioned earlier. Trillions of permutations and combinations are possible, in the path of karma. So, please do not look at it two dimensionally. Look at it objectively, as one of the numerous possibilities.

This is a real life scenario, hence I cannot disclose the person's identity and have concealed it as much as I could.

A dedicated life . . .

Malaysia, early 1900s. Sue Ann was 28 years old when her husband died. He left behind some debts and a baby boy. The boy was almost one year old when her husband died. Sue Ann was strong willed, disciplined and intelligent. She never surrendered to silly emotions or others words. She decided to fight it out on her own and bring the child up. Her husband's family blamed her for his death, even though he had met with an accident in a remote place, far away from home, while working in plantation fields, and could not be taken to a hospital immediately due to the non-availability of vehicles. By the time they could take him to the nearby clinic, he was breathing his last, due to loss of blood and some allergies.

Sue Ann received the body of her husband, one evening, after she had bathed and put her child to sleep. She did not know what to do. She was helped by her husband's colleagues in the farm, and they buried him in the nearby church cemetery in the early morning hours. Sue Ann was understandably numb about the whole thing and forgot to inform her in-laws. Luckily, someone told them and they joined for the cremation, but, did not talk to her nor share her grief. They did not even look at her son. This was an inter-caste marriage out of love and their whole family was against it.

When Sue Ann was young, her grandmother used to tell her: "you must pray to Buddha to come into our family, he will come as your son." Ever since, she used to make this her daily prayer. And subconsciously, she considered her son as Buddha.

Sue Ann was a thin woman. She was of medium height. She always dressed elegantly and carried herself with dignity as well as humility. She lived in the rural area. The terrains of that locality were hills and valleys, with a single lane metalled road running as a garland around the village. Her house, and all the houses in her neighbourhood, were on flattened land cut out from the hill. All had plantations in front of their houses till the edge of the road, which was about 50 feet below their houses, and also had plantations on the backside of their house for about 50 feet till the middle of the hill. Thus, their house was in the middle, with plantations on both sides and road running in the lower portion. Sue Ann's late husband had bought this property on borrowed money, made a small one bedroom hut in the middle of the property and started cultivation around it. He said: "It is for the sake of self-sufficiency". Sue Ann continued this legacy. They had some debts to clear, which she continued to repay after her husband's demise. Since she was paying well, banks did not bother her. Apart from plantation, she also had some poultry and a sheep.

She was an introverted person, who kept away from everyone, as far as she could. She doted on her son. Her son was everything to her. She looked after him without leaving any details unattended. He was a quiet boy, occasionally naughty. But, he turned out very well under the watchful eyes of his loving mother. She was not connected to her late husband's family and since her own family had disowned her when she married him, she had no friends or relatives. An old woman who lived two houses away was perhaps the only occasional visitor to her house. She was a kind woman and considered Sue Ann to be her daughter. She was living alone too. She always reminded Sue Ann that if she let go of her youth, she would suffer during her old age.

Despite her poor existence, Sue Ann was self-reliant. She not only dressed up elegantly, she always kept herself and her house clean. She also made sure her son also learned the habits of perfect hygiene. The house and her person were always neat and clean. She stayed up until late hours, after putting her son to sleep, cleaning and tidying up the house. They did not have electricity. She was using oil lamps. She was always careful about her expenditure, though she never cared about money, where her son was concerned. She provided him everything she could. He was a sensitive child and in his own way, he loved his mother deeply. He was never quite demanding in any way. He was more or less happy with what he had. Moreover, the neighbourhood children were also not rich or affluent. Everyone was more or less even.

She never would get annoyed with her son, no matter what he did. Sometimes, when he would not eat the food that she cooked for him, she would calmly make him understand that food is God, that food should never be dishonoured, and diplomatically, she would make him eat. He was a good boy and he usually obeyed his mother. She always made him nap in the afternoon after he came back from his school, which was in the neighbourhood. His school was so small and he had only a few hours to spend there everyday. Sue Ann dropped him there and picked him up after classes every day. She would carry him when he was sleepy and reluctant to walk.

The old neighbourhood woman tried her best to convince Sue Ann to remarry. Sue Ann refused all such proposals point blank. She was completely pre-occupied with her son. The old woman told her: "You are like my daughter. Now you are in your thirties, men will still want you. You are elegant, neat and clean and I know that many men are interested in you. Today, you may feel that you need no man's company. Tomorrow, when you become like me, who will look after you? You see how I exist! I can hardly walk a hundred steps. I have to cook, wash and do everything alone. If I call for some help, I have to pay money. I am just managing an existence. If one night, I fall sick and need to see a doctor, who will help me? If one night, I die, who will know that I am dead? Understand all this clearly. You are still very attractive and we can get you a good groom. Its four years since your husband died. You should not be staying like this anymore."

Usually such discussions happened in the afternoon, after lunch, when her son would be sleeping in her lap and the old woman usually sitting leaning against the wall. Sue Ann's house was very small and had only one proper room. It was a kind of tiny hall, with three windows and a door and sufficient light and air flowed into the room. There was no furniture, except for a chair. Both the mother and child slept on the floor, on a bed made of cotton. Sometimes, when it was dark, the son feared about ghosts and thieves. Then, Sue Ann would lock all windows from inside and keep a lamp burning till morning for his sake.

She still had her small altar with the statue of Buddha, even though she had changed her name and religion when she got married. When her son refused to sleep, usually because she had him nap every afternoon, he would be very energetic at night, so she would tell him stories and sing songs until he slept. After she was convinced that he was asleep, she would get up and go back to kitchen to do her domestic chores. She worked hard, day and night, for her son. She had no other aim in life.

She was averse to travelling and speed always made her stomach churn. She avoided all kinds of travels. Except for the old woman, nobody bothered her routines. She liked the old woman, because she was kind. Sue Ann told her: "One day, my son will become an officer. At that time, we will leave this house and property. He is intelligent. I will give him the best education and he will become a big officer in government. People will respect him. I will also get him a beautiful wife. He will give me a peaceful life, when I am older. I have no other aim in my life".

She was a reasonably stubborn woman. She always kept to her agenda. She never stopped at anything, when it came to her son's matters. She provided him with everything she could possibly afford. She would not even allow her son to go out and play alone. He had to cross the road to go to the playground. She always accompanied him, in the evenings if it wasn't raining; and she never left his hand while walking in the rain. She always feared, that since they lived on uneven terrains, he could slip, fall and injure himself. She was careful and she never allowed her son to be away from her eyes reach.

Her sister-in-law was vicious towards her and even spread rumours that she was prostituting herself for survival. Some of her relatives and her husband's relatives believed this, as she had refused to re-marry, and stopped the advances of some of them, very effectively. She was even dishonoured in public. She suffered all humiliation silently and never retaliated. She would not even cry in front of her son. She always kept him happy and positive. She swallowed all pains. Her son was too young to understand what his mother was going through, anyway.

Sue Ann suffered all humiliation silently and concentrated on her son, fully. She cared for nothing else. Her son was growing well.

He was close to 7 years now. He was doing very well in his studies. One afternoon, after he returned from school, Sue Ann saw that her son had fever. She gave him some medicine that she had kept handy. He slept immediately. By evening, the fever intensified. She somehow took him to the nearby clinic, with just two beds and a visiting doctor. The attendant admitted him and the doctor checked the boy the next morning. He prescribed some medicines and he left. The boy kept telling his mom to take him back to their home. But, the doctor asked them to stay in the hospital for another night. By evening the next day, despite the medicines, the boy became unconscious. Sue Ann was praying with all her energy to all the Gods to heal her precious son.

Late in the night, he opened his eyes, and looked at his mother who was gently stroking his chest, holding his right hand in her left hand, sitting on his bed. She saw that he was crying silently. Tears were flowing from his eyes. She wiped his tears and told him not to cry, as she was sure that he would be healed by the next morning. He gently closed his eyes. Sue Ann realized that his hand had become cold. The fever had vanished! She checked his feet. They were cold too. She checked his face. It was still. He was not breathing. There were tears still on his cheeks, which were not fully dried as yet. With a shock, she knew the truth. Her son had left her and gone!!! The look of tears that he gave her was his final good-bye!

She kissed the tears from his cheeks and hugged him and lay with his body for some time. She did not know what to do. Whether to accept the truth or end her life. The attendant saw her lying in the bed with the patient. Since it was not allowed, he told her to get up. She was crying silently. The attendant checked the pulse of the boy and knew that he was no more. He made Sue Ann sit down, gave her a glass of water, and told her to try to relax. Sue Ann's whole life was over. She had had no other aim in life than to bring her son up. Now, everything had gone. The whole dream was over. Reality was too stark. She sat there numb, praying to the same gods that she asked to heal her son, to at least look after the soul of her son.

The next day, the doctor arrived, completed the formalities and released the dead body. Sue Ann buried him in her own property. No church or Buddhist cremation. What caste or religion does a small innocent boy have?

She continued to live till she was 52, alone, praying for her son's soul and working as hard as ever on her property, without depending on anybody. She never complained about anything. She worked hard till her last day. She died peacefully, in her sleep. Three days later, her neighbour, not seeing her outside for two days, came to check and found her dead in her bed!

The story continues . . .

In a small village in the Philippines, to an unmarried couple, a girl child was born. She was called Maria. She was the second child of three siblings. Her elder sister and her younger brother had nothing in common with her. Her father was a wounded soldier and her mother a housewife. They never found time or necessity to get married. The sickness of her father affected the entire family. He was gravely wounded in a war and he survived even though the war delivered him disabled. He had an addiction problem too, which landed him and his family into many troubles. Even their relatives kept a distance from them because of this matter. There were lots of calamities amongst the parents which affected the children emotionally.

Even though her father respected Maria, she could not recognize him as her husband of her past life. Whatever Maria said, her father obeyed. While her elder sister displayed lot of immaturity, right from her childhood, Maria was very matured and balanced. While she never had the privileges of the eldest or the youngest, she never complained and found her way without stepping on anyone's toes. She was liked by many and envied by many. She had faithful friends and the strengths of her character were her honesty and willpower. She even advised her mother who felt compelled to listen. Thus, right from early age, she displayed exemplary maturity. She did most of her academics on her own and in order to study at the university, she had to leave her small hometown and move to the capital. She stayed there with her uncle and paternal aunt out of necessity and compulsion.

She was not really welcome nor was she appreciated. Her aunt never lost any opportunity to abuse her or ridicule her in front of her friends, who occasionally came to her house to prepare for examinations together. This gave her so much agony. One day, she was accused of stealing money and was thrown out of the house in the middle of the night. At first she was shocked and cried because of the hurt of her ego, prestige, and dignity. But, her real independence began at that moment. Out of sheer necessity, she decided to take life head on. She moved to a friend's place and continued her studies till graduation. She worked day and night and made her own path. She also landed a job on her own and moved to another land, far away from her hometown.

She was popular with her colleagues and her friends. She was also respected by her clients. Her boss respected her, for her integrity and even though she was only 23 years old, even her senior colleagues confided in her, their deepest secrets and sought her advice. She had no craving for money and spent it freely. Her only weakness was coffee and an occasional beer. She never drank out of control.

She always dressed elegantly and could read through men. She knew their intentions and handled them carefully. She kept a serious, determined and almost a tomboyish attitude. She only had two lovers in her life and that also did not proceed beyond limits. Her father had warned her against losing her chastity before marriage and she was determined to stay that way. Even though most of her friends were boys, she was well respected and never taken for granted, by any. She never allowed anyone to run over her.

She did more than her boss expected and this got her good recognition.

Their organization was conducting a global meet and she was one of the key coordinators. She went into micro details so that no gaps were left in hospitality and coordination. She personally received many guests from the airport and dropped them to their hotels. All the guests were senior executives of reputed companies from around the world and her elegant approach was well appreciated. She spoke very little and listened more, as she knew that the cultural differences demanded more listening than speaking. She was well aware of cultural positioning. Everything went very well. The last of her guests were two officials from a location almost eight hours away by flight. She picked them up in the evening and dropped them at their hotel, as scheduled.

Right from the moment she welcomed the two guests at the airport, one of them caught her attention. She thought that his eyes were familiar. It could not be. This was the first time he was visiting her country and he was more senior, at least 20 years older. She discarded her thought and quickly moved on with the prescribed schedule.

Again, that evening, his face came back to her mind. "Who can that be? I have seen him before. I know him. How do I know him? He belongs to another country. He is the top executive of a multinational organization. Where have I met him before?"

The next day, they had arranged a tour. She happened to be guiding the tour that this gentleman was taking. It was again a surprise or coincidence. She noticed that he was silent, soft-spoken and elegant. Again, his eyes seemed too familiar. The more she looked at him, through the corner of her eye, she saw that he was reserved, silent and quite simple. She felt no reservation or barrier with him. Even though she was not of an imposing nature, she felt that this man needed guidance and protection. He was withdrawn and never cared for anybody's attention, even though she observed that he was being watched by many.

He was even reluctant to cross streets and chose to walk longer to use the designated pedestrian crossing, or over-bridge. He was rather shy and she thought that he detested any kind of risks. She held his hand and walked him to the other side of the road and he joked: "I am not as old as you think I am". They both laughed. Again, he was his silent self, withdrawn and disinterested. She even thought that he was terribly absent minded. Every time they had to cross roads, she found herself holding his arm and guiding him, whether he liked it or not. She was doing it as a duty which surprised even her. She even kept herself between the traffic and him, as if it was her duty to protect his life. He always smiled and joked and even gently protested that it was not necessary. She did not know why, but, she took on the responsibility of his well-being. She also made sure his special dietary requirements were met. So, out of courtesy, he invited her and other guides/organizers for breakfast on the day he was leaving, after the conference. The conference had actually ended the previous evening. She had an urge to come and meet him the same evening. She called him on his mobile phone. Shy as he was, he reluctantly agreed. She offered to show him the city and he went along. While walking through the old city, they spoke a lot. And he expressed his surprise at her treating him as an old man. She corrected: "No, a small boy". He laughed and laughed. She was even surprised to see him laugh. She told him that the way he carried himself, she couldn't see him as a senior official at all. In her eyes, he was a small boy, vulnerable and shy.

He laughed aloud. He could not contain his surprise and amusement at this strange young woman considering him as a child in an alien land. He also told her that he had never experienced such a situation in his life.

He said many things about business and life abroad, as well as his impressions of her country. She listened carefully. She was surprised that she craved for every word that he said. It was as if an eager mother was listening to her little son's big stories, expressing amusement and surprise at every word that he spoke. It was as if she was waiting eagerly since ages for these stories.

She almost knew what he would say next. It was like everything was pre-scripted. They had breakfast the next day and he was as formal as ever. He had a kind of silent elegance in his mannerisms and he displayed a cool respect for her always. Was it motherly or respect towards an elegant host?

He left the following day, and they communicated further. He always maintained his surprise at her treating him as a child, even though he was older than her. She always maintained her self-proclaimed mom's status. She would demand attention from him during his busiest of times and he would give it, even though amused. She would make sure that he slept on time, ate on time and even dressed up properly through expensive long distance calls. He started calling her mom. He would say: "yes, mom", "I shall do it, mom", "don't worry, mom". She became even a bit possessive about him, just like a mother would be, about her beloved son.

After many months, he told her: "I am adopting you. I will help you climb up the ladder of your career." Thus, the son adopted his mother of another life. She changed completely, after she met him. She became more bold and confident. She was sure she could tackle her sorrows more easily. She had no expectations from her son now. She just wished and prayed for his well being. The mother's love was pure and past the boundaries of time. Her soul knew very well that she had got her long lost son back. She had waited for many years, to see him again. The soul recognition was instantaneous. The mind always created questions. The son who had left her half-way in her dream had come back to complete her dreams. She had hoped that during her old age, her son would give her peace and happiness. Her son came back to give her that peace and stability in this life, in a different way. She wanted nothing but protection from this man, even though he lived so far away. She had to migrate to the new place far away from her home town to meet him. Her receiving her son of previous life at the airport was no coincidence. Her helping her son to cross the street was no coincidence. She had done similar things before. Even meeting her ex sister-in-law, her aunt in this life, was no coincidence. The sister-in-law/aunt was also consistent in her behaviour. She accused her of prostitution in her previous life, and accused her of stealing money in this life.

Now this girl of strong character is living her life in peace and happiness. There are many more comparisons and details between the past and the present. I shall not explain anymore because it is my duty to keep the privacy of this individual.

This whole story was meant to portray how character traits get carried forward, beyond time, space, country barriers. How souls unite and come together and how they help each other, over generations. There are no coincidences. There is only a grand symmetry. A larger play in action.

Checking Karma Accumulation

Our subconscious mind takes all matters literally. It does not discriminate between emotional gas and real substance. This is the truth. So, what we think or feel is very important. We are creating our destiny at each moment.

A person who repeatedly says: "I don't care about money, for me richness is nothing, we cannot carry money with us when we die," will eventually bring in poverty consciousness followed by poverty in reality. He will become poor either in this life or the next. Hence, respecting money while not being emotional about it is essential. Greed for money and indifference for money are both karmically bad. Gratitude is the solution. Being grateful for what has been given since you deserved it, and being compassionate and 'giving' is the right way to exist. Gratefulness checks karma accumulation, compassion helps cleansing too.

The shift from emotions to intellect needs a strong will. The shift from intellect to spiritual realm an even stronger will. Determination is the key. Mind will get drawn to emotions automatically. This is the nature of the mind. Remaining pure inside could be achieved through benevolent thought, words and action. Service is the best way to achieve purification. Selfless service. Talking ill about others poisons your mind first, and then those of others. It eventually poisons a generation's mind.

Prayers will certainly help. Prayers of thanks and gratitude are the best of prayers. Prayers for something will project your insufficiency. Thus such prayers will bring in more deficiency

Exhausting Karma

Q: How do we excel in our karmas?

M: Karma cannot be excelled. It can be created and exhausted. Excelling in something is a terrestrial matter. We could excel in education, in a career or in our actions. In karma, we are passing through time, parallel to time, exhausting karma and also, in most occasions, accumulating fresh ones.

Free will is to choose the higher from the lower at the given point in time. Free will is to know the truth and express it truthfully. Free will is limited. Free will is to know and express who we actually are!!! Free will is to break the bondage of endless births and deaths and attain liberation, here and now.

Enlightenment is being-ness. Enlightenment is liberation. Again, there are different levels too. Realising the self and being one with the self is the first level, after we cross the barriers of our sheaths or koshas. Once we are one with the self, we still have a body and requirements of the body. Slowly, when we detach from the elements and essentially the body, the need of the elements for our survival also gets diluted. Savikalpa Samadhi, Nirvikalpa Samadhi etc. are such states in awareness. Asamprajnaat Samadhi or Nirvikalpa Samadhi is a higher state where there is complete merging with Ultimate Reality. There is no consciousness of body or individuality left. Again, desires or vasanas, even minor ones from many distant past lives, could bring the saadhak or aspirant back to the terrestrial plane. He will need more sadhanas to break the various levels.

The soul keeps going up and down. Even after all karmas are fulfilled in this life, the soul is still pulled down. The hangover from past lives. These are called samskaras. Slowly and steadily the yogi comes out of the samskaras and after various attempts, he breaks free. The final binding is the binding of mother earth. When all things are complete—no samskaras, no karmas, no vasanas—the yogi has attained absolute purity. He takes off and the mother earth unbinds or releases the soul from herself. The complete moksha, mukti or liberation happens. Till then, there is always a struggle between soul and matter. This is the real struggle of every life. All other struggles are insignificant.

Being in the present is the first step. Being-ness in all conditions is the path and liberation of the true nature and merging with the infinity is the result.

Sense Control

Controlling senses is not easy because the very nature of senses is to go external. Senses pull the mind to external objects like a child pulling his parents towards an ice-cream shop. The senses often come back, but the mind gets stuck with those objects and moments. Just like when you see a beautiful painting or even better, a pastry. The visual impact is good and the mind recognises that this has to be something so good. The mind harbours the feeling, lingering long after the actual encounter with the sense object has occurred. Controlling of senses amounts to controlling of the mind. That is not easy.

The nature of mind is like an intoxicated monkey. Heavily restless. So, mind cannot be controlled through direct attack. Mind needs to be controlled through indirect diversions or facilitating detours into something higher and more meaningful. Control is not the right word as in reality we control nothing. Mind cannot have any vacuum. We need to fill it with higher thoughts, such as the nature of the soul or your true self, and develop contemplation (manana). Contemplation happens in the peripherals of intellect (buddhi). This allows a shift from mind to intellect. And when intellect gets tired of contemplation, it shifts to meditation—dhyana. When the shift happens to dhyana, the senses are inactive, and mind and intellect also become inactive, in a thought less state. Doingness shifts to beingness. As you progress in dhyana, the mind also stays inactive. Patanjali says: "Yoga, Chitta Vritti Nirodhaka". This means that yoga eradicates mental imaginings, or the internal debates. Automatically, mind is calm or even absent, and senses minus the aid of mind do not have any effect.

Deliberately denying senses will amount to Karma. For example, imagining that eyes must be controlled because they're luring you to pastries or blindfolding to aid control over eyes—if this was consistent enough, it would lead to blindness in the next life. This is because the subconscious mind gets the impression that you do not like to see anything or you do not want to see. So, direct 'tackling' is dangerous. Indirect way of managing the senses is the most effective method. Substituting a nagging desire with something higher is even better.

Vasanas are based on karmas. Only when there is a karmic push will there be a vasana. A person who has no inclination towards alcohol will never be tempted even if placed amidst the best brands of alcohol. If it is not in his karma to drink, the thought will not occur and naturally the action will not take place either. Vasanas will be eradicated only through their exhaustion or acting them out in this world. The karmas that provoked a birth also have a definite road map for their exhaustion.

Those who are not eligible to read this, will not get to see this. Those who are casual readers will not understand this. Those who were awaiting this message will take cue and take the next step for sure. Thus, nothing is accidental.

Higher awareness will eradicate most of the base vasanas. Higher vasanas will get dissolved as the soul gets dissolved in the supreme. Till then, objectivity and awareness are the best methods. Being aware of each thought, word and action. Nothing is unconscious. Karma cleansing takes place because you are in the present.

Trust I have made this clear.

Good And Bad Karma

Q: People suffer in life mainly because of their bad karma. But why is it that sometimes we are punished although we haven't committed anything bad? Like some people have a lot of money, maybe they are born with it and they don't have to struggle at all for money. On the other hand many other people have to work hard just to meet their minimum requirements. Similarly, many people get good partners, good children, career, name, fame, etc. whereas many others are unlucky.

M: People suffer in life because of their ignorance. Suffering means ignorance. Having pain is karma. Suffering due to that is non-awareness. There is no such thing as good karma or bad karma. Karma is just one. We categorize it as good or bad based on our limited faculties such as mind and intellect. This is also influenced by social, educational and political conditionings. As far as the soul is concerned, all happenings are just experiences. There are no classifications. All discriminations are happening at the mind level. And only in the conscious mind level.

Understand that the senses connected to the mind are churning and procuring lots of data. Usually the conscious mind does not discriminate the inputs. We gather data from everything through every sense and feed the impressions into our own subconscious mind. That's a huge data bank. It has data from all your lives still stored there. Its capacity is huge. It will store data without discriminating. So the deeper the residue, the easier it is to turn into what you call karma, or the capacity for an experience related to that. So, when we go into the world and virtually experience various things, the subconscious that does not discriminate, will consider it as real or something you wanted to store or experience and keep a residue for further, similar experiences. There are no punishments. It is only what you chose to experience 'subconsciously'.

Your experiences will depend on what you have in your bag. Children are also individual souls with individual karmas. Your feeling of ownership is only as long as you exist in this body. The more you exhaust karmas with objectivity and awareness, the fewer are the complications. When confusing data is fed into your subconscious, confusing results will happen. Detachment to everything and assuming the nature of your soul, as a witness, will take the suffering away from your pain. When someone asked Bhagawan Ramana Maharshi: "Do you feel pain?" (Maharshi was suffering from cancer.) He said: "There is pain, but there is no suffering." This is witness-consciousness.

You only get what you deserve and not what you desire. This is one of the fundamental laws of our existence.

Right or Wrong Behaviour

Q: When we behave badly with someone that adds on to our bad karma. But how do we determine what kind of behaviour is wrong? For example, if I am a manager in a company, I have to make sure work gets done smoothly. In this process, I might have to take to task certain employees who are not doing their job properly, and scold them time and again. Similarly, I might have a maid working in my house, she might be lazy and she might do the same mistake again and again, despite repeated corrections. So obviously we will have to scold her. Similarly we might have lots of arguments with other people to stand by what we believe in. So in such cases, will such behaviour constitute bad karma?

M: Karma is produced through thoughts, words and action. These are the three levels of our playing with energy. Energy is released through thoughts, words and action. There is nothing wrong nor nothing right. It is highly relative. If you feel good with a certain action, if it expands your heart chakra, that's good for you. It all depends on what you want to experience from life. If you want to experience love, you must release love consistently. The world is like a mirror. You see what you choose to see. You can put on masks or you can stand naked. This is your free will.

While existing in the corporate world, be careful, your inside should remain unaffected. Anger, if pretended, is your strength. Ego, if pretended to prove a point, is your strength. This does not increase your palpitation. This is the sign that you must watch. If you are genuinely angry or egoistic, then that's your weakness. When you have weaknesses, your self-esteem is highly affected. Others can take advantage of you. It's the same with expectations. Our expectations from people create negativities within us. We often fail to see that the other person is just acting out his/her karma, which may not suit our expectation. Every action creates karma, unless all actions are performed in perfect witness consciousness or objectivity without emotions. Just like petrol behaves in a car. It does its job perfectly well, but does not influence you on your journey. This is exactly the attitude of your soul too.

So, there are no bad karmas, just sundry experiences.

Karma, New or Old

Q: While we are going through the present life, how do we know whether we are accumulating new karmas or exhausting previous ones?

M: This is very difficult to understand. The karmas which provoked a birth will also find fulfillment in the course of life, one way or the other. This is because when the soul takes the body, it chooses from millions of permutations and combinations. It would be wrong to say that just like we sit at the table and choose our food, the soul chooses an existence. The soul automatically navigates towards the platform where it could unburden the karmas that it carries. It takes a suitable body to accomplish that, at the right location and time.

What remains unfulfilled at the time of death, if that can be quantified at all, is to be acquired in the next life. Otherwise, the karmas from the past life (prarabdha) and the newly acquired karmas (aagamya) join together like milk and water. It is very difficult to separate them. In the way the Paramhamsa (celestial swan) drinks only the milk from the mixture of milk and water, the wise one refrains from accumulating too many new karmas. Karmas provoke vasanas and vasanas provoke thoughts, thoughts provoke words and words provoke action. This is the chronology of action.

When the senses are disciplined, when they are detached or not running after sense objects, when the mind is always with the predominantly active sense at any point of time, totally rooted in the present, karma accumulation will be minimal. When tongue is at work, that is, when you are eating, when the mind is with the tongue absolutely, then you are in the present. You will be totally conscious. When this existence is repetitive, unconsciousness vanishes and consciousness takes root. Men become rooted in the present. Consciousness leads to conscious awareness, which in turn leads to the awareness—bliss state, the turiya state.

So in short, it's not easy to separate between the brought-forward karma and the daily accumulation. This is especially true since karma happens through thought, words and action. So, even an inactive man creates karma at every moment.

Money, Comforts and Karma

Q: Many men who are 'rich' (in terms of owning land, houses, properties, money, irrespective of the way they might have earned it) are enjoying power and luxurious lives that gives the impression that only money leads to power and comforts in life. While thinking about how to make more money, they're losing all their morals. This also gives the impression that the man who is poor, or not rich, has no value in society. How to make up our minds? Living in this kind of society, how can we move on with 'awareness', 'love' and 'bless the world'? How can this be made effective and known to the world? How much time will it take to change? Or is it possible that change may not happen?

M: This question is apt for our time. Perhaps it has been apt for every time. We shall analyze the questions together.

We will start by ignoring the maya factor, just for clarity's sake. Prarabdha karma is the cause for taking a body. This consists of the seeds or engrams: deep impressions left in the canvas of the previous life, plus whatever impressions we have retained from all the lives of the past. The sum total of it provokes a new life, at a time and space suitable for acting out these incomplete vasanas.

Thus the child is born to a particular set of parents, with the sole aim of exhausting his/her inherent prarabdha. It has no other aim. Once the child is born, the parents and the relatives will name it, tag it and make it realise as it grows up, that it is part of a particular family, particular society, particular country and even a particular class, subclass and other categories. Therefore, the child gets branded. As it gets accustomed to the world outside, it forgets about its past lives and its mission. It sets foot on the soil as a fresh individual. The life begins, as a new name and a new form. It starts out acting its own new life, which is guided by its prarabdha karma. It does not know that, as it cannot see its past. Nor can it see the future. So in a way, it is blinded.

Apart from an able body, it possesses a strong and overpowering weapon called the mind. The mind starts interpreting good things and bad things according to the available data of happiness, sorrow etc. along with the inevitable social conditionings.

The society effectively programs the child as a social being and social status becomes important. He/she works out a social status through hard work and luck, which is nothing but prarabdha in disguise, and sets out to exercise his/her power. Ego works there. Status is translated into ego. He/she shouts and roars for recognition. A new lion has landed!!!

"Parame Brahmani Kopina Sakta" (it is surprising that nobody considers the only permanent 'brahman', the soul inside man).

The electricity that runs this engine is ignored and a society-programmed, unconscious existence gets executed. He embarks on a money-making spree, which means money, power and control. He executes his power at will. Ego blinds his vision. Ritualistic worship (and even that is to show his mettle or ensure supremacy) become a habit. Religion and worship—both become tools for expressing his pomposity.

After living a life of this kind, time arrives for his exit from this soil—time to die. Slowly, the realization dawns—nothing can save him. Money, power, position, relatives, friends, property, gold, are all left behind. He is leaving empty-handed. As he dies, he rewinds his life to the beginning. "What have I experienced? What did I do?" None of the material concerns really matter then. It's only the spiritual connectivity with the Higher which will help him see the 'bright light'. The exiting soul, after leaving the gross, goes through a confused state. The first feeling of lightness is confusing. After living for so long in this gross body, the soul does not know where to go. There has been no meditation or higher experience ever in life. It moves around, looking at the body that encased it once, looking at the crying relatives, looking at the property, cars and other things, which are absolutely meaningless to the departed soul. A soul which is constantly in touch with the higher realms through meditation, will touch those realms the very moment it leaves the physical sheath. So, this is the essential difference.

Life is a continuous stream from death to birth and birth to death. The propulsion is due to karma. Material possessions are based on your karmic access. It's as simple as understanding that those who starve in one life, take birth in a place where food is abundant, and crave for food. This is visible in daily life. Likewise, poor can be born rich in next life, just like those who feel guilty of having money can be born poor in the next life. The cycle is self-created.

All in all, each person is experiencing his/her karmic agenda. There is no good or bad. It's not the mission of elevated beings to convert anybody. They only work as road signs, as neutral pointers, and those who choose to use the road signs will reach the destination. Those who ignore road signs might reach the destination, but after many detours and delays. That's all. Greed for money is part of one soul's karmic agenda while benevolence is also part of another soul's karmic agenda. What you need to follow depends on what you are born to experience. If you craved for money and power in this life and could not reach it, you will achieve that in the next life. It all depends on how deep your craving is.

Hope I have done justice to your question.

Children and Parents

Q: My daughter is getting increasingly indifferent and erratic. I will turn 62 this year. I do not have the strength to fight her. I never treated my parents like this. She is involved in rehabilitating old people in the street, but she does not care about me, her own mother. Why is this happening to me? What can I do?

M: Understand that your daughter is essentially a karmic being. You never chose your daughter. Once she appeared in your life, you started considering her as your daughter. Then, you started being possessive. Then you started becoming increasingly protective, even at the cost of restricting her movements. She started revolting, because as an adult, she thinks she knows what she wants and how to get it. Whether this notion is true or false is not the question. The fact that this notion exists is the fundamental truth.

As a child, she had to obey you, or else . . . As an adult, she has carved her own freedom. The balance slowly tilted in her favour. You said, your age is bringing in weakness. She is stronger than you now. This is what you are experiencing today.

Two points here. Over-possessiveness or over-protectiveness will not help relationships. Likewise, over-indifference does not help relationships either. There should be love and care. We must understand that a soul came into our family because it knew that it could exhaust whatever agenda it brought from the past, through this platform. The child is pure. We start conditioning them. We start burdening them and pressurizing them to create the 'competitive edge'. We and society, hand in hand, create stress, anxieties, fears and guilt in them. Thus, we 'break' the child to the 'standards' of our society. The child is under stress and when it becomes an adult it becomes irritable or insensitive. Karmically speaking, the child deserved it because that was probably its agenda. Socially speaking, we just created another brick on the wall!

Each person strictly undergoes his/her karmic agenda, whether they are related or not. Karma is predominantly individualistic. People come together on one common platform such as family, society or country, because they have a similar karmic agenda to exhaust. Karma propels life. Karma-less situations propel exit from life, which we call death. Lack of karma is not always the cause of death, it is also accumulation of karma that cannot be exhausted with the current infrastructure, such as body, mind, intellect and circumstances. The soul then needs another body at another location, to exhaust the newly accumulated karmas as well as the past hangover.

The next main point is that, our possessiveness happens also due to our insecurities. The more possessive and restricted you are about your child, the higher the chances are that the child will rebel and break free. This is also because you are restricting its karmic freedom. At the same time, just letting them loose in careless abandon, might not be the right way either.

Love is the remedy. Kindness and love will strengthen relationships. Keep displaying unconditional love and feel love towards one another. Also, grow beyond your immediate family and spread your love around. The more you display love, the more you will get. The more we give, the more we get.

If you suppress affection and just keep having expectations, you will only create frustrations within. If you also embark on projects to assist the downtrodden, I am sure, you will develop a special bonding with your daughter. You will be talking her language.

The concept of fighting her will not work, whether you have the strength for it or not. Only love will work. Understand that the more you fight, the more your ego will be active, and the more you will suffer. Fighting does not solve anything. Wars create destruction and devastation. Love is the balm. Love unconditionally. You will also receive love from various other people. You will not feel lonely anymore. In today's world of induced competitiveness, we need lots of love as an antidote for all the established negativities and habits. If you start loving and participating in her humanitarian projects, in a few days your relationship will flourish. Also, please remember to trash all the past grudges or differences in opinions. If you bring the past emotional wounds to the present, it will spoil the present as well as the future.

Love all, Serve all. Love anyway. Love and only Love.

Samskaras-Endless Lives

We have had numerous lives. Each soul has assumed many bodies and has experienced many situations and conditions, happiness and sorrow. Every situation has created numerous impressions. Some impressions stayed and some vanished in the course of time. Impressions of events along with their corresponding emotions created karmas. Impressions without corresponding emotions disappeared into oblivion. Thus, our soul travelled up and down through birth and death.

The soul has never been polluted. It remained pure. It can never be polluted.

The impressions that the soul carried through lives became the character or the personality. The present environment perfected or adapted the basic traits. The basic traits always existed, through time and eternity. This also means some habits, some attachments, some emotions, some fears, some insecurities, some phobias, so on and so forth. Not knowing or not being aware of the entanglement of all these impressions, man lives his life. In the waking moments, the immediate name, fame and social position dominate his existence. He becomes that. At night in sleep, he nullifies all these unconsciously. While in deep sleep he forgets his name, gender, location and position. Thus he assumes distinct roles and nullifies them every day. Yet, the truth lurks between these two states. The soul sees the truth, but never interferes. The subconscious triggers realities based on the data that it gets to digest, which the heavily under-privileged conscious mind feeds. The sum total of a regular man's existence is a kind of un-mindful helplessness or in other words, complete oblivion.

The only time perhaps he gets to see the reality is at the time of his death when he feels the lightness of being and feels a state of non-attachment to every object that he thought was essential for his survival on earth. The soul never had a doubt. And it acted only as petrol in the car. When the petrol is finished, the car must stop. It stopped. The soul carried the backlog of the existing samskaras and went in pursuit of the next womb to launch another life. Birth, death, re-birth, re-death . . . the story continues.

A woman had many children and she cried a lot and created a deep impression that she wanted to have no children. Since that was not possible in that life, she took birth again to experience a life without children. In that life, since she did not understand her past life with lots of children and her associated agony, she craved for children. Since her previous agenda was different from her present craving that she developed in this life, she comes back again in another life, a third life, to have several children. When will this end? One needs to have higher awareness to get out of it.

One person hated another so much that he told him in extreme anger: "I will come back only to kill you." They both died and both took birth in the same mother's womb as siblings. Right from childhood, they fought with each other and made each others' lives miserable. They almost killed each other and eventually one caused the other's death. We must be careful about what we think, say or do. It can all become our samskaras.

One person was a servant in a rich man's house. The rich man had a bar and this boy used to serve the man and his guests exotic wines. He never got to drink any. He took another birth, that of an alcoholic and his main agenda of existence was drinking alcohol. Nobody could change him. He died young.

A starving man became obese because of overeating. One who thought that having plenty of food at home was 'sinful' because of the starvation in the world, was re-born amongst poverty. One who was a butcher became an animal in his next life and got butchered and suffered extreme fear and agony of death. One woman who had forsaken and humiliated many men enchanted by her beauty, living a life of arrogance, in her next life got married several times and in all these marriages, her husbands abused her.

How many lives!!! How many combinations!!! What are we running for? All people seem to be terribly busy. All seem to be slaves of their own minds. All people seem to struggle in their every existence. A few break free. Those wise men did break free, but their society could not understand them. Society sometimes even tried to kill them, because it could not understand them. Men conquer everything except their own mind and often lose everything because of their own mind. It's perpetual agony.

A story . . .

Alexander the Great was getting ready to 'conquer the world'. Before he set out on his journey, he went to seek the blessings of his teacher Aristotle. He asked Aristotle: "When I come back, what would you like me to bring for you?" Aristotle said: "If you can get me a truly enlightened saint from India, I will be truly happy." He replied: "No problem, if they are available there, I will get you many."

He went around, conquered many a lands, many a kingdoms and reached India. He conquered whatever was ahead of him, defeated kings and established his empire and called himself Alexander the Great. He decided to return back and remembered the promise to his teacher. He asked his chief of army to fetch him a 'good quality saint'. The army chief asked all wise men and they all said that there was one such saint inside the forest—a true saint, an enlightened Master. He sent his army to fetch this man. They found him sleeping completely naked on a rock right under the sun. Both the sun and the rock were burning hot. They were confused. How could this naked and obviously mad man be a great saint? Anyway, they caught him and brought him to the city. They covered him with some clothes and presented him to Alexander. Alexander was not at all impressed by his appearance—shabby, long matted hair, unbathed, unclean and unshaven. He discreetly made sure that his soldiers had not made a mistake. Everyone confirmed that this one is of good quality.

Alexander tried to impress this saint by telling him about the riches of his land. He tried to develop a conversation.

The saint kept saying: "Take me back to my rock."

Finally, Alexander was fed up. He asked: "What do you want from me?"

The saint asked: "What do you have?" Alexander said: "All the land from here till eternity belongs to me. I am the world conqueror." The saint laughed aloud to Alexander's greatest annoyance.

He asked: "Show me what you have conquered."

Alexander said: "It's spread out and I cannot show it just like that." The saint asked for a wooden ruler and a wooden plank. Someone brought both. He placed the wooden ruler under the wooden plank, like a see saw. He asked Alexander to stay balanced on top of it. Alexander could not.

The saint said: "All that you 'seem' to have conquered has already returned back to normal life. You cannot conquer any people, any places, anything. If you felt you conquered anything or achieved anything, it is only a burden of your own ego. There is only one conquest which is worthwhile—that of your own mind. You are far from conquering that. All other conquests could stay with you only till your grave, at the most. So do not be so proud of yourself."

Alexander was furious. He commanded the saint to be 'thrown back into the forest'. He went back without any saint from India because he did not want to carry this unwelcome annoyance and botheration back to his country of birth.

When he reached his teacher's house it was early morning and Aristotle was meditating inside his room with the doors open, facing the young sun. When Alexander came to the door, the sun was blocked and Aristotle opened his eyes.

Alexander said: "I have come back victorious but I could not fulfill your wish of bringing a saint from India. They are all so ugly and rude, they are not worthy of presentation to a noble soul like you. Please tell me Master, what else can I give you?" Aristotle simply said: "Move away, let the sunshine fall on me."

Alexander walked away in utter dismay. He could not understand why his teacher was not impressed at all. He said: "All these saints are alike. They always manage to annoy me."

I do not know whether this story is true or not. Just do not worry too much about the names of the characters and their historical importance. Just look at the context and understand the message.

Selfless doing

Q: You said being in perfect witness state doesn't create any karma, is it the case even if the deed I am doing is not good?

M: In perfect witness state, you are not the doer. You will be just an instrument. So all your actions will be selfless. You will see yourself responding to situations and doing whatever is best from your side, without emotional attachment or craving for glory. This cannot be negative at all.

Dropping desires

The three levels of creation are thought, word and action. The fourth level of creation is collective consciousness. Thoughts, words and actions are coming from vasana, basic inherent desire. Constitution creates thought, word and action. Behind the vasana is the karma. This is the clock: karma—vasana—thought—word—action, and again it creates karma. That is why we keep taking one birth after another. We cannot stop it because we produce new karma every moment. Then we have more desires, and more thoughts happen.

If someone does not have a desire to smoke, he will never smoke. If you suppress something, it will sprout at the right point in time. You cannot suppress anything in life and move ahead. You cannot suppress anything for a long period of time. It is like a spring, if kept suppressed for some time, it just takes one time that you take your hand out and it springs up, bounces back. Similarly, whatever you suppress, that desire will spring up and will become a reality in your life at some point of time. You must experience things and move on.

Each person shows expressions based on the consciousness that they exist in. If you require lot of knowledge to satisfy intellect, then you will read a lot. You will join classes to acquire knowledge. You will be provoked to attend classes. Desire makes you move from one place to another. Desire for an ice-cream will take you to the place of ice-cream. When you want an ice-cream you also pull your friend with you. You come together because karma brings you together. Otherwise you cannot come together; you will not express anything together.

The place where you are born, the events you went through, everything is predetermined through your prarabdha karma, the karma which provoked your existence. Unfulfilled desires at the time of death provoked this existence. You went to the right womb and right place, where you can start the journey and effortlessly complete this journey. We take birth and simply go through the journey. While we are going through life, we add more karma. When we do not have enough petrol to complete the added journey, as our agenda increases, we take another birth!

What is jnyana (gnyana)? Jnyana or knowledge is only for the mind or intellect, mostly intellect. If jnyana becomes a rope to climb higher in spirituality, then it is good. If jnyana creates ego, it becomes a burden. Craving for understanding the fabric of life is in everybody. When we take birth, we operate from limited consciousness. The intellect (buddhi) is from this life. The consciousness is from the other lives. The soul, which is like the petrol of your car, cannot operate on this level if you do not allow it to. How will you reach your soul? The same mind which goes out with the senses should be brought back. It should penetrate sheath by sheath. Then it can reach the soul. That is why sadhana has to be intense. Desires may be intense in the beginning, then they will drop off. When you achieve Shiva, there are no desires.

SOUL

Soul's Purposes

Q: You had mentioned that every soul has a purpose in taking a birth. So before taking birth, will the soul be aware of all the experiences (good and bad) it will have to go through once it has taken birth?

M: Every soul carries baggage, which consists of various impressions, from various lives, which provokes more births. This is also what we call prarabdha. Otherwise, the aim of the soul, if left alone, would be a complete merger with the Supreme Father, which is perpetual bliss state. Soul has no discrimination between good and bad. This is just the problem of your conscious mind. Even when you exist in your sleep, you are not discriminating. In the deep sleep state you are 'more or less' experiencing the state of the soul. 'Less' because you have neither 'I' consciousness nor awareness. Soul has awareness. This means, at that level it has the capacity to witness events. In the timeless state, the past, present and future do not exist. In that state, all you might experience in the future has already happened. This is what Krishna explained to Arjuna in the 11th chapter of Bhagawad Gita, through his Viswa Roopa Darshana (through the display of his cosmic form).

Q: I understand that the reason we meet people is also because of a residue which helps us to recognize souls, and I guess I'm asking for only the good and constructive memories and happy soul connections. Is it possible to leave behind the destructive stuff?

M: The soul is always neutral, like the petrol of your car. Soul does not wish to have any baggage, just like human beings detest all burdens. Every thought, word and action creates vibrations. They stay in the ethereal plane. Then later on they become our realities.

There are various koshas or sheaths in our system that stores various impressions from our everyday life. The major sheaths are physical, emotional, mental, pranic, etheric, causal (a very important one, because this is where the seeds of all your past engrams, deeply imprinted subtle impressions, are restored), nirvanic etc. Various impressions are carried in different layers. When the seeds are burned in the causal layer, there will not be any birth because the soul departs with no baggage. After all the engrams are exhausted, the soul will not come back. Even if it comes back, it would be based on higher karma which would be like leading lots of people to higher awareness etc. True saints are mostly in this plane. This is called a dharmic existence.

The supreme aim of every soul is to get back home, which is the lap of the universal father, the Almighty. The path to reach this status is perpetual witness consciousness. Good and bad are part of the discriminatory faculty of the conscious mind. Equanimity will be achieved through the wisdom that we are essentially the eternal spirit, pure and divine. All the baggage then, both good and bad will vanish and instead of doingness, beingness will take its place. It's total detachment from the fruits of your actions, irrespective of whether it's good or bad.

Understand Yourself

Q: I cannot understand you, Mohanji. You are confusing me.

M: Ha! Ha! Why do you have to understand me, my friend? Understand yourself first. Only then can you understand another. Why do you worry about my physical frame or the words that I utter? Understand your own thought process. Then you can see mine. Why do you worry about my action? Be with your own action, be conscious. Love yourself, then you can feel love everywhere. Your own soul is your greatest guru. When you understand your own soul, you will understand all souls. They are all one.

The World

Q: Why is the whole world reeling in insecurity?

M: The world consists of its children, its inhabitants. When a soul decides to take a body, it knows very well that its existence in that body is temporary. There begins the insecurity. So, insecurity has its root right at the existence level. Therefore, in order to remove the root cause of insecurity, you must get back to the soul level. I hope this is clear. Secondly, since the world consists of people, the world will reflect the thoughts, words and action of the people. Emotions accent insecurity and insecurity breeds emotions—it's a kind of a vicious circle.

Q: How to get out of this vicious circle?

M: Only through higher awareness. Only through conscious understanding of how the system functions.

While on Earth

Some fish can exist only close to the surface, in lesser density, but they are also more vulnerable because they can easily become a prey to birds. Fish species in denser waters are safer, but they can't easily come up — the lower density water does not suit them. They always exist in the dark, deep down in the ocean.

Just like the fish that swim on top of the water cannot exist in a denser level, a soul that has come from a much higher plane, cannot exist in a denser plane for long without adapting to the density and forgetting its higher being state. Invariably, if you look at the outside world, you can see many such people being considered a failure in the material plane while the denser souls (who know how to 'play the game' of density) have terrestrial success. So the success and failure comparison has no meaning that way, unless we know where we have come from. The soul that exists in the subtler realm is already a higher being which has come here out of compassion and though it cannot compete with another denser being, it can always easily relate with higher beings and succeed through their Grace. This kind of soul will be internally craving for the company of the higher entities, for communion with higher entities. It will naturally look for activities like Kriya or other sadhana (like Bhakti Yoga, Karma Yoga etc.) through which it can elevate itself. So the tejus/brightness is already there, and though the soul recognizes it, the 'substratum', the mind and intellect, cannot recognize it.

So what happens when a higher soul decides to come to the denser plane and why does this happen? First of all, the other souls from that plane are always aware of this soul's decision and they make sure this soul is aware of what it's getting into, and what to expect. The differences between these planes are so huge. Here are some examples:

1. Multiplication—on higher planes, souls multiply at will. 'For example, if they need to create another being, they just expand and segregate themselves into another being—they make another being out of themselves. Unlike the denser plane, where you have to go through the process of physical union and then gestation, in subtle realms beyond the earth, there is instant multiplication at will.

2. Communication—since words are denser than thoughts, on that plane of thoughtless state, a thought itself is a conversation. A thought itself is loud enough!

3. There is no ownership on that plane—in this denser plane, relationships mainly boil down to ownership. In that plane, there is no ownership, it is all complementing. Meaning, you exist and if you don't need to exist separately, you can also merge into another soul (just like one box can go into another box and another box etc.). So let's say ten people can merge into one—that's possible. Because the bliss state is absolute, and only and completely an energy state. So these souls are always experiencing the Father, what in India is called the Parabrahma state—this is Heaven.

4. Oneness and duality—on this earthly plane, there are always dualities (man and woman, night and day, etc). So wherever dualities exist, it will always be difficult and you have to go through the process—creation and demolition, joy and suffering, physical decay, etc. It is therefore natural that there is so much confusion and lack of clarity on this plane—how to go about all this, how to go through all these experiences that are so unlike what the soul remembers from the higher planes? That is why higher souls make those souls who are about to go to a denser plane aware: "It's fine that you want to go to a denser plane out of compassion, to help as many terrestrial beings as you can and elevate them to higher awareness. But you also will have to experience all these problems too! If you still want to do it, then do it." But then what makes one get stuck in the denser plane are the RELATIONSHIPS (my father, my mother, my, my, my . . .). Thus,

relationships become a catch, emotions become the glue and those souls cannot go higher than the astral plane—they lack the lightness that would take them to their original realm, but have to oscillate between the astral plane and the physical plane again and again until all the karmas are worked out. In that way, many deaths and births come to be.

However, fortunately on the higher plane, time and space do not exist because there is no duality. So the number of lives one had before final elevation, does not really matter all that much—it's all amounting to EXPERIENCES.

Therefore, the more one exhibits compassion, selfless service, unconditional love, he/she will be serving the soul's purpose of relieving itself from the density and coming finally home.

In this process of shedding the density while on earth, denser souls catch hold of the lighter souls to help them elevate themselves—in the way a basket connected to a helium balloon of lesser density, one gets to float up. Likewise, it is also possible that in the way a drowning man clutches and sometimes pulls his rescuer down to the depths of the water, the rescuer could get trapped too.

That explains also the importance of being in the presence of the elevated beings, the true Masters. Among the Masters currently present on earth, there are differences. Some are like balloons with helium, and some are like rockets! Anything is possible. Everything is available.

Conscious Mind and Character Difference

Conscious mind has limitations. First of all, limitations about space: this is usually related to the person who occupies that mind, limitations of actual external space, space of the mind (capacities), these always confined to waking hours. Conscious mind is usually related to one terrestrial existence. It is used to experience only the current existence. The emotional residue from the current existence gets stored in our subconscious. This is what the soul carries at the time of death. Conscious mind can access whatever is stored in this life. It cannot access what is stored from our other lives.

The soul that enlivens our conscious mind has done so over many lives. It has enlivened many conscious minds, as many as the births that one has taken. Each conscious mind has been independent. Each conscious mind has been individualistic. It has never consciously shared any characteristic from any other life that the same soul has enlivened. Even though conscious mind is individualistic, it still expresses the habits, nature and characteristics that this soul has faithfully carried over many lives. This is why some children display distinct diversity in character from their parents. A child born in the clan of academicians, professors or scientists could eventually become a sailor, a completely different profession, to the utter dismay of the whole members in that clan or family.

Song of the Soul

In the spiritual heart of everyone, there is a deep craving for expression. It gets sidelined, nullified and even distorted in the mental confusion of terrestrial existence. True expression is that of our real self. Man searches for temporary glories and paltry achievements. Man rolls through these short-lived glories till death and continues again in another life. We fail to understand that our mind is lingering in temporary happiness given by trivial pleasures while searching for permanent happiness. Time after time, life after life, many wise men have tried their best to get man out of his illusions. They tried to guide man to himself or oneself. Still, man cannot understand who he actually is!!! Many got stuck in ritualistic spiritual practices. Many wandered on the intellectual plane all their lives, which gave them a false feeling of spiritual supremacy and social elevation, mistaking intellectual knowledge for spiritual experience. Many tried to categorize and compare. Very few reached the other bank of the river, using the available boat and the boatman. Their only possessions were faith and patience. So simple. That was enough to cross the river.

The deepest craving of every man is a sincere spiritual expression. Since it is intangible, man sought tangible terrestrial expressions as a substitute for the real one. It never gave him lasting happiness. It also gave him false appetite which eventually hindered one's spiritual digestive system.

I am the source. I am the powerhouse. I do not become tired or depleted, ever. I am just like the candle that can light many candles and still maintain the same glow and glory. Just like one sun gets reflected in many objects without losing its intensity and energy, through the cycle of generation, I exist. I am the string that kept the generations together. I am the only imperishable entity in this highly perishable earthly existence. Sun, moon and stars are formed out of me. Galaxies are within me. All forms of deities are formed out of me. Darkness is non-existence of light. Being me is non-existence of maya or illusion. I am everything. I am the in-dweller of all beings. There is no hierarchy or supremacy. I exist with the same intensity in all beings. Beings are different, in looks, in feel, in characteristics. I am the same. I am changeless. I am everywhere. I am one-ness.

I have no form. I assume the form of the vessel that contains me. I assume the characteristics of the being that encases me. Even though I remain neutral always, I empower actions, words and thoughts. No one can touch or feel me. One can only realize me. One has to become me, reach my subtlety, to realize me. One has to shed a lot of gross-ness to reach me, recognize me and understand me. I have no agenda. I assume the agenda of the being and, like a faithful and non-interfering servant serve the embodied entity till the end. I allow myself to be trapped in the body. I assume the body. I allow myself to be called the body. I even pretend I am the limited body. I never interfere. I liberate myself at will.

Possessions and money cannot buy me, because I am that. Relationships cannot bind me, because I am that and beyond that. Whatever you offer me is mine. Whatever you cannot give me is also mine. All are expressions of myself. Nothing is ever separate from me. You can only achieve me by being me.

Over time, I have expressed my essence through a multitude of characters in the divine play that I created. I chose the characters. I chose the drama. I have been both, the demon and the saviour. I have also been the worshipper and the worshipped. My intense form is considered as god. My weaker expression is considered as embodied beings. I am not attached to any of the characteristics that the body portrays. I am beyond all afflictions that the body and mind are vulnerable to. Just like the rain, I enter terrestrial existence. Just like the water becomes vapour, I dissolve in thin air. I come and go at will. I exist at will and exit at will.

Those who have found me, recognized me and become one with me, become all powerful. They will be freed from all terrestrial needs. Elements will not bind them or bother them anymore. Earth just becomes a platform for their seemingly gross expression and existence.

Those who only pretend to have become one with me, will reveal their anxieties and fears time after time. They will crave for name, money and fame, using my name and status called self-realization. I cannot be achieved through books or rituals. I cannot be reached by searching outside. I can only be reached through introversion, introspection, contemplation and meditation on one's own self.

I can only be reached through constant elevation of one's deserving levels. Deserving levels cannot be elevated when terrestrial pulls are equally strong. A man who has firm desire to reach me, but also cannot leave the terrestrial vasanas, will reach only the lower branches of the tree, and will never attain the fruit situated at the higher branches. They may see the fruit afar, and even boast that they have got the fruit. However, desire cannot become deserving level and it will definitely show, if the society that entertains such people has keen eyes to see the reality. One can only wake up those who are actually asleep, not the ones who pretend to sleep. Only those who have eyes will see. Blind cannot and will not. And this is fine for them. Leave them alone. Do not disturb them.

When a man sees his own reflection in all beings around him, and due to that, when love and compassion overflows from his heart, he becomes me, he realizes me. When a man sees his own reflection in the eyes of all beings around him, he becomes one with all the beings. His personality merges with them and theirs with him. All differences disappear. All forms disappear. Then that which remains is pure consciousness, only oneness. In this oneness, all identities vanish. The man becomes me, my form. The man becomes one with the universe. He moves from the ignorance of limited existence to the vastness of super conscious existence. There are no aspirations anymore. There is only awareness of who he is, of his full stature and the associated bliss. Ignorance is darkness. Bliss is awareness. Man merges with all entities to form one universal entity.

Deserving levels are increased through detachment from all that earth can offer. Being happy, non-resistant and staying beyond expectations makes one fully liberated. For such a person existence becomes bliss. There are no worries about one's physical defects or discomforts. Those people fall in tune with the rhythm of creation. When expectations leave the mind completely, I fill in. When resistance leaves the mind, mind becomes subtle and I fill in. When needs of the body are not quiet, I cannot express fully. In the profound depth of silence, the only voice that you will hear is that of my heartbeat. This is the father of all the sounds. The sound and the listener becomes one! When the sound becomes the listener, we come back home again and realise—I am THAT.

SPIRITUAL PROGRESS

How to Measure Spiritual Progress?

SIMPLICITY IS ONE criterion. Reduction of dependency on external elements is the second. Change in the type and quality of friends is the third.

Simplicity: the thought process becomes simpler. There will be fewer complications in lifestyle and you will prefer a simple but elegant existence. This includes simple food, often only a vegetarian sattvic diet, simple clothing and simple lifestyle. If you force yourself, it will not work. It should happen to you, based on your evolution levels. Simplicity is godliness. The closer you are to God, the more simple you become. You become more independent. You will have fewer terrestrial needs.

Dependency: the more spiritually evolved you become, the more self-sufficient you become. You will automatically drop external gadgets for your internal gratification. Dependency will reduce considerably and accumulation will also stop. Accumulation of anything, including wealth, knowledge or even relationships. Life becomes simple and elegant. Mind becomes more objective. Thought process becomes clearer and unbiased. Saints and higher Masters start appearing in your life, because you became eligible to receive them. Whether a particular type of food is available or not, you will be the same. Whether a particular environment is available or not, you will be the same. Thus, dependency on anything, even people, will steadily reduce and you will become more and more liberated.

Friends leave too: as we evolve into a new stage, new friends appear. The old ones drop off, unless they also evolve at the same pace that we do. Usually, people evolve spiritually, at their own pace. So, it is likely that those who cannot understand or recognize this aspect in their friend will cease to communicate with him. This means parting. So, when friends drop away and detach themselves, it could be a sign of your evolution. A different set of friends will appear at each stage. Even in a family each person's evolution will be different. Husband, wife and children will have different levels of evolution. They also get alienated from each other. This is only natural. Even our own relatives will become alienated from us, because our tracks change at some point in life.

So, not everyone may understand your spiritual growth. Hence, take it easy. Do not expect them to. Just let them be. Just let it go. Be kind to everyone. Help all. Love all.

Q: I have been observing someone close to me and I do not think that there is any spiritual progress. After spending so much time with God, why is the person not progressing spiritually?

M: First of all, do not judge another person's spiritual progress. You do not have the authority to do that. Nobody has the authority to judge another person because they cannot see his / her karma which makes them progress or get blocked. Secondly, what do you mean by spending time with God? Is God an external entity? What is your concept about God? Does God experience loneliness, does he ask someone to give him/her company? Understand that God is omnipresent. God is beyond all forms and is all forms. There is no separate God away from us. All are God. All are aspects of God. I believe what you meant by the expression "spending so much time with God" was ritualistic worship or chanting. It is true that rituals hardly produce evolution. Rituals are usually habits. A ritual easily becomes another habit without which we feel incomplete. Unconscious habits cannot help spiritual evolution. So in that context I am not surprised that the person is not evolving. But I still would like to appeal to you to avoid judging another person as well as yourself. You do not know your karmic agenda either. Remember that. Also, comparison is not possible in spirituality. Everyone is walking his/her own path to the same destination. Lastly, God does not need your time. God needs nothing. We need God because God is the final destination of every soul. God has no insecurities in your absence or indifference. We have that issue. Let us not compare God's consciousness with our waking state. So everything is for ourselves. Nothing is for God. Understand this clearly. God Bless You.

Feeling Lost

Q: I feel really disturbed. Never before had I such a feeling. I don't want to talk to anybody, don't want to see anybody. I feel I have had enough. My gains in life are a big zero. I had dreams but I have not achieved anything. My mind does not work the way I want.

M: The mind is a magician. It can create a situation which would seem extremely real. And it makes you believe that it's real for sure. It's like a dream. We need to wake up to realize that the nightmare was false. We have not been affected. Likewise, an average human being goes through the swing of happiness and sorrow each day. Sometimes the swing really catapults you to extremes. When we do repetitive action every day, tedium builds up. This is also called 'ennui' which means tiredness due to repetition. When you work for hours and days, on and on, this happens. What is the remedy? Escapism is definitely not the remedy. Waking up is the remedy. That has to happen from within though.

If you feel mentally tired, enter into some physical sport and exhaust your body. This is a sure way to tackle the mind that injects ennui. Whenever you feel dull, go out and exhaust yourself physically.

A second tedium-repellent is water. Take a dip, swim or do something like playing in water. It does not matter if you feel that others might think you have gone mad. Everyone is mad; the only difference is that some people know how to hide it effectively! So, even take a shower and feel fresh.

Start observing yourself, as if you were watching a movie. See yourself playing various roles. And as you will not see yourself doing that act on screen, please see yourself as a witness to your own acts. You are watching your own life as a movie. Enjoy it.

Also start concentrating on your breath and catching the breath, slowly, inch by inch, descend through your spine. Be spine-oriented. Usually, we are sense-oriented with 120 degrees vision. Now, become back-oriented and shift your focus to your back side as if your eyes went to the back of your head. Start observing. Feel the change. Always cling on to your spine. You will slowly develop a 360 degrees vision. Then you will not feel any stress at all.

Lastly, whenever you are walking or relaxing or at work, keep breathing on the count 1, 2, 3—1, 2. This means breathing in (inhaling) for three seconds and breathing out (exhaling) for two seconds. Keep doing that automatically. If you constantly practise this with awareness, you will be fine in a week's time.

Spiritual Awareness and Spiritual Evolution

Clarifications *(in response to an email):*

A. Intellectually you have understood you are God. Have you understood that experientially? Intellect is often a barrier, same as ego. Ego is the root for arguments. Fr. Anthony de Mello says: "One who is proud of his intellect is like a prisoner who is proud of his prison cell." Knowledge should be a means for higher evolution otherwise it is useless. It is only a burden. It breeds ego.

B. In Bhagwad Gita, Lord Sri Krishna is talking from
    a very high plane of existence, and that existence
    is well beyond intellectual understanding. Intellect
    has limitations. Book knowledge will give artificial
    comfort and elevation. It also tells you that you are
    God. Experiencing this is the most important thing
    though. Who is eating, drinking and sleeping? Is it
    God—your atman or you, the physical entity? Leave
    theory aside. Are you able to experience that state?
    Are you able to convey that state to others? Words
    and book knowledge will give you only intellectual
    supremacy. Only experience can take you spiritually
    higher. This is why rituals are often just ineffective
    and usually unconscious repetitions.

C. Spiritual awareness is a state which is well beyond
    intellectual awareness. It is beyond all senses.
    Usually, in that state, people will become spine
    oriented and third eye oriented. This will relax all
    the nerves. It will settle you in absolute peace.

D. Spiritual evolution is not the same as the theory of
    evolution by Charles Darwin. It is not adapting or
    evolving for survival either. Spiritual awareness is
    being aware of the truth, the eternal truth. The truth
    is that duality exists as long as there is ignorance.
    Total eradication of ignorance is self-realisation.
    It is not about knowing that you are one with the
    Father. At all points are you able to feel the oneness?
    If the answer is yes, if you are experiencing that
    every moment, then there will be silence within.
    There will be beingness or non-doingness. All
    actions will be on karma yoga basis. This is the sign
    of evolution. The kshethra (*here meaning* the body)
    and kshethrajna (*here meaning* the in dweller or the
    soul) become one. This is also the 'Sada Shiva Bhav'
    meaning a perpetual bliss state.

E. Prarabdha cannot be changed. It is your original shopping list that you brought when you came to earth. This is what you used for taking this body. It can be diluted through sadhana or penance. You can choose your future by being in the present. Prarabdha is the cause of every birth.

Regarding your mail, I feel that mostly, you are trying to prove your point and you are not actually looking for answers, are you? If that is so, this communication will neither help you nor me. Intellectual arguments amount to ego. Nobody wins here. I am glad you are opinionated and if it is helping you progress spiritually, I am more happy. There is no need to debate on that. You are welcome to convey your knowledge, which I am sure will benefit many. You can do that, without asking for my opinion. You do not need any endorsements, do you? Need for endorsements is often a sign of insecurity.

I would like to quote a story . . .

A learned man went to meet an old Zen Master. He was in a hurry to put forth questions. The old Master said: "Let's have tea before we start discussing." He gave the visitor an empty cup and started pouring tea from a mug into the cup. The cup filled up, started overflowing into the saucer and yet he continued pouring. The tea started spilling onto the floor. The visitor informed the Master: "Sir, the tea is overflowing." The Master said: "What can I do, if the cup is already full?"

The point is: if you want guidance, there should be some space for that. If you come with a full cup, what is the benefit? All knowledge will overflow. If you feel that I am not capable of answering your questions or guiding you, this is also fine. That's a good enough reason for not asking. There is a difference between a genuine seeker and one who comes to test his own or other's knowledge. A genuine seeker takes cue and evolves. The other one stays where he is. He accumulates knowledge based on others' words and remains where he is. That kind of knowledge only develops ego. It will not help his spiritual growth.

I am more than happy to share what I know. If you want to share your knowledge with others, please use your channels and convey it in your own way. Who will stop you? If you genuinely want clarification, please be specific. I shall answer. I get many mails every day; not only spiritual ones but also those concerning charity, the meditation group (see appendix), official ones and others. So, it's only natural that I would like to use the time as precisely and meaningfully as possible.

No offence intended.

Love, M

Challenges

Q: Apart from ego, what is the most difficult thing to tackle in the path of spirituality?

M: It is EXPECTATION. Expectation is the biggest treason that mind clings on to. It's subtle, you may not be aware that it exists. You may control anger, fear, hatred and everything else. Unless you tackle your expectations, liberation is impossible. It also means existing without the craving for results of action and accepting any result for your action. And it means extreme flexibility.

Q: What alienates me from you? Sometimes I feel connected. Sometimes I feel detached from you.

M: Your conscious mind and its doubts. Mind poses doubts which alienate people. Connection is the same at all times. Mind is not the same. Emotions are not the same at all times. Ocean is the same, its waves are different. This is the difference that you are experiencing. Mind plays various games. It creates doubts, confusions, questions, faithlessness—and all these create alienation. Ego also alienates. Highly egoistic people are usually loners. Humble and kind people will never be alone. Kindness attracts. Ego alienates. So in order to stay connected, you must go beyond your mind and catch the energy plane. There, you and I are one. Same energy. Same soul.

Q: What's the main hindrance in spiritual growth?

M: Tendency to swap our own experience for other people's words hinders spiritual growth. Man stagnates because of constant detours. Any kind of attachment and binding also hinders spiritual growth. This includes habits too. Liberation from everything is the aim. In order to achieve that, we should start accepting ourselves the way we are, with all our deficiencies, pluses and minuses. We should also accept our experiences, whatever they are, with gratitude, own them and be free to express them. It does not matter even if the entire world laughs at you and considers you a dreamer. Your own experiences should be cherished and honoured. Belief in them is essential to transcend them. This does not mean that you can develop attachment to them. You should accept them as a personal experience and keep walking further. Never care for others' opinions about it, unless it is coming from a higher Master. Once we accept ourselves, we can detach from anything. Otherwise, resistance to everything will bind us to all that we resist. This is often why we tend to stagnate. We may not know where or why we are going wrong. Look deeper and you will see that you are resisting something. You are against something. Whatever we energize, stays with us. This includes the problems in our relationships.

In relationships, the fear of losing invokes attachment. It creates so much bondage that we come back again to live together, through time into eternity. Familiar souls come together to exhaust their karmic vasanas. Their roles change, yet they do get together. In short the emotion element attached to any thought, word and action essentially comes back as karma. The emotion element adds the impression of an incident to your checklist of things to do. This becomes the agenda of your next life.

If we perform each thought, word or action without emotions, objectively, mind fully with it, there will not be any backlog. A job well done and well completed. We can easily move on. Mind will not stay with it anymore. Mind will stay with you, because you have moved on. Mind will stay with your present moment. Past is well performed in the status of dharma.

Changes

Q: How can spirituality cause physical changes?

M: If your mind absorbs itself intensely on a particular object, your body also tends to get tuned to that object. Nikos Kazantzakis almost became Buddha after studying Buddhist teachings day and night and unconsciously observing ahimsa and conversion in his food habits. One who is absorbed in Jesus' teachings eventually becomes one with His consciousness. When the intense connection happens with any higher entity, the physical signs also can happen, at least in a subtle way. What prevents that from happening is our own ego and attachment to our own name and fame. Alienation of the mind from the entity that we worship causes separation or non-merger. Complete surrender and non-alienation will make your physical also become the entity that you are associated with. There will be no difference. When we become totally fluid, extremely adaptable with complete surrender to the shapeless entity, you can become any shape, at any time. Trust you have understood the science behind metamorphosis.

Creating Internal Awareness

Q: In one word, can you tell where to start?

M: Breath.

Deserving Levels

There are numerous questions on inequalities on all levels, hence I am generalising. I know that generalization will not help much to give clarity. But I hope it will give a broad understanding.

Masters over generations have taught us, that:

You are what you think.
You are what you eat.
You are what you believe etc.

Tradition has given us various paths for liberating ourselves. We have chosen some and chosen to ignore some. We have always displayed our individuality in this aspect. All of us are unique combinations and our choices also reflected our uniqueness. We lived what we are. We saw things as what we are. We heard as what we are. We never saw or heard what actually is, but we saw only according to what we are. We can only understand a matter according to our faculty and not as what that matter actually is. Hope this is clear. This is one of the fundamental limitations of our existence in the sensory levels.

Grossly speaking, the driver of the vehicle was the mind and we seldom knew the path, though we were vaguely aware of our destination. Even the awareness of our destination has been created through books or words of others. We were always unsure. So, navigation of life was impossible. The driver took us through what he thought as the right path. He did not forget to stop at the right restaurants and other areas of traveller's relief. We were generally happy. At least there is movement, if not progress, and we are generally comfortable. How do we measure our progress? Is it the tangible distance that we covered or the seeming proximity to our destination? Road signs were right. But wrong choices and detours on the way, delayed the progress. We decided to check with pedestrians or seemingly reliable people on the way about the way ahead. They gave us their opinion, which gave temporary satisfaction. Some opinions helped the progress. Some were grossly wrong and took us back to square one. We moved on. There was no way to ascertain progress. Some were happy that the change in scenes at least destroyed the monotony. Finally, we decide to end the journey. This was because either the fuel was finished or because we could not travel any further.

Refuelling and resumption of the journey. Thus we have been travelling through generations, with our mind as the driver. Mind cannot have absolute clarity about the destination. It is following signs and assumptions. It is also following many opinions from seemingly superior minds. Some of them have vested interests and selfish motives. We always failed to understand that. This was causing delays and diversion.

When clarity is lacking, progress is slow. When clarity is absolute, progress is better. We know that. Travelling is easy when we don't have much baggage. Less luggage, more comfort. Shedding happens periodically, whether we like it or not. Benevolence and explicit expression of love and kindness brings forth an easier transit. More people will aid your journey. Self-centredness and selfishness slow us down. Thus life goes on.

Inadequacies take birth in our mind first and then get reflected in our life. Life is only a reflection of our own subconscious mind. Emotion plus action becomes karma. The stronger the emotion, the deeper the imprint in the mind. Repetitive thoughts, words and action will strengthen the chance of a tangible result. Continuous negation brings complex results. When we keep shifting from positive to negative thoughts, words and action, results will be complicated. Thus, we create our own destiny. The soul never interferes. Positive and benevolent action without many thoughts will reverse our mindset. JUST DO IT. Too much intellectualisation and postponement of action will destroy one's self-esteem. Silence and inaction due to indecisiveness will lead to decay in self-esteem and mental depression. Silence due to inner abundance leads to complete enlightenment. It is that simple. It is not through doing that you can attain enlightenment. It is through being. Life is not complicated. Purity of thoughts, words and action can never lead you to depression. Due to these, even if there is failure on terrestrial terms, you will still have the inner strength to survive the failure. No doubt.

All sorts of positive emotions help create positive results in the future. Action happens now, results might be delayed. Every action has an appropriate result. The residue of all actions gets stored in the subconscious and gets transferred to the next life if it could not be fulfilled in this one. Since the data stored had all the ingredients to create a great drama, it gets played out in the next life. The reason for the script is unsure. Your exact role is unsure. The scriptwriter's identity is also unsure. The actor plays his role, within the permitted lines.

Inequalities are a matter of the mind. The soul has nothing to do with it. Mind compares between the past and present, and also between one another. It breeds discontent, based on inequalities. This creates fear, anxiety, jealousy and many other things. It has the potential to destroy oneself and also all others. Wars happen in the mind first and spill over into the nation. With peace, it is the same.

So, acceptance of oneself is the necessity. It gives peace of mind. Shanti.

AUM

Poornamda Poornamidam
Poornaat Poorna mudachyathe
Poornasya Poornamaadaaya
Poornameva vashishyathe.
"That is complete (the Father), this is complete (the son);
From completeness, formed completeness;
When completeness is removed from completeness
All that exists is complete too."

Remain complete. Remain blessed.
Love all and serve all.

Knowledge and Clinical Understanding

Q: I found the path of knowledge is the best so far. Do you
have any comments?

M: You are a jnana yogi and hence you like the path
of knowledge. Unless you convert the knowledge into
awareness, it will become a burden for you and you
will develop insufferable ego from knowledge. Of all
paths, the path of knowledge is tricky because it works
on your intellect, which is supposedly superior to body
and mind. Intellectual gratification always provides an
artificial feeling of supremacy. Understand that acquired
knowledge is borrowed knowledge. It is not born out of
your own experience. Unless you convert the knowledge
into experience you will not evolve. Shedding is liberation.
So, avoid accumulation. Keep shedding and evolving.
Knowledge must be used to evolve further. Liberation should
be the purpose of your existence. Sometimes books also help
escapism, just like TV. This is tamas, inertia. So, be aware.
Be careful. Knowledge becomes a burden if it's not used for
evolution. There are some people who suffer from lack of
confidence. You can see them in our society. They either buy
beautiful cars, houses, dogs or books to position themselves
in society. They do not have their own stature. They need
the assistance of these gadgets. Minus these gadgets, they
become insignificant. So, be careful. Be real and live real,
always. Live in absolute consciousness.

Q: Does clinical understanding help? Is it necessary?

M: Well, it depends on your individual constitution. Clinical
understanding is a necessity for an intellectual, a jnana yogi.

Overall awareness is perfect for a karma yogi. It depends on where you stand, individually. Some are satisfied with a general understanding while others cannot sleep properly until they get to the bottom of a matter. Discoveries and inventions are nothing but recognition of the existence of an external matter or situation. Inventions are essentially modifications. When we say we discovered something, it was already existing, well-covered, somewhere there before and we happened to discover that. If possibilities do not exist for a chemical reaction, there is no invention. So time, space, characteristics, intellect and awareness are given to aid a particular situation which in turn creates a result. Invention takes place. Events get formed. Thus, we are only one of the ingredients of the whole show. We are perhaps better considered as catalysts. You may disagree. I know where the question has come from. So, understand this as my opinion. You are free to have your own opinions.

Gross and Subtle

Gross cannot understand subtle. Subtle can understand gross. Energy conglomerated is matter. Matter cannot understand that. Energy can understand matter. Likewise, gross people merely know that subtle exists, just like we know that infinity exists. We do not know what infinity is, until we become that. Infinity needs to be experienced, not understood. So, please do take everything in your stride.

Q: Right and wrong. Gross and subtle level. How far? How long?

M: Right and wrong are relative terms. This is from the discrimination of the conscious mind. These are not absolute. That's why we see so many different and contradicting customs in the world. I am not telling you that eating meat is wrong. I am telling you to understand that meat has come from animals or birds who have suffered pain and fear when they were forcibly killed to fulfill your appetite for meat. Whatever you do with full awareness, rather than unconscious repetition, is good for evolution. I have said earlier that some of the saints ate meat. They did it with consciousness. My job is not to distinguish between right and wrong.

For example, the soul whose sole agenda is to merge with the Father or the Universal Soul that it came from, has no interest in the tours and detours of terrestrial existence. Soul never interferes in your activity and never stops you from doing anything. We do not even know that a soul exists until the time the soul leaves the body, which we call death.

As for the senses, they thrive on sensory pleasures. That is their agenda. For the mind, emotional satisfactions and ego satisfactions are the agenda. For the intellect, intellectual fulfillments, qualifications and the related supremacy is the agenda. Thus, man is a mixture of various agendas put together. We are quite complex.

The gross level is the visible level of existence. The subtle level is the invisible. Gross is heavy, subtle is light. Gross is perishable while subtle is imperishable. Our mind is more subtle than our body. Intellect is more subtle than the mind. Soul is more subtle than the intellect. It is the subtlest of all.

What we are trying to achieve through these communications is clarity. What's right and wrong is up to the individual and his agenda. He can choose what he wants to express in this world or let's say, his world. Hence, every man will express his agenda. It might be complementing or contradicting to other people or even society. A karmic man just goes around and expresses it. If eating meat is part of his agenda, come what may, he will do it. The same with alcohol or drugs. The same with love or hate. Repeated actions become habits. The first level is conscious action. This is taken over by the subconscious and then action gets converted into habits. Habits become character. Just like you driving a car. After learning to drive, within a few days you learn to drive without thinking about where the brake pedal and gear are. This is one example of how the subconscious takes over. If we get it back to doing things with full awareness and conscious mind, we will live in the present. This is one sure way to avoid indiscriminate data entry of our varied impressions and emotions, into our subconscious mind. Our hard-drive will remain reasonably unclogged. Distinctions become thinner and thinner as we go more and more subtle.

Q: As we go subtle, things become more and more intangible. How do we know it is real?

M: Through your own experiences. Experiences will become extraordinary. You cannot fake it, can you? If you are faking it, how long will you fake it? Someday, you have to come back to the real, right? So, intangible experiences must be accepted in their own way like you do not expect the air that you breathe to have the same tangibility as the ice-cream on the table. Subtle must be accepted as subtle and gross must be accepted as gross. We must maintain maximum adaptability. We must be extremely open and receptive too. Energy cannot do any changes in closed minds. Faith is the key that opens closed minds.

Disowning your own experiences would be the highest dishonesty. Especially, if you follow others' words or books and compare them with your own experience or even disown your experience. That would be the biggest disfavor that you can do to yourself. I have seen people talking book-knowledge or others' words profusely. They are convinced too. They themselves do not have the personal experiences. They create harm to themselves by hindering their progress. Book-knowledge is transferable knowledge. Experiences are not transferable. It is easy to acquire book-knowledge. It is difficult to amass experiences. When experiences dominate, books will drop. That is why there is a saying which states something like this: even the Vedas should be burned once you have crossed over. That means, information should be used to attain experiences or else it becomes an unnecessary burden.

There is also a saying: "Those who knew will never talk and those who talk never knew." Those who are completely and fully god-realized will slip into silence and bliss. And those who are not there yet will keep talking. How can those who are not settled in the being level themselves, guide a student into the being level? Acharyas (regular exponents of knowledge—not the enlightened Masters) carry portable knowledge. They teach what they have learned. They have to learn more to teach more. There will be nothing of their own, in what they teach.

True Masters impart wisdom from the Divine, as they exist in absolute unity with the Father. Even if there are a thousand people in front of them, each person will get what they need from the Guru. Shirdi Sai Baba, Ramana Maharshi, Parthi Sai Baba, Akkalkot Maharaj and many other Masters are examples of this. This is the difference between acharyas or teachers and gurus or true Masters.

Responsibility

Q: Am I responsible for what happens to me?

M: Yes. But understand that we are not consciously choosing unwelcome events of life. Nobody will choose diseases or poverty, right? We do not even know what our next thought will be. Often, there is no logic in our flow of thoughts.

The results are due to indiscriminate entry of various impressions into our subconscious, which produce confused results. In order to have control over the events of the future, the unwanted files must be deleted from the system. This means, we should go above the emotional plane and reach a no-mind status. So you ask if you are responsible? Yes. You are responsible. Also understand how you are responsible.

Can you change what you do not need? Certainly you can. Again, only when you go higher, will you be able to sort out the lower. By just suppressing desires, karma will not be cleansed. Evolution cannot happen.

Troubled Soul

Q: Mohanji, I can only see darkness. Where is the light?

M: Choose to see the light. You will see it. Darkness is a state where light is absent. What you experience will depend on what you choose. Choose love by expressing love, not waiting for the elusive love without giving any love. Unless you sow, you cannot reap. If you try to reap what others have sown, it will never belong to you. You can express love by choosing to express love under all circumstances. You can choose romance by expressing romance to every object around you. Romance is not restricted to a man and woman relationship. You can also express beauty by choosing to admire beauty. Happiness and sorrow are experienced by the same mind. Beauty and ugliness are the same. If you choose beauty, you can see beauty even in utter ugliness. If you choose love, you can see love even in the height of hatred. If you choose light, you can see light even in darkness. All these are relative things. Nothing is absolute. What you choose to express becomes you. That becomes your character and destiny. So, choose love. Choose romance, choose beauty. Choose light.

Receptivity

Q: I want to thank you for visiting and blessing us at the meditation on January 23rd. It was wonderful to see you. After you hugged me I felt a sudden surge of energy which stayed almost for three days. I did not even want to sleep. I was so energized, all those three days. I was also consuming less food. I have never experienced this kind of a cleansing with anybody before. Biba told me that you constantly remove blockages in people and 'change the software' in people. I had a pain in the back, which completely vanished and till now it has not bothered me. While I thank you for this great blessing, I am developing a fear that soon you will become completely inaccessible. I am sure that many more people will recognise your stature. You will become more and more busy. How can we be still in touch with you?

M: Thank you for this kind mail.

Transfer of energy is real. All of you have experienced it in the past. (Whether I am doing it directly or I am doing it through others, it's the same.) In my expanded state, when I hugged you, your shells of negative coatings were broken and you experienced high energy. The energy which you experienced has always existed. When the sheaths were removed, which has been blinding you from reality, you started physically experiencing the higher energy. The potential to experience that energy has always been there in you, all it needed was some fine-tuning. I do not hug anyone just for the sake of hugging. I hugged you to cleanse your aura and chakras and you actually experienced the result. That is why when I hug, I hold for a few seconds to allow the energy to transfer and merge completely. When you are in the higher energy plane, sleep or food is immaterial. So, the hugging was not just an expression of love. It was a complete chakra and aura cleansing. And you experienced your ailment disappearing too. This is because when there are no blockages in your system anymore, there is no room for such physical ailments. Receptivity is as important as faith. When there is faith, there is receptivity. What you get from me or anyone else will depend on your level of receptivity. It depends on how much you can receive. How open you are.

As far as the future is concerned, what we will be, is in the future, right? Let us be in the present. I'm very much accessible to you today and you are accessible to me now and that's our present reality. Who knows, in the future, whether I will be existing in my physical body at all? Who knows, in the future you may not need me at all. You will perhaps have become self-sufficient. This is what I want to see as well. I would like to see people evolve and shed dependency. My job is to liberate and not bind anyone to myself.

As I had mentioned earlier, memories of good experiences stay in the mind less easily than memories of bad experiences. If someone cheats you or insults you, it will stay in your mind much longer than the memory of someone helping you. Even if someone helped you a 100 times, if he scolds you just once, that bad experience will overpower all the other memories of goodness that this person expressed before. This is human nature. So, even though I respect your love and kindness, I am very well aware of human nature and I do not expect anything. I stay well beyond expectations. Whether many people want to meet me or nobody wants to meet me, I will remain the same, with zero regrets and zero expectations. Understand that you and I are one, in the absolute sense. I would rather have you achieve perfect understanding of that unity.

It is human nature to judge people through our capacity of understanding. Every human being has a different constitution. They are unique. So, it is better if we just live moment by moment, with gratitude for all the experiences that life has given us profusely. Expectations spoil our present. This is always the truth. Acceptance of the gifts of life with open arms, irrespective of where or through whom they come from, is important. Life is full of thorns and roses. Often we have to accept both. Because both are part of our own creation.

Faith

(Continuation of the above reply to the email)

Faith can move mountains. No doubt. Lack of faith in anything makes bundles of burden for oneself. Faithless actions are always a burden. That action lacks life, lacks inspiration. So, take time, but develop firm faith in yourself. Then the faith in the divinity that resides in yourself and that helps you read these words, makes you think and even runs your life. Respect that divinity and understand that it is timeless, while all your current thoughts, words and actions are impermanent. No external guru can take you to yourself, if you continue to be a reluctant child. All true Masters are only doing this—introducing your Self to yourself. Belief in oneself is essential. Concentration is essential too. Watch how divinity makes things happen for you. Do not cling onto your past. Do not over emphasize yourself either, which is indeed a burden for you. Selflessness is good. It lightens you. It makes you feather weight. Expression of selflessness will transform you. No theories can do that for you. More than belief or faith, it's the intensity that matters. Faith does not matter as much as its intensity does. If your faith is weak, the corresponding results will also be weak. So make no compromises, my friend. Faith is the key. Have firm faith.

Consciousness is Everything

Once upon a time, there was no you and I. There was no earth. There was no cosmos. There were no galaxies. There was no life as we see it around us now. There was no up and down. There was no black and white. There was no darkness. There was no duality. There was no relativity. There was no time. There was nothing. There was only consciousness. Undiluted supreme consciousness.

In the womb of the absolute consciousness, in the depth of silence, began the song of silence. The deep hum. It pulsated within the consciousness. The sound of life—the heartbeats. Energy started to move and conglomerate. In the intensified hum from within, energy exploded into trillions and trillions of pieces. It further conglomerated into matter. Duality happened. Space happened. Relativity was born. Consciousness saw itself in multitude.

Consciousness saw itself in everything. It allowed the multitude of consciousness to awaken into positions that were suitable for each. When duality happened with the internal explosion, time began. Consciousness could measure itself from here to there and beyond. It could see itself as separate from the other. Relativity got transformed into more tangible relationships.

Relativity gave billions of options for creativity to take place. One consciousness in many forms. Then the challenge became to come together, come back and become one consciousness again. The option was always open for experimentation. Each unit had its power as it was essentially one with the supreme consciousness. However, in the darkness of duality, it had forgotten its true identity and was wandering in search of its home. The supreme never interfered in its pursuit. It just allowed the experiences. The free will of the present combined with the destiny of past karma, formed lives, existence and terrestrial experiences.

Consciousness experienced itself in various levels. The devil and angel were two sides of the same consciousness. From the barbaric dense state to the supreme consciousness state which was all-encompassing, the options were huge and varied. The denser it went, the deeper was its alienation from the supreme. The lighter it became, the easier it was to get contaminated. Consciousness never experienced any happiness or sorrow. It was always supreme bliss of perfect awareness. There was no form and no death. There was only the detached state of witness-hood.

Embodied beings cleanse themselves over lives and elevate themselves to higher consciousness. Yet, when they cease to express gratitude to the beings that helped their existence, they come back to pay. They pay their dues, sometimes over lifetimes and when they finally get the 'no objection to travel' from the mother earth, they elevate themselves to the lighter zones. Once that is achieved they never come back to exhaust their karmic agenda, because they have none. However, they may come back— out of compassion—to elevate a few more to the lighter existence.

In the varied levels of consciousness, from the gross noisy existence, a soul grows into the zones of silence. Words are gross there. In still lighter zones, even thoughts are gross. Those zones deliver absolute bliss of silence. They are not reachable until years of shedding and existence based on detachment that deeply segregate the embodied into a state of seeming disembody-ness happens. It is called the Avadhoot state. The detachment is applicable towards everything that is gross, which includes food, weather, air, earth and even space. When the elements are won over, the body is in control. When the body is in control, coming in, living and going out of it, is part of one's free will and not destiny which amounts to past karma.

Denser consciousness is lived out through fears, possessiveness, hatred, revenge, soap operas (ha! ha!), so on and so forth. The ones who get attracted to a particular object, person or a lifestyle usually have a similar level of consciousness. It is easy to recognize. Some attribute all enviable qualities to themselves. They are living in a borrowed state of consciousness. They do not have their own identity. Their consciousness is limited.

Our universe is full of beings with diverse consciousness. Each is expressing it in its own way all the time. Birds of the same feather flock together. Similar consciousness attracts similar beings. They come together and create events. Consciousness creates events. When a generation is glued to television and watching soap operas narrating stories of hatred, treachery and deceit, people will carry the same consciousness to their next lives too. This is their existence. They are part of the role-plays. They live that and they experience that. Some people cannot agree with one another, and some people feel too alienated from a particular society because of the difference in their levels of consciousness. Thus, consciousness is much deeper than it seems to be.

Furthermore, physical beauty or appearance has nothing to do with inner consciousness. Great saints may look like nothing— too ordinary. Ordinary people fall for physical appearance and vocabulary. Even an avid reader can be a good speaker at public functions. He also can handle portable knowledge effectively. If we assume that his gift of gab represents his actual stature, we will be terribly mistaken. Consciousness has its own compatibility. A boy in lower school can never fathom the thought process of a graduate student. He has to rise up in stature through hard work spread over a period of time, in order to understand and fathom the higher consciousness. Some people believe that cramming-knowledge will give them stature. No way.

It might get them status—definitely not stature. We respect

intellectuals because they are visible and tangible. Intellect believes in constructing. Being spiritual amounts to demolishing or destroying even own identity. That is the essential difference. We are eternal deconstructors.

Men of higher consciousness are usually not street-smart on the gross terrestrial plane. They might even be considered as failures or misfits in the gross society. Gross works well with gross. When subtle has to coexist with gross even for the sake of providing duality, the subtle always gets shoved around. We can see many people with superior consciousness levels not making both ends meet. They indeed brought this reality upon themselves because they are in an alien land!!! They do not belong here!

Different species are in different consciousness planes too. There are still high and low amongst them. Leaders of the pack display higher consciousness than their subjects. An ant has its consciousness. An elephant, a lion, a leopard, a whale or a dolphin have their own consciousness. Men also display different consciousness. Some are base and barbaric. Some are born to lead. Some talk too much and add to the sound pollution that is already plaguing the world. Some pretend and display stature which they do not possess. Some are silent, quiet and effective. Some dare to be different even at the cost of their own existence. Some dare to walk alone. Some are greedy, some benevolent. Some love. Some complain . . . , so on and so forth.

There is collective consciousness too. A group of people thinking alike creates events suitable to their consciousness. In daily life itself we can see the 'mob-effect'. A group of people nullifies individual consciousness and displays collective consciousness. They often display in groups, the kind of courage and determination which individually they never display.

People of lower consciousness dwell as victims of the up and down swings of life. Their life goes on like a pendulum. For those who are of higher consciousness, there is no resistance. They have no tragedies. They consider everything as experiences, as lessons. Life is only about experiences. Consciousness is everything. That is the only thread that runs through all our states, such as waking, dream state, deep sleep state, as well as the turiya state. That is the only thread that runs through all our lives. That is the only thread that began before time began, and that exists in the absolute plane of timelessness. I hope I have given you sufficient food for thought.

Those who understood this have already found the thread. Those who contemplate on it will find the thread. Those who ignore it will be caught up in samsara. Everything is fine. Everything is life. Everything is consciousness.

Q: Why can't they understand me?

M: There is a huge variety in levels of consciousness. In that context each one is in their own sphere. Those who bother us are those who cannot reach or understand our level of consciousness. Forgive them and love them. Soon enough they will see what we see. It can also be the other way—we may not have the capacity to see their realm of existence. Then we tend to disagree with them. We fail to understand them. Nobody is perfect. We are all walking the same wide earth seeking varied experiences. We all are trying to understand this existence, using our faculties, through the senses and mind. We are all enveloped in different levels of consciousness.

Q: Talking about collective consciousness. If I feel good with a certain action, it's good for me. But what if that action does not go down well with the other person? So while doing things to make ourselves happy, it makes someone else sad in the process. As long as collective consciousness is not there, I will not be affected, is that correct?

M: Collective consciousness is literally the unity in consciousness of a multitude of people. A tsunami had an impact on a lot of people and it created similar emotions in many at the same time. The emotion can be happiness (definitely not in the case of the tsunami), sorrow, anger, hatred, helplessness or a mixture of many emotions. When people consistently dwell in misery, they crave for a messiah. The result will be the birth of a redeemer. When a society dwells in ego and insensitivity, mad and ruthless leaders can come up and control them. Any given society gets rulers it deserves.

One action of an ordinary individual and its corresponding impact cannot create any events or lasting impression in the wider world. Its effect will be individualistic. (At the same time, one thought, word or action of a leader can affect the entire country. In that context, he could be the mouthpiece of the collective consciousness of that specific generation of the country who elected him.) When others talk negative things about you, as Shirdi Baba says: "Your karma gets cleansed." If others are criticizing you it is good for you. I am not suggesting that you should create situations for others to criticize you. What I mean is, that if your intention was pure and others criticized and blamed you, the effect will be positive for you. Every thought, word or action from everyone is creating and un-creating karmas at some level. Hope this is clear.

Thinking

Thoughts do matter because they have the potential to become words and action. Thought is the first level of creation. Energy gets released. Similar thoughts from many minds have the potential to create events. So, thoughts do matter. While I never advise censoring your thoughts, I would definitely advise observing your thoughts. Observation of thought is equal to spiritual sadhana and can be considered similar to meditation. If you keep observing your thoughts, you will see them dropping off and you can reach the realms of thoughtlessness. In this emptiness, you can listen to the sound of silence. Perfect silence. And you can listen to the voice of god. This is a great realm to be in. External search must stop and internal observation must begin. No need for any guru. You can do it yourself. Remembering and respecting all the masters who graced your life will certainly get you their Grace, for sure.

Q: Talking about others? Thinking about others? Gossip?

M: All are unnecessary and anti-spiritual. When you talk about someone behind their back, you are indirectly and unknowingly licking up their karma.

You are pulling yourself down with that. It is always better to confront the person in question. If you have any dispute or difference in opinion, ask, clarify and move on. This will keep you and others pure in mind.

Thinking about others benevolently is a positive thing. Again, thought, word and action have the potential to create karma. Emotions attached to all these are the reason for karmic binding. Hence, being in the present, loving everyone, irrespective of their response to you, and doing things objectively, without expectations, will keep you clean and pure.

Good and Bad Deeds

Q: It is said that good and bad things happen to us because of our own deeds. When we do bad deeds, bad things happen to us, and when we do good deeds good things happen to us. People are trying to do good deeds and not hurt other people so that good happens to them. So someone who hasn't done many bad deeds, why would he have to suffer?

M: Good and bad things are from the discrimination of your conditioned mind. The same thing can be good and bad for different minds. Meat could be bad and unacceptable to a pious Brahmin. It could be the most acceptable thing for another. Good and bad are relative terms. Experiences happen due to our creation through thoughts, words and deeds. They all produce results, both tangible and intangible. Energizing negative thoughts almost always makes sure negative events are given to you. Thus fear of theft will bring you that reality. Doing good things should become your nature and character. Only then will the results be consistent. For example, taking an external bath and purifying your body while keeping a mind full of hatred and anger will mean that you are still impure. No real cleansing has happened. Our meditation is meant for this purification. Consistent selfless action will give you immunity from all kinds of happenings in your life. You will have many experiences, but you will have no sufferings. Your plane will be that of higher awareness.

While watching TV or being 'on the internet', you are creating virtual realities. There are many games which bring out the sadist in you. You may not be killing a living person, but you kill many in the internet games. For your poor subconscious which cannot see, this is its reality. That data is also stored in your data bank. It's good that you are not physically going out and killing a villain. But virtually, you are doing that. Likewise, witnessing torture, rape, killing animals and all other kinds of negative things, will leave residue in your subconscious. The deeper the engram, the more likely that a similar experience gets enacted in this life or at least the next one. Understand that the subconscious is like the engine room of the ship. It's not witnessing. It's only perceiving what the conscious mind sees and participates with the senses. It takes everything literally, so whatever impression the conscious mind got out of a picture or story or a sadistic game, the subconscious stores it as an experience. Thus, once again, every thought, word or action can and will create your character and thus your destiny.

Expecting Results

Q: Are positive results guaranteed in your meditation?

M: Doubt is the enemy of spirituality. Doubts block progress. Doubts block faith. Blind faith is bad, just like emotional criticism. But creative criticism is good. Criticize something with the purpose of gaining more clarity about it, not criticizing with the mind based on destruction or negativity. So the results are up to you. How consistent are you? How dedicated are you? Are you fast-food oriented or do you entertain patience to cook and eat a healthy meal? Do you read hair-raising fiction or books on the lives of saints? Do you keep your house filthy? Do you procrastinate? Do you walk around with a filled cup of intellectual trash? Is there room in your mind to take on new experiences? Are you brave enough to experience or daring enough to jump upside down into spiritual experiences? Do they scare you? Are you guided by your own experiences or others' words or book knowledge? How deep is your devotion? Is your devotion transactional, that is, does your devotion end when results are not satisfactory? Do you get all what you expect? I have to ask you all these questions. You are expecting me to deliver experiences all the time. I am doing that too. But, what are you doing? What is your contribution to yourself? You are expecting a lot from me. No problem, I will give as much and as good as I can. What can I expect from you? At least sincere practice and faith? Whenever you expect a lot from others, just for a moment think—what are you giving to them in return? I do not want your money or goodies. All I want is your wholehearted attention and openness to receive. Do you think I am arrogant to ask such questions? If you consider me so, it does not matter to me because my intentions are unselfish. Results are directly related to your capacity and openness to experience other realities. Everyone gets what they deserve in our meditation. This is for sure. This has been our experience for more than 3 years. Many come with filled up buckets of spiritual expectations and trash. What can I give them? Even if I give them something, unless they trash their junk, how can they carry it home? I shall deliver, provided you can receive and save. All meditations are certainly powerful. Just let go, unburden yourself and come to me with empty minds. You can take home the celestial nectar. Nobody can eat the whole buffet. You can only eat as much as your belly can accommodate. Eat only as much as you can digest. Overeating will lead to stomach disorder. In spirituality also, walk the strides that you can easily take. Never walk or run to keep up with another. If you do that, it will be a BIG mistake. Whenever you approach a Guru, do not go there to test your mettle against His. You should meet a Guru with an attitude of surrender. A willingness to receive and the ability to assimilate the pearls of wisdom that you might gather there. No words happen by accident. No thoughts are unnecessary. They all come out of the substratum which makes you and your expressions. They are important for you. So, with faith as one leg and patience as the other, walk to the glory of spirituality. You will reach the realms of your Father effortlessly. Destroy expectations. Destroy ego. You will see the light. Nobody can give you experiences until you are ready to receive them and experience them. Hope this matter remains clear in your mind, always. This is important to remember.

Q: I have been practicing rigorously, but lately I got the feeling that I'm not evolving. Why?

M: Doing easily becomes a ritual. You will be chanting, but your mind will be musing on other matters. There is no evolution possible this way. Conscious efforts happen only as long as it takes to learn a mantra or practice. Then the subconscious takes over. It becomes a ritual. Conscious mind does not need to bother anymore. There is no evolution in this process. This is what is happening to most people. If we do not know exactly what we are looking for, we will keep searching unconsciously and will not find anything. The remedy is conscious sadhana or practice.

HUMAN ATTACHMENTS

Role Play

"THE WORLD IS a stage" is attributed to the wisdom of Shakespeare. We all are actors. Actors keep coming and going. The show goes on. When an actor plays the role that has been given to him or her in a detached way, he or she will not be affected. When actors get too involved and cannot detach from the role that they play and believe that the role is more real than their own selves, they suffer the agony of existence and essentially become confused.

The same actor comes back in different roles, constantly. Sometimes the actor pretends to be the role that he has played and tries to live it as if he and the character were one. Eventually, he has to remove his makeup and see his true face in the mirror. He may not be able to accept his real face from the pretentious one. Some cannot accept realities without the support of makeup. They can never come out of their pretensions. They suffer a lot because of their resistance to reality. They take their makeup home with the belief that, without its support, their life is incomplete.

The show goes on. The director has the complete view of the show. He knows the story. He stays in the background, sometimes guiding some actors who are surrendered to his will. Otherwise he never imposes himself, once the show is on. No one even feels his existence, as only the actors are on stage. The one who made the show always stays in the background, watching and witnessing the show.

Actors also change according to times. Old faces perish. New faces appear. There is no eternal tragedy. All appearances and disappearances are part of the show. There is nothing permanent. Every situation is temporary. Every emotion is temporary. Those who hoard emotions and keep them, suffer. Those who let the emotions go, stay light. All sufferings are temporary.

When the role-play changes, a man could also become a woman or a dog. A father could become a son or a wife. A beggar could play the role of a king in the next scene. All scenes are temporary. When we give lots of importance to each scene and start comparing, we fall into the trap of delusion. We suffer due to impermanence and uncertainty. Accepting the scenes as they are is important to truly enjoy the show.

There are critics of the show. They never created the show. They are also actors who are playing the role of critics. All should be considered as actors and all roles are important. If all roles are not played or if some actors are missing, the show will become incomplete. This can never happen.

Some actors feel more important than the director. This is their ego. The backdrops, curtains, all the objects on the stage add to the flavour of the scene. They provide the inevitable fragrance and reality. They also are important. As important as the actors themselves. And as important as the makeup the actors wears and as the stage itself where the show is being performed. Every object has its importance. Every object is equal to any actor. All have come out of the imagination of the director. Only the director knows the whole play through past, present and future. The director uses time to set his play and to create relativity between scenes and relationship between characters. He remains beyond time in creation, running the show as well as its conclusion. He stays immune to time. He only uses time and relativity for his expressions. Relationships are his power of expression, which knit scenes and actors together. Actors are not as important as the show. The show is watched and enjoyed by the director, without interfering, while the show is on.

He is objective. He has no favourites. He never discriminates. The actors who have understood the mind of the director play their role very well. Others only imitate others or perhaps express their limited understanding. Whether an actor performs well or not, the show goes on . . .

Guilt

Q: If I haven't done anything wrong to someone, but feel guilty wondering if what I did was wrong. Will this get inside my subconscious mind and—even though I might have done the right thing—because I am feeling guilty, will I be punished because the feeling of guilt in my subconscious mind?

M: Fear and guilt always go deep into the subconscious. All negative emotions do. This is the nature of negative emotion. Positive feelings never bury too deep. Negative ones certainly will. A good rose plant needs nurturing. A parasite weed needs no nurturing. This is how positive and negative feelings work in your subconscious. The only remedy is the removal of ignorance, and the understanding of who you really are. Once you know that you are the all-powerful soul, your guilt and anger will go and you will reach God. You will stop discriminating and start accepting realities as they come. No expectations, better living. Guilt should be removed through awareness at that time or at the event. You could not have done any better. You did your best. Do not look back. Do not repeat. Just handle your today well, with purity and honesty.

Greed

Good and evil are two aspects of our own existence. What pleases us and makes us happy, we call good. What affects us or others adversely, we call bad. Likewise, whatever action we do using our intellect, usually produces benevolent results. Whatever actions are done using emotions, produce results usually of negative nature. When a person is angry, emotion is at work and intelligence is kept shut and sealed.

Good and bad are two options that every human possesses. It is at each one's discretion on how to function in this world. When a person is guided by the soul or is one with the soul, he will stay beyond dualities and life will be good, on the evolutionary path. When the person is driven by emotions, he/she will always be like a pendulum swinging between happiness and sorrow, which are both temporary in nature.

All the soap operas are catering to the emotions of people. Most of the advertisements are designed that way, too. They use every tactic to make people react emotionally, especially when it comes to spending money, which one usually regrets later. Selling emotion is the name of the game in today's society. Angry characters in movies who destroy establishments are considered heroes, while in reality those who have conquered their own minds and attained the soul are the real heroes, because they achieved this great success within this lifetime.

Once a saint asked Alexander the Great: "Who are you?"

Alexander was surprised by this question as he thought that everybody knew him!!! Controlling his ego and anger, he replied with a sarcastic smile:

"I am Alexander, they call me the 'Great' because I have conquered most parts of the world including this land that you are standing on. All these places belong to me."

The saint who was standing completely naked, took one step backwards and asked: "Oh, really? I did not know that this piece of land is yours. Where are the other lands that you just said you have conquered? Can you show me?"

Alexander said: "I have appointed able people to look after those lands." And the saint asked: "And why can't you carry them with you if they are yours?"

Alexander replied: "Obviously, you cannot transport land. Ha ha. What matters is that they all belong to me anyway."

The saint asked: "You cannot carry with you what you say you have conquered because all these conquests are outside of you. This means all the conquests were wasted as you can effectively carry only what is inside you?"

Alexander did not understand. The saint explained further:

"All the people at the places that you say you conquered have already gone back to their old habits, as soon as you left those lands. You are not in their lives anymore. Greed can never conquer. Greed is self-destructive and negative. You can actually conquer nobody, because people are not their physical body. Body is only a shell. You might be able to subdue them temporarily, using force. But you cannot conquer their souls. That's the only real stuff in them. All bodies are highly perishable!

The lands that you say are yours existed well before you, and will exist well after you. So, how can you say that you own them? You never created them. You might be a temporary custodian of that land.

The only real conquest useful to you would be that of your own mind. Obviously, this greatest conquest is not yet done, so according to me, you are not eligible for the title 'Great' and according to me all your conquests are illusions, nothing but a mere ego satisfaction. And just to satisfy your ego, you have unsettled many innocent people who never intended to fight. All you have been successful in doing is only to disturb the peace of all the places that you visited with your army. You have managed to accumulate the curse of peaceful people, all along the way. In that aspect, instead of being called 'Great' you are eligible to be called a 'Sinner.'"

Obviously, Alexander was 'greatly' upset. He shouted: "Take this mad fellow away and throw him into the forest!"

The chief of the army said: "Sir, we fetched him from the forest for you, because you told us that you wanted to see a great Indian Master. He will be comfortable there. Should we lock him up for insulting you?"

Alexander said: "No. Put him back to where he belongs. His looks and speech irritate me. I do not want him anywhere in this area."

Truth is often irritating. Yet, they are truths and only truths can survive the test of time. All the great Masters the world has ever seen were completely based in truth and only in truth.

Greed can never survive for long. It definitely can temporarily unsettle the lives of many.

And collective consciousness certainly works. All agonies and ecstasies over generations have created and uncreated events. Let this story be understood and digested properly. Be good, do good and love all. This will help establish a good life.

Money

Q: Kindly elaborate on people's issues with money.

M: Why do we think that money is bad? This is a wrong notion. Money is good. Money is matter. Matter is made out of energy. Elements are also matter. Our physical body is made out of elements. It is the same with money. Money is good. Emotions attached to money are bad. This includes attachment and ownership. And this is what makes you happy or sad. Both are to be understood as bondage to money. There is a saying: "If you have a handful of currency, you own it. If you have currency till your neck, it owns you." So be in a state where you act as a custodian of money. Be grateful for that role. Money will stay with you and will be useful to you. The moment you shift your stance and become a watchman for your wealth, you will start suffering because of the associated attachments and anxiety. Money should be considered primarily by understanding its nature:

A. Money is a terrestrial transactional tool. It travels from hand to hand. Nobody owns money and we are always only a temporary custodian of money.

B. If you hoard it and if it is out of circulation, it stagnates and loses its potential.

C. Attachment to wealth creates anxiety and fear.

D. Non-attachment along with gratitude for wealth creates liberation within. Money flows.

E. Money develops ego and if that is checked, we stay free and liberated.

F. Money has no value to us at the time of our birth and our death and neither during sleep.

G. Money enhances power and social standing. If ego, attachment and greed also grow accordingly, we will have a spiritually poor existence. If humility, compassion and Grace grow with monetary richness, we gain a lot in life. Wise men handle money with detachment and gratitude. Ordinary people handle money with ego and pride. They remain extremely poor inside, while rich outside. They trade love for money, in other words, they fall into isolation and lack of love from the world because of their fear and anxiety of losing their wealth. The wise men gracefully handle their money and use it for the well-being of themselves, their family and society. They will then earn love and Grace from the world too. Only they are truly rich. The one who has a rich heart is the real rich man. When we are capable of bringing happiness and solace to at least some people who are not immediately related to us, our life becomes meaningful. Otherwise, as anxious watchmen of our own wealth, our life gets wasted. Usually for such people, their next generation will waste their hard-earned money.

The new generation does not know the emotions behind this money. They will squander it in wild abandon. This breaks the heart of their fathers and usually they die heartbroken and helpless. What they predominantly carry on to their next life will be this helplessness. The graceful rich one leaves behind a legacy of selflessness to his children and they learn by the example of their father. They also learn to give. These graceful fathers die a peaceful death after a life well-lived. True happiness is in giving. Give only what you can give. But learn to give without inhibitions and emotions. Give to the needy without any feeling of doership. You will stay liberated and peacefully happy.

Image

Q: Do you think image has value?

M: Image has value for the seeker, not the sought. For the seeker, image is a means or a door to enter the realms beyond the image. For the Guru, if he is image-oriented, it might represent subtle ego. Some Masters have deliberately distributed their pictures with the purpose of bringing the attention of seekers to one point, that of absolute attention. This cannot be considered as ego. This is only an effort from the Master to bring the attention of sundry seekers in order to enable them to transfer knowledge or energy. This is also an effort to contain the wandering attention of the followers and to bring forth single-pointed concentration in them.

Image is a good tool to focus on and go beyond. The danger would be to get stuck with the image. An image is a reminder as well as a reassurance of the presence of the Master or God. The visible signifies the invisible. All images are temporary. Not many are able to understand the energy realms. For them, an image would be helpful. Image attains value through constant attention and energization. It becomes alive and a guiding force.

The value of an image will depend on the attitude of the seeker. The smaller the ego, the higher the value because the attitude of self-surrender would be strong. Self-surrender is towards the higher entity of which image is only a representation.

Q: I read that you do not care about maintaining an image. Why?

M: Images are highly perishable. People are too eager to create frames and put one inside. People would like to look at two dimensions and ignore the third dimension of an individual which is more real. People like finite objects while true personalities are infinite. Even our own life is infinite. Soul is infinite. Every moment we are changing. Every cell is changing within a period of time. Body changes, mind changes, emotions change, situations change and beings die and take new births. Change is the truth of terrestrial existence. Amidst all these changes, what image could we keep? What for? Why don't we just let the changes take place and be an impartial witness of all those changes, happening within us and outside of us? No complaints. No judgements.

Secondly, sometimes images are created out of insecurities. Some people are afraid to change their image because others might get disillusioned with them. Some are afraid of any changes. A life of conformity is very easy. A life of non-conformity and fearlessness is very difficult. People say that one who born in fire or moulded in fire is not affected by the scorching heat of the summer sun. He has no fears.

If you look around, images are worshipped so much in a conditioned way that often people cannot get liberated from them. They get stuck inside the cages of their own mind. They deny everything else due to mental conditioning. Their soul attains that image that has created a deep impression in their own subconscious. Or sometimes they stagnate and get disillusioned.

My aim is to not to bind people or blind people—instead my effort is to liberate them if I can. I am glad if my existence helped a few people to get liberated. I am just doing my duty. Not conforming to any image is my way of staying liberated. It becomes difficult for people to put me in any frames. So, they will also stay liberated and unbound. People who are heavily conditioned will go away. This is fine. It is not yet time for them to break their boundaries. Those who can 'see' will stay.

I also do not believe in becoming a statue in a garden. It amuses me infinitely to see 'great men' standing in a garden or public place in all their glory, as toilets for birds. I am sure birds love such grand toilets!

Many people have walked on earth. Generations have trodden on this soil that you tread on today. They all lived with the same emotions, love, hate, anxieties and fears. They all believed that they are better than anyone else.

They all believed more in making money than in living meaningfully. So, we are no exceptions. We are not different from them.

All that matters is what you can do in the present. No image matters. Just purity of action matters. The world is your oyster.

Pride

Q: However much I read, I cannot control my pride or ego. I am really proud of my achievements, even though I am not particularly proud of my wealth. Many people have appreciated my achievements, and at my age I feel I have done well. Is my thought process wrong? Please guide me.

M: Be proud of everything. First be proud. That's for your emotional satisfaction. Then get to your intellect and start analyzing. What exactly am I proud of? This ever changing body, upon which I have no control? This ever changing mind? This ever changing intellect? Ever changing possessions? Transitory money? Rented house? Decaying possessions? Fragile relationships? If you go deeper and deeper and bring all your pride to your own faculty of analysis, it will start dropping away. Finally, your pride will rest on your soul. This is fine. Be proud of your soul, which is subtle and invisible to naked eyes. Only through introversion can you shake hands with it. Once you do that, all your external pride will vanish. Ego will take rest. You will feel liberated. Ignorance and wrong attachment cause pride and ego. Awareness and knowledge of the self will wipe it away.

Expectation and Dependency

Dependency on something can be called a habit. Repetition of one activity continuously for a period of time becomes your character. So, if you choose actions, thoughts and words of kindness and love, you will become that. Each cell of your constitution absorbs that nature. If you express selfishness and deceit, you will become that. It is up to us to choose what we should be and program our actions accordingly. This is based on our inherent trait or vasana. The more dependent you are on something or someone, the more attachment as well as corresponding expectations gets formed. When expectations are high, vulnerability is high. The tendency to get angry or frustrated will be very high. Expectations breed anger and frustration. Then, intellect shuts itself down. Emotion will be running the show. It would be like the office boy running the institution while the CEO is away. We should have absolute clarity about how our system works.

Reduce dependency through constant introversion and introspection. Move towards a witness state where you are witnessing your every word, thought and action. Then you are aware of everything and without conscious awareness, nothing is happening. The first step is to keep observing your breathing pattern, when the breath shifts from left to right nostril and vice versa. When all your unconscious activity ceases to exist, you will be detached from external dependencies. Then, you will stay liberated. Whatever happens outside, will not affect you much. Whether it is turmoil or peace, you will be the same.

We can see that in the first part of their life, children are completely and helplessly dependent on their parents and they usually take each other for granted. In the later part, the parents become dependent on their children and again, usually they take each other for granted. Often, new entries like a son or daughter in law appears and the room of heart needs to be expanded suddenly to accommodate more heads. Sharing the son or daughter with the 'inevitable intruder' becomes painful and uneasiness takes root. We usually fail to accept this inevitability. Anxieties, hatred, frustrations follow and eventual cold and hot war. This way, the family splits up into pieces. Family consists of different karmic beings in coexistence. This fundamental understanding—about diversity in relative unity—does not exist and hence, the issues happen. If love, objective support and non-dependency are the base, the relationship will stay firm. Expectation and dependency kill relationships.

All children must be looked at as karmic beings, with equal importance as adults. They should be respected as adults. This is because their karmic intensity is the same as the adults. We can never underestimate any being on their karmic intensity. It's the same for all. So, be aware of dependencies and expectations. Use your intellect more. Avoid emotions. Avoid resistance to your current situation. You will be calmer and much more peaceful.

Weakness of Character

Aristotle talks about a tragic flaw in human beings. This is real. Out of all the merits, one flaw in the character pulls the whole man down. He might have hundreds of good qualities, but one weakness causes the tragedy. The usual tragic flaw is lethargy, laziness, tendency to delay things without any reason, tendency to procrastinate, tendency to lie, jealousy, greed, insatiable craving for sex, insatiable craving for money, insatiable craving for power, recognition, ego and position etc. Everyone has one or some of these, and one quite predominant. I do not think any human being who walks on earth is immune to it. If someone claims he is immune to this, he is lying. Hence there is no point in comparing one with another. It would be like comparing common fever and the flu. Both are ailments anyway.

Understanding a tragic flaw is the first step. We must accept ourselves along with our flaws. Circumventing or isolating the flaw with higher interests is the next step. If you have the tendency to fear the future, replacing it slowly and deliberately with higher understanding, that the future will happen whether we worry or not, will slowly anchor you firmly in the present. When you are always in the present and your mind is not oscillating between your past and future, then guilt and fear will die a natural death. You will feel more complete and satisfied. We should handle ourselves more sensitively and with good care.

Agonies and Pains

Q: When and how do we feel wounded?

M: Mainly on three levels. Injury to the body, injury to the mind and injury to the ego. The degree of impact is also in the same order. Bodily injury will be eventually forgotten, unless there is an emotion attached to it. Emotional injury will be harboured forever. Injury to ego will get converted into venom and revenge in the course of time. Forgive and forget. Empty your trash each day. Stop carrying generations of trash. You will have to come back to settle scores. It's not worth the trouble.

Q: Which is the worst of all attachments that gives maximum agony in life?

M: All attachments eventually give agony because detachment is essentially the path for liberation. We do get detached from all our worldly possessions at the time of our death, in any case. All attachments, sooner or later will start giving pains. The best way is to be detached in attachment. This means, do love, but always be detached and keep reminding yourself that you are not this role-play that you are effectively performing, and you will eventually remove your makeup one day. Detachment in attachment is the path for liberation. Perform your given role to its perfection without expectations of any kind. Acceptance of reality as it is. Non-resistance. Zero escapism. These will reduce the intensity of attachments and eventually liberate you from perpetual pain.

Injustice

When we do not know our true 'deserving level' and when we consider our desirable level to be our deserving level and try to live it, or when things do not happen as per our expectation, we feel blatant injustice. When we understand clearly that we will get what we deserve, and that what we got was exactly what we deserved, there will be no feeling of injustice. Desire forms out of circumstances. It is our mistake when we feel that we deserve what we desire. We have to raise our stature to be in the deserving level of whatever we desire. Again, desires constantly change and we need to keep upgrading ourselves. It continues through lives. Our deserving level is our actual reality, while desiring level is only our wish or imagination.

Self-Respect and Ego

Q: What is the difference between self-respect and ego? I think the line between them is very thin.

M: We are essentially living for ourselves. We are here to exhaust our own karmas—all of us. In that agenda, some other souls are also a part of it, especially the souls that we call parents, brothers, sisters, cousins, children etc. Emotions bind relationships and even create ownerships while in reality we are already liberated souls handling individual karma. This also creates agony and anxiety which further intensify the karmic binding. Energization of any emotion is like watering a plant. When you water plants, sometimes weeds get nourished too. Thus, energization of emotions breeds many negative effects.

We have come alone, and we will go alone. All these attachments will be left behind at the time of our death. The more conscious we are about what others might think about us and what we think about others, the more we limit ourselves. The moment we decide to express our true nature and decide that we are a liberated soul and express unconditional love towards all beings, we will realize and live the liberation. Then self-respect will not be interpreted as ego.

As you said, there is only a thin line between self-respect and ego. Ego exists in all beings as ego is the skeleton that gives shape to our character. When it gets over-emphasized, it creates a problem for others. If it stays within its own boundaries, it is good. Excessive ego is self-destructive. Excessive ego destroys at every level, especially relationships.

Self-respect is your personality. The way you present yourself to the world. The consistency of your behaviour pattern. All these tell the world who you are. Respect has got to be earned through consistent display of unconditional love, selflessness or benevolence. Our existence becomes meaningful when many lives benefit from it. Otherwise we will just live and die like a parasite thriving on the fruits of Mother Earth, taking everything but never giving anything. We will have contributed nothing to the world.

It does not matter what others think of us. If our conscience is clear, if we have purity in thought, word and action, the war is won. Others can interpret us the way they choose. We cannot do anything about it. We will suffer, if we are dependent on their interpretation. Not every apparel size fits you. And you cannot wear each outfit you are given. You can only wear the one that suits you and your constitution. So take care in that. Expression of ego to convey a message is your strength. Expression of uncontrollable ego as your nature is your weakness. This is the difference that you should be aware of. Analyse expressions, be aware. Do not censor. Be aware.

What Others Might Hear Or Say

Q: Mr. A. said that you think he was narrow-minded. Surprisingly, he is not offended. Why do you think he is narrow-minded? Isn't that statement a sign of your arrogance?

M: Mr. A. is not offended because my intention was good. It's not malevolent. I told him clearly why I thought he should be more open-minded. Why did you not ask him? Whether this statement amounts to my arrogance is up to you to decide. I have nothing to do with such questions. Whatever you think I am, I am that. Nothing more, nothing less.

I posted this message just to let people understand how some people interpret my words and messages. Instead of taking the positive, we cling on to the negative. This message is an example. We dissect a positive message and misinterpret something negative. Another important point: sometimes it is the witness who is offended, not the one to whom the message was addressed. This is a typical issue. The person whom I spoke to has taken the message with Grace. The other person who listened to it—a third party listener—is more offended and is spreading venom. This is how negativity spreads. Negativity breeds by itself. It needs no nurturing like positiveness does. To slip into the negative is very easy.

I wanted to highlight this aspect of our existence. We can only see through our eyes. Truth remains the truth. Interpretation of the truth differs from individual to individual. This is how the world works. As you rightly said, personal insecurity is one reason for gossip. All are interested to know what the celebrities do. This is also part of our sadistic minds. When a celebrity falls, we are interested. We like to see people falling. All these are naked truths of our social existence. I am trying to show a mirror to the face of the society. Two aspects: 1. Taking offence on a third party affair and owning it. 2. Gaining confidence or popularity through spreading venom. Both are heavily negative. My advice to you is to have nothing to do with it.

Material and Spiritual

Q: Why is it that gaps in the materialistic world get filled so quickly for people who have lower vibrations? I've noticed people who just wish for situations and they get them fulfilled even in a very short time. It seems like they have no need to go through any difficulties.

M: Material world is denser than spiritual world. There is gap between material and spiritual. Consider that as the gap between 2nd floor and 10th floor, for understanding's sake. When you are fully immersed in the material plane, your energies are single-pointedly integrated into that aspect. We could compare it to a magnifying lens: we could burn materials with this lens if it is focused properly on an object against the sunrays. When your focus and intensity are accurate, an event can happen — a wish becomes fulfilled. It is the same in spirituality. The same mind that goes out partying with the senses could stay home and bring forth great inner awakenings and revelations. The partying mind and the domestic mind are the same. When the mind goes out partying, it seems like a different entity. When it stays home, it is insignificant and even dissolves into the magnificent soul. The supreme mindless state gives you nirvanic bliss.

Your wish becomes command to nature, when you graduate to the level of effectiveness. It is the same on all planes. Material achievements are more tangible and hence visible. They are also aplenty because the gross is easier than the subtle. Subtle is intangible and the mind always poses questions which tilts our faith. When you decide to move towards subtle, the road becomes rough. It is rough almost till you reach your destination. The need to move into the subtle is a need of the soul, which is tired of these unending births and deaths and being a garbage carrier. Otherwise, there is no liberation for it. It has to keep carrying the karmic baggage and it has to keep coming back to the earth to exhaust the never-ending wishes and dreams.

All of us go through a variety of situations over lives. Fortunately, our conscious mind does not understand this as we do not have awareness of our past lives through our conscious mind. Our subconscious stores it all.

So, the power of materialising your wishes exists in all planes. Consistency of thoughts, words and action are the key. Conviction is a necessity. Confusion is the hindrance.

Sins, Status and Stature

Dear Friends,

Guru Poornima is a great and auspicious day. I wish you could get the maximum benefit from the auspiciousness in the environment for your spiritual progression. Let me use this time to answer a few questions that are welling up in your mind.

About sins:

We are destroying numerous entities when we cook, when we breathe, when we walk and even when we sleep. This should be considered as nature's way of recycling life. Do not take ownership of something that you have no control over. Nature uses a tsunami to wipe off a coast along with its people and captive animals. Nature uses a tiger to control the deer population. Likewise, nature has its means and ways to control life. We cannot take ownership of destruction on that level. We are only instruments in the master plan. Do not entertain guilt for the role you play. Always live with gratitude. Every aspect of your existence is helping your evolution, whether you know it or not. If you plot and kill someone, it's different. If you deliberately destroy anything at all, it's different. If you entertain greed, jealousy, anger, hatred and all such destructive emotions, it will destroy you and others. Lack of understanding of your true nature in one lifetime amounts to a life well wasted. How long will you chase these vain glories? How long will you chase all that glitters? All that glitters is not gold. If gold has to happen in your life, whether you chase it or not, it will happen. Thank your existence and increase your deserving level through non-resistance or by accepting your present reality and conforming with it. Nothing exists forever. Every role-play has a duration. Everything changes. Just have patience to keep playing the role till the end of a scene. Impatience only adds to the agony. I hope I have answered your question on sin, on that aspect.

About status and stature:

To some people, status is given irrespective of their eligibility. For example, becoming a prince, a princess, a lord etc. happens when a person belongs to a particular family, such as the royal family. There are honorary doctorates, conferred out of respect or gratitude. While status can be conferred, stature is always earned. You cannot buy it. Stature is transferred through lives, like samskaras or basic traits. People can buy status with money. This is the usual progression of material existence. First there is the money, then the power, then status. Thus one greed leads to the other. Status such as president or CEO can be conferred based on one's social standing or money power. Stature cannot. Stature can earn status and then it is permanent. Borrowed or purchased status is temporary. It is perishable, highly perishable. Status due to stature is imperishable. The equation is between the deserving versus desiring levels. Stature deserves status and it happens.

Status due to greed is desire and it is perishable. Desire can exist only at a particular space and time for a particular person. Stature is permanent. Stature also could remain undisplayed. This is individualistic. Shirdi Sai Baba, Ramana Maharshi and many Avadhoot saints living in the forest who have, and had stature, never cared about it. This was their personal will and choice. In short, status and stature are different. Status can be bought, stature cannot. Stature can only be felt and perceived. Status can be more tangible. When one achieves stature, status is automatic.

Please understand the difference clearly. Operate sensibly.

HUMAN CONDITIONS

The Right Path

DOUBT IS PART of human constitution. We doubt everything. This is mainly because of our insecurity and fear of failure. What if the society calls us 'dumb'? What if history calls us a failure? All these doubts are blocking everything, especially our progress. We always live in perpetual fear, one way or the other. Fear of exams, fear of losing image, friendships, appreciation, love, self-esteem etc. We are a bundle of numerous fears. This is the opposite of love. The absence of love is fear.

Many of you have asked me numerous questions about the right path. My answer is simple: it is the path that you are currently travelling on. You could not have travelled another path. It is not a coincidence that you are sitting here and reading this mail. It is not a coincidence that you are born at a particular location, to a particular set of parents and lived your life along with a particular set of people, education, job, location of living at various points in time. Making money, losing money, falling in love, falling out of love etc. Everything was part of your script and agenda before you set foot on earth. If you have doubts if this is the right path, while living that agenda, it only amounts to insecurity and fear of the unknown which you have acquired in this life. In simple terms, we come here because of our prarabdha or unfulfilled wishes. We keep coming back in various shapes and names at various locations only for the same purpose. So, let's not be too proud or too sad. A man who was a beggar constantly craved to be born in a palace. That was his next birth. He was penny wise, pound foolish, because of his past life impression of saving it all for the rainy season, and not spending. The signs of poverty existed even in his palace life. But he was a royal! Similarly one who was oppressed in a past life, when he became a royal, was extremely benevolent to his people. You can see many such examples around us, including ourselves. Our attachments can easily disclose our true nature. A man craving for alcohol had in his previous life died without having enough of it. A Casanova or Don Juan was perhaps ugly and unwanted by women in his past life. A voracious eater may have been starving in another life. A lean man was probably very fat in his previous life. So on and so forth.

My request to you is, please do not compare yourself with someone else. Trust in your path. If you deserve to shift your path at some point in time, it will happen. The environment will set it right for you. Never worry. You are definitely a divine child. Insecurities of others also need not bother you. Many of you asked me about the right way of worship. Worship whom? Is God outside of you? If yes, where is he? What is your concept of God? The picture that you see on the wall? So what are you, in relation to him? When will you get closer to him? Only when you become another picture on the wall?

You are him, right now and right here. The right way of worship is through consistent benevolent thought, word and action. No God needs your money as he produced all matter. We are temporary custodians of a small part of his huge estate. Also remember that our earth is only a very small part of this whole estate! Lack of awareness makes us believe that we actually own it all, because we have some papers to prove our ownership. No God needs your praises. He is not your judging and punishing dictator. God is love. When you wholeheartedly express kindness and compassion, continuously, you become him. You have to become him to know him. All theories are useless. All methods or worships are useless, if they only become an addition as another of your rituals. By doing, you cannot reach him. By being, you can be him. His state is egolessness. So how could he become a punishing and judging God? Natural calamities are not his plan of revenge. That's your given result of the consistent abuse of nature. Why do we blame God for a natural disaster? Why did we cut all trees and pollute the atmosphere to obscure the whole universe? Our own senseless creativity chokes us. How can we blame God for that? He has always been like petrol in your car or electricity waiting at the switch to serve you. No intentions of any kind. He just aided you to accomplish that. It does not matter if you worship him or not. Be him. Express his character, which is unconditional love. Castrate fears and install faith. The key that will eradicate all fears is the complete awareness that: "I am imperishable and indestructible". I am THAT. You are that.

My dear friends, the path that you are travelling now, is the right path for you. The moment you think that there is an inadequacy, understand that it's the play of your mind. There is nothing wrong. It is the nature of mind to create these feelings and push man to the edge very often in life. Of course others also help you to feel inadequate. Do not fall prey to that. Please maintain an attitude of surrender to the will of the Almighty without resistance: this means surrendering to the agenda that you prepared for yourself before you set forth on this journey. In reality, the Almighty had nothing to do with your agenda. He just poured the petrol in your car, sufficient petrol to take you till the end of your journey in this life. He made sure you are able to fulfill your agenda, perfectly. If you could not understand the pattern you set forth and do not remember what you fed into your personal navigator before you started the journey, what has God got to do with it? If you wanted detours because you saw many more interesting things on the way which were not part of your original travel plan, what has God got to do with it? If the petrol was insufficient to complete the new travel plan, what has God got to do with it? He will help you to stop this journey and allow you to plan another one. No interference. Just assistance. God behaves like a faithful servant. True God's children also behave in the same way. God never operates egoistically. If His children do, at that time they are disowning God's nature. God has nothing to do with it. He knows that the estranged children will get beaten in life and with their ego thus annihilated, they will come back home. Where else can a wounded child go? He has to come home! God waits to embrace and heal them.

If I say that only my path is the right path, I am being insincere. My path is the right path for me. Your path is the right path for you. We all are in our own personal right paths. No need to compare or criticise. It is the same with religions. For each one, the religion or faith that he follows is the right one. Conversion is only like changing the attire while the person inside is the same. It has no meaning. It only shows the helplessness of man. Truth stays beyond religions.

Some read lots of books in search of portable knowledge and get applause from the public. Knowledge is a burden if not converted into wisdom. Accumulation of knowledge is like emotional eating. Most of the food that we consume goes to waste because the body does not need it. Or indigestion happens. Read what can be easily digested. It will help progress. What you could not read was not necessary for you. Understand that. When you need to read a certain matter, it will reach your hands. Be clear about that. Never feel that you missed something in life. You have not.

Some people do all sorts of things on earth to gather attention. Everything perishes at death. Sometimes all that was earned through wrongdoing becomes the reason for the downfall of one's descendants. The residues of actions never die. They exist, conglomerate and become events. Sometimes these can be strange events, because we cannot see or understand what combination of karma created it. Some get carried away with applauses and accolades. When the applauses that sustained them stop, they fall flat onto the ground and break their bones. What glory are we chasing? What are we trying to prove here? Where will we take it all? Eventually, the bright smiling face that shone amidst people will become a grinning skull in some graveyard. We may still smile through some pictures in frames, which nobody will care for as they have become used to such pictures. Or new pictures will replace the old ones, including your image. Both can happen. It's not worth the race. Be aware of it.

Dharma is important. This is duty in its perfection. Karma is important too. When you wipe off karma, the body also gets wiped off—unless the transition happened into the non-karmic state, and you decided you might as well continue with this body for a few more years.

The following is a compilation of answers to many questions.

Friends, I cannot do anything about other people's method of operation in the spiritual field. I do not endorse anything. If you want to experience various cuisines or taste variety, please understand that you have no chains around your feet or neck. You are free to proceed. Please do not expect me to endorse or criticise. Also, I am very objective in what I am doing. I am looking at all this purely as my little bit of service for the children of Mother Earth. I am her child too. Mother is looking after this body too. I think it's my duty to serve her. Mother is happier when her children are served and when they are happy and peaceful. This is why I am constantly requesting you to serve the helpless creatures if you want to do something for me. Serve Mother Earth: a mother's blessings are enough to liberate you. Mother Earth's blessings are necessary to liberate you. Gratitude is a must. If you live here on earth and just exit thanklessly, you will have to come back to express gratitude. Be aware.

I give all that I have to anyone. I have always done that. It depends on your capacity to carry what I give. Bring larger vessels to carry it next time. Increase your own spiritual capacity. Spiritual capacity has got to be earned. It cannot be bought.

Unhappiness

I get many questions about life. Unhappiness about current life, life patterns, thought patterns or intellectual capacity and discontentment about other things. My answer is pertaining to that.

Respect your constitution. This is fundamental. You are a

unique being. There is none else like you, at exactly your vibratory level and constitution. Understand your own constitution in three levels: physical, emotional and intellectual.

Physical: I am what I am. I cannot change into another's shape and there is no need to change either. I am unique. This is the fundamental acceptance that we must create within ourselves. The height, colour, shape and all aspects of our physical constitution have been part of our agenda for this existence. This life. We did not choose this consciously. Yet, all the variety of data that we fed into our own subconscious mind created this shape or physique. If you deny and are unhappy about your own physical form, you are denying your own creation. Whether you are beautiful or not-so-beautiful, whether you are tall or short, whether you are fat or slim, whether you are black or white. You are what you are. Accept whatever you are, as it is. There is nothing to compare with another. Comparisons are futile. Acceptance of your own physical constitution is the first step towards finding peace in this existence.

Emotional: The emotional constitution is also created by you. You are what you are. There is none exactly like another. There could be someone similar, but not alike. Accepting the emotional body as normal and accepting it as part of your constitution is essential. If you cannot come to terms with the nature of your own emotions, peace will elude you. Whatever your emotional nature is, accept it as it is. Keep telling yourself: "This is the way I am and I am happy with my way". The more you resist your own inherent nature, the more you will suffer. In order to understand your emotional nature or your nature of emotions, you must observe your response patterns closely over a period of time : the patterns in which you are responding to this world. An external observation by somebody else or external comments by someone will not help you here because those comments are given by another person and hence could be biased. You must observe yourself. Recognize your own emotional patterns over time, objectively and without bias. Understand this is the way you are responding in this world. Accept that wholeheartedly as the gift of the Almighty. You will be peaceful. The observation of your own emotional pattern will also identify flaws in the pattern, such as lethargy, tendency to delay things, over-reaction for the sake of protection, desire for attention and sympathy, anxieties, fears etc. Then it becomes easy to handle them and correct them in the future. If diagnosis is perfect, treatment is simple.

Intellectual: right from childhood, a child is subject to comparisons on intellectual competency. The average child undergoes tremendous pressures that affect his self-esteem. Acceptance of intellectual levels is fundamental. Everyone is different. Variety is the core of terrestrial existence. There is none higher or lower in any way. Flavours are different. Life patterns are different, and so are lifestyles. We must accept our IQ level as it is and should never compare it with another's. Comparisons lead to agony and feeling of inadequacy. We always compare ourselves with someone who is relatively superior. This creates jealousy and unrest. Hence, it does not matter whether our intellectual capacity is the best. It only matters whether it is useful for your current existence. The current intellect that you possess is what you had demanded when you came into this life, from the past life. So after taking birth and after a lot of comparisons made by yourself, your family members or even your teachers, if you come to a conclusion that this IQ level is inadequate, it only means that you are dissatisfied with yourself and in a way that is utter nonsense. You cannot move on that way. You have to understand that there really is nothing to compare with. All have their inadequacies. Everyone is an individual with a unique constitution or pattern. You are similar. Just accept that. Be peaceful.

Finally, the set of impressions that created karma and that created a new life for you are exclusively your own. Nobody imposed anything on you. You were living a life, which had a set of relatives, a set of friends, a place of action and a physical, mental and intellectual constitution to facilitate your existence and actions. You lived that life and collected various impressions (just like you are doing now) and whatever you could not satisfactorily fulfill, you brought forward into a new life. The soul has been the same. The impressions were carried forward. The new pattern was created according to what you wanted to achieve or exhaust. Accept that first before you attempt any changes. The events in your life are according to the available impressions in your subconscious mind, brought forth from your past lives. You could not see its existence, since data stored in your hard-drive stays invisible, unless brought to the screen of life. Hence you could not truly understand the pattern of events that happened in your life and why. Every thought, word or action had a root. They all were provoked by the inherent desires. Some are carried forward from other lives and some are acquired in this life.

All these are collectively called your personal constitution. Respect that constitution first. Observe it very closely as a witness. Understand yourself first and stop comparing with another. Once you start respecting and honouring your own constitution, there will not be any internal conflicts. Internally, you will be at peace. External peace automatically happens.

Resistance to any aspects of yourself will lead to agony and suffering. And you will not know the reason why you are suffering. Internal unrest will overflow as anger, jealousy and hatred. You will carve your own hell. You will suffer and many others will suffer. Hence, take the time and understand your own constitution. Respect it. Observe it closely and correct whatever you want to correct, subtly and gradually.

Happiness

Q: We are all in the pursuit of happiness. We seem to miss it between the cup and the lip—why?

M: This is mainly because of two reasons. We are looking for highly temporary external happiness, which means sensory gratifications.

People do not understand that there is a true possibility of permanent happiness through liberation. They get pulled by society, media and advertisements. They usually cater to one's senses and emotions, and definitely not to one's spirituality. When the urge for something higher emerges in someone, he often gets trapped in cults propagating capsulated spirituality, which is easily available, and becomes a victim of a vicious cycle. This is almost like jumping from the frying pan into the fire. Instead of providing means for liberating oneself, the cults bind man for their benefit and suck him into their black holes. Afterwards, there is no external world, as this prescribed world becomes all-encompassing. The cults control people through creating fear or through creating comfort zones or continuous feel-good programs. The poor seeker never understands this trap and blindly follows the group that guides him. He lives and dies in this make-believe world, unfortunately.

And while we are enjoying this conquered happiness, our mind is elsewhere so we miss out on enjoying it when we have it.

Sensory happiness is temporary. Just like eating food. Food has only visual and olfactory appeal when it is on the table. When the food touches your tongue or the taste buds, you can enjoy the taste. If there is no saliva, your taste buds will not do their job. After you swallow, there is no taste either. So the feeling of taste is just when the food is transiting through your taste buds. Neither before nor after. Likewise for all other sensory gratifications. Even a piece of good music repeated many times continuously will lose impact or appeal. External happiness also depends on our mood of the moment. If we are in stress, even the best quality food will not appeal to us. We will not even register its quality in our mind. Just imagine a man who will be assassinated in a few hours time, and he comes to know of this. Even if you give him the best dinner, can he eat at all? Will he enjoy food? The fear of death will be predominant in his mind. His only craving will be for life. He will need nothing else.

Also, if we have not slept for days on due to work, then we are too sleepy and if someone offers us a great dinner, we will opt for sleep rather than dinner. Thus, our mood plays a major role in our enjoying any happiness. Happiness also depends on time, space, environment or situation, capacity of the enjoyer plus his mood.

All through his waking hours man goes from one happiness

to another and compiles a lot of temporary happiness, even developing dependency on some, for example a morning tea or coffee, and the like. And minus this thing, life becomes incomplete for him. He becomes nervous or sad.

Another aspect of elusive happiness is when you are enjoying your favourite food, perhaps you will also watch your favourite game on TV. This distracts. And you fail to enjoy your favourite food as well as your favourite TV program in fullness because your attention had been constantly divided. Thus the unavailable mind is one of the main causes for non-enjoyment of a sensory object when we are at it. We can also call it absent-mindedness. This is dangerous. It can cause serious accidents and even death, for instance if we are at the wheel and our mind is absent from the act of driving a car.

Permanent happiness happens only when we are not dependent on external gratifications. It is not easy to just cut it off like that. Suppression is also not the right way. Increasing awareness and replacing habits with higher pleasures could eradicate the interest for certain habits that we have formed without thinking.

The first step is to disallow all unconscious activities and replace them only with conscious activity. Be aware of even a slight movement of your hand. Be aware of your breathing. Be aware of the food while eating. Be aware of its taste. Be aware. This is the way to shift from unconscious existence to conscious existence. Then life becomes enjoyable, because your mind will be present when you enjoy any sensory object. This will also eventually eradicate dependency. This will definitely trash many habits too.

Confusion

Q: So many things are bothering me. I am confused as to what I should do in the current crisis.

M: You cannot change certain situations in life. Accept this. You cannot go to the past and rectify or change something that you had done earlier. Accept it. You cannot go to the future and do something there either. Accept it. All you have is NOW. The present time. You have this time in hand along with the present facilities, current knowledge, infrastructure, time and space. Do your best now. When tomorrow happens, we will tackle it then. There is no benefit in harbouring anxieties, fears and regrets. These are all waste materials that you have been carrying on your shoulders for generations. At least in this life, you can consciously discard this burden. Can't you? Regarding the crisis, you never created it. Do not take ownership. The crisis has taken place and you are dragged into it. This means it was part of your karmic agenda to go through it. Go through it in a non-attached way. This will not destroy you. This is just another phase. Also this will pass.

Anxiety

Q: How can we tackle anxiety?

M: Through understanding. Through clear understanding of the truth or reality. Higher awareness is the only way. When we look from below, the mountain is unconquerable. For a mountain climber, that is only one of the challenges that he has encountered in the course of his life. He will conquer that too. It is the way you look at it. Anxiety happens due to the fear of unknown, or the unknown fears, especially about the future. Since the fear exists now, the future essentially becomes clouded. In other words, if we do not use our NOW wisely, the future will be murky. Understand that nothing belongs to us. Just look around. Your house, your car, the clothes that you wear, the transitory money in your hand, your own relatives, even your own body . . . , you own nothing. Everything came to you, to give you experiences and everything will leave you at some point or the other. Your body will be trashed too, after death. So what is there to hold on to? Your soul. Only your soul, which is the only permanent entity in this impermanent world. All the wars and fights for possessions and power are all useless. They are unnecessary. All you need is love. Just love. All anxieties will go. Whether you are anxious or not, the future will happen and you have to face your future. There is no escape. We might as well face it bravely. Head on. That's the way to live life.

Those who commit suicide might feel they escaped problems. Bigger karmic problems await them in the next life. Problems will be much more magnified and multiplied in their next life. Escapism is not a solution to anything.

Q: Why am I anxious?

M: (a) Pressure from society to perform in a prescribed way. (b) The targets that you have set for yourself. (c) Comparison with other people. All these are unnecessary. You are yourself. There is no one like you. No need to compare. No need to prove anything. If you are working in an organization or running your own business, you will have targets to achieve. If you are not able to achieve that, it could be either because:

1. The job is not suitable for you and you are doing it out of some kind of helplessness. Or, you have set for yourself targets which are well beyond your capacity.

2. Mind is elsewhere when you are doing your job. Distraction.

3. Lack of confidence.

All these need to be tackled using different methods. Nothing is unachievable if you concentrate on it. Multi-tasking dilutes concentration on everything. Do one thing at a time with full concentration, which is equal to meditation and move on to the next. This is why we say, work is worship. Perfect application of yourself without expectation of returns is Karma Yoga.

Analyze what makes you anxious, because it is individualistic. Analyze what materials you have in hand now. Use the same materials to overcome anxiety. You cannot use anything that you do not have. Do not cry over what you do not have. Use what you have and overcome situations. Fear takes away more than 50% of the chance of you winning any situation. Fear makes your heart sink. Fearlessness is the key and for that you should understand that you are not this limited body, mind or intellect. You are the imperishable Brahma, utilizing this body, mind and intellect for a particular duration and purpose. Every situation is momentary. Every situation will change. Anxiety should be tackled through awareness.

Q: Anxieties are not going away. Fears are increasing. Times seem to be bad. Please help.

M: It is essential to understand the situation fully in order to overcome it. Walking the path, you must. I shall explain an average human existence:

A soul takes birth as a human body (in this story, as a man). His childhood is spent in blissful abandon, as a child immersed in seeking playfulness and fun. He is ignorant of his true state. He is also anxious about proving himself and being better than his friends.

Then he becomes a youth and spends most of his adolescent years in a struggle to gain recognition and position in society. Adolescence puts him in a kind of no-man's-land. Neither here nor there. He struggles to carve an image and position for himself. He is also keen to have a girl of his dreams as his partner—a lot of time and energy is spent in fantasies and daydreaming. He is anxious about proving himself in every aspect of life.

As an adult, he is busy with carving out a life for himself and his family. He is also immersed in earning money, educating his children, building a house for himself, securing his old age etc. He runs all over the place in a struggle or race to create the life of his dreams, forgetting to enjoy the present and always being anxious about the future. As he grows older, helplessness increases and so does associated anger and frustration. He also builds up expectations about his children and if they do not fall within the frame of his expectations, he is disappointed and disillusioned. Sometimes he also pampers his children too much and in turn they kick him around.

He prays to his gods ritualistically, offers a part of his earnings to appease the gods, expecting tangible favours in return. He lives in a world of dreams and expectations, in a continuous struggle and anxiety.

Old age: he is retired. People are not respecting him as they used to, as previously the respect had come out of compulsion or due to his official/social position, and not due to selfless service rendered to society. He has become insignificant and is now simply existing in his hard won home, which has already been taken over by his children. He is often a babysitter of his grand children, or a temporary watchman when his children travel. He often feels like a doormat. He is weak and helpless. He craves for his past glory and yearns for respect. He is anxious about his relatives going away and is not sure whether he will be properly attended to. Sometimes he also fears that he could be dumped into some old people's home as an unwanted burden. Anxieties rule him. He silently nurses his sickness too. He spends sleepless nights filled with fears and anxieties, but during the day he puts on a mask of overconfidence, rigidity and grumpiness. Whenever left alone, he secretly cries over his helplessness. Silently during one such night, he leaves his body.

At that time, he realizes how all the ego built on the sand castle of his achievements and possessions over the years actually meant nothing. He realizes how futile everything was. He regrets that not for even one moment did he ever connect to his own soul. He had forgotten everything in the struggle to create an existence, name and fame. It was only at the time of death that this profound realization had dawned on him—the only thing that ever mattered was his own soul! The soul was in charge. The soul was running the show. The very reason why he had assumed the body was to fulfil the mission that his soul had—but he never even bothered to introspect and enquire what this mission was. All of this was a late realization, as it had come at the time when his soul was already leaving the body. Too late for any correction now.

This is the story of the existence of an average man. Unconscious youth, egoistic adulthood, anxious old age and the most certain death. Unfulfilled wishes and another birth in another womb. The continuous stream of birth and death. The soul carries on, without complaints.

Please be aware: even the child born today will not be existing on this earth in a hundred years from now. There will be a completely new set of people. Many souls have walked on this earth before you, with the same feelings and emotions, and many souls will walk this earth after you, with the same feelings and emotions that you have now. Understand your significance in these relative terms.

Now it is time for introspection. What was worth it and what was not? Observe your life from the perspective of your soul. Even when attempting to understand your relationships, see them from the perspective of the soul. All relationships are as important as relativity and are a matter of inevitability. Are you that, or are you beyond that? This question must be pondered on. Nobody owns another person in any way—even though you may disagree with me on this aspect. Even if two people are married, they do not own each other. They came together only because their karmic vasanas were similar. That's all. An individual is essentially an individual and an independent karmic being. This must be clearly understood in order to curtail expectations towards others. A person will perform up to your expectation only if your wishes and his/her karmic agendas tally perfectly well. Whether it be your parents, wife, husband, daughter or son, the same rule applies. Be aware of this.

Awareness of the macro existence will take anxieties away. Anxieties are only in the mental plane. Mind likes to hold on to fears for its own existence. At your soul level, there are no anxieties or fears. Soul has no guilt either. All this exists only in the conscious mind, as well as on your hard drive, the subconscious. Subconscious only stores impressions. It never discriminates.

Good or bad times are derived out of collective consciousness. When a generation of people lives in fear, hatred and anger, they are only inviting agony into their own lives, one way or the other. When a generation lives in love and kindness, they create that reality. Therefore, there is no point in blaming the times. Times are created by all of us, collectively. As thought is the first level of creation, energy is released. If thoughts are negative, they conglomerate with such similar thoughts and become an event. This is how events are formed.

We have to tackle good and bad. Have faith in yourself—yourself, the non-perishable entity, the god that lives within the temple of your body—your very soul. Also have faith in the supreme entity—the God or the Supreme Soul. This kind of faith will diminish your anxieties and fears. You cannot leave the mind in a vacuum state. It must be substituted with faith. So, start contacting your soul through your breath and slowly internalise your focus. The less external you are, the lesser your cravings will be. The lesser your anxieties will be.

Emotions

When emotions are active, intellect is absent. The result is what we call reactions. This is the space where regrets and guilt are produced. Reactions are spontaneous responses where a consultation with the intellect has not taken place. Whenever intellect is absent, responses cannot happen. Only reactions happen, which we regret later. Observation is much more important than meditation here. Observation can begin with observing our own breath. Every 60 minutes the nostrils alternate, each one comes alive in turns. By observing this you can slowly control each and every thought process. All agonies are formed out of uncontrolled mind and senses. This is the bottom line. Observation is associated with intellect and the more you observe yourself, the better you will be at responding to situations. Through observing yourself, you can also develop a witness consciousness. This happens automatically. Through witness consciousness, you will automatically burn seeds of karma. For easy understanding's sake, start with observing yourself getting, angry, sad, happy etc. and start detaching from all emotions and expectations. Then you stop accumulating further karma. We shall take it from there. Actual satisfaction can happen only when you attain soul realization.

Q: I have had situations where those whom I trusted and loved, betrayed me. I cannot forget the hurt. Please help me.

M: There are no coincidences in life. If a certain situation happens to you, you have subconsciously attracted that situation. Situations happen in life. Allow it to happen. Do not attach yourself to the emotions attached to a situation. Emotion plus situation creates a file in your subconscious. Emotion is the glue that sticks the file of each situation to your subconscious. This stays in your hard drive and creates a reality again, in the future. Understand that such an incident has taken place, understand that it was supposed to happen and it was no fault of yours, understand that there is no point in crying over spilled milk and spoiling your tomorrows. Buy another bottle of milk and keep moving. Be objective. An incident took place. Fine. It's over. Now, take the message out of the incident and keep it in your reference file. Discard the incident as dead and gone. Move on with better clarity and understanding. Past is past. Present is the only reality. Future is yet to be. Never stay in the past. Never stay with silly emotions. If someone cheated you with money, who knows, you may have owed him that money in another life and could never repay it in time. Or, understand money is transitory and it never stays in one place for long. It moves and you are only a temporary custodian. Another aspect of karma is that you can never choose to not pay a debt. So pay, and finish your payables.

You must forget the bad experience through higher understanding and acceptance. If you keep energizing your negative past, it is likely that it will happen again one way or another. This is because you are reinforcing that reality through constant energizing. Lastly, you must also pardon and forgive all those who harmed you, as they came into your life to strengthen you, to give you those experiences. All these gave you knowledge and further maturity.

Do not keep a lot of expectations in relationships with others. The general society works on conditional love, while only saints and the Almighty work on unconditional love. People will love you, provided you conform to their expectations. If you choose to be different or independent, they may not love you. Leave this room and all your relationships, so that you will not be too depressed with people's behaviours towards you. Take every smile and every kindness as a gift from God and reciprocate appropriately. If tomorrow it does not happen, you must remain the same. This quality must essentially be cultivated. Avoid letting emotions spoil your day and also pull you down. Understand that each person expresses himself in this world according to his character and conditioning. It may not be the same as ours. Allow in your mind, room for that variety to exist. So you will not be 'hurt' by any kind of behaviour. If someone decides to walk naked in the street, we will not essentially do that. He expresses his culture, we will express ours. Bear this in mind.

God needs nothing from you. Do not add stress to yourself. It is up to you to connect with God for your own sake. God is unconditional. Everything belongs to Him. What more can you give Him?

Be happy. Pardon all. Lead a pious life. Love all and respect all. You will be fine.

Q: What's the main cause for anger? How can we control it?

M: Main cause for anger is ego. Second cause is expectation. You can decrease it by observing it as a witness. Be aware that you are getting angry. Be aware that you are becoming egoistic. When you observe, automatically, it will start diminishing.

Responding Vs. Reacting

The main difference between intellect and mind is this: intellect is the unemotional discriminatory factor of our constitution, while mind is the seat of emotions. From an activity point of view, the intellect leads to responses, while emotions lead to reactions. The difference between free will and destiny also should be considered in this context. Destiny is prarabdha karma, the karma that created this birth. The karma that provided us with this constitution, including the mind, intellect and character. Free will is the available choice in a given situation. Sometimes the choice could be whether to have breakfast or not. But in totality, deviation from destiny is difficult. Yet it is possible, when you push the limits by non-resistance to any situation, acceptance of yourself as you are and others as they are, nonviolence in thought, word and action—even if our constitution demands otherwise. This 'non-frictional' existence will push your awareness levels towards the omnipresence. That will help you to detach. You will also automatically shift to the company of unconditional people. You may engage in charities. You may also opt for silence more than regular reactions. Thus the signs could be many. The essence is that dependency will be less and detachment will be backed by a purposeful inner peace. This happens, it cannot be created.

The right moves are those formed out of intellect. But as awareness grows, the intellect also performs better. It is like climbing up higher and higher: you can see better. As the intellect understands the vastness of creation, its existence and its relevance in the collective sphere, it starts guiding differently. So it would be better to stick to the intellect and respond rather than react with emotions.

'Easy is right' is a beautiful statement. It is the same as 'simplicity is godliness'. Easy is a state of mind. Resistance makes things complicated. Easy means non-resistance. Mind is telling us whether something is easy or difficult. For a person completely surrendered to the existence or his/her guru or God, everything is simple and easy. Devotion makes everything simple. Lack of faith makes things difficult.

Q: I feel that each situation will not necessarily become 'easy' by surrendering. Isn't it sometimes better to just withdraw oneself from too complicated and uneasy situations? For example if there is a trauma or issue like co-dependency in a relationship. If one realizes that a situation is not going anywhere and entanglements are getting worse, shouldn't one get out? Or would non-resistance also be the way forward here (difficult to imagine that as a solution!)? When is it right to surrender and when to take action/responsibility? Would the intellect be the correct instrument to make that decision? Intellect might tell us to get out of a situation, but the heart hopes and wants to stay. Or is this hope then an attachment (thereby having nothing to do with the soul's guidance)? Could you please describe the collaboration of one's heart and one's intellect?

M: Intellect usually never overrules the heart. Emotion overrules intellect. Emotions lock the intellect up and make it unavailable. A man operating from his emotional plane all the time is like a pendulum. Completely at the mercy of the given situations. He has no control over himself. He enacts more and more ridiculous situations because of his emotional outbursts. Intellect is always kept locked up. We can see that in ourselves, when we get angry and emotions run wild. We will regret our own actions later. This is human nature.

The one who operate from the spiritual heart will always be balanced, will have objectivity, unselfishness, determination for selfless service, no anxiety and complete peace within. Their inner space will be relatively clean. Spiritual heart is the same as soul. Soul is above mind, body, intellect and ego. It is beyond everything. It is the only permanent entity existing in our substratum. The spiritual heart is the expressive side of the soul. You can also call it your higher self. There are no confusions there. No regrets either. Spiritual heart is synonymous to detachment in action. All the actions that it provokes will be for the general well-being of the person and the society. There will be no selfish motive ever. So, rising from emotion to intellect is very important. From intellect plane to the plane of the soul is further elevation. The yardstick is difference in awareness.

Do not confuse the spiritual heart with the heart which is the seat of emotions. The word 'heart' is just a word to demonstrate the seat of emotion or the location from which the person operates. Spiritual heart is different. It is the expression of your soul. Spiritual heart's guidance is soul's guidance. That happens when total surrender to existence happens. Avadhootas are prime examples. They surrender to existence completely and accept whatever comes their way. They kill expectations in every way possible. They also kill fears through confrontations. Thus, sheath by sheath, they liberate themselves from all impressions from the past.

Simplicity and toughness are a matter of attitude. Attitude is an offspring of our mind. When we say we have the right attitude or attitude of surrender, it means that the mind is in acceptance of the given situation. So, any situation can be simple or complicated depending on your attitude. Also, any complicated situation will not be painful, if we have the right attitude. Surrendering should not be taken in the passive sense. Surrendering to any situation should be out of deeper awareness that each situation has been created only by us, using our own faculty to think, speak or demonstrate and act, along with adding emotions at each step. When we know that we created the given situation, when we know that we are responsible for everything that we are and that has happened or is happening in our life, we feel a surrender to it. This surrender is not out of helplessness. It is out of awareness or ownership of our own thoughts, words and actions. This helps liberation. Running away from a problem takes us nowhere. We cannot run away from anything. Escapism is only postponement. You must face it sooner or later.

You can walk out of relationships. This could also be because the joint karma is over. You may meet the same person again. This could also be because at another space and time there is something to be accomplished together. We cannot take situations and assess them each with the same yardstick. Each situation is unique and so are the individuals. You cannot go anywhere. You have to do it right here, right now. And when you surrender to that reality, you are home.

Intellect is always better than emotion when taking any decision. Emotional decisions have weaker longevity.

Quarrels and Shouting

Q: I live in a joint family set up. Recently my cousins lost their jobs. We witness constant quarrels and complete uneasiness at home. Too much anger and shouting. The children are scared and frightened. What can we do?

M: You cannot do anything except for bringing them to understanding.

You can only bring the horse to the water, drinking the water is up to the horse. Resistance to any situation causes anger. Accepting realities as they are and using the intellect without becoming emotional about it, and finding the best solution is the key for peaceful co-existence. Since you are in a joint family situation, burdens also can be shared. Both blaming, and taking more weight than one can handle, are destructive to oneself and the relationships.

Obviously, self-esteem is low in a situation of joblessness. They would react violently to any situation, because emotions are at work and inside they are like a volcano ready for eruption. Using intellect more is the key remedy here. When emotions are at work, stepping aside and switching the intellect on, is essential. Collective thinking can help in such situations. You are lucky that you have a joint family.

When hearts are apart, the volume or sound of our communication increases. We shout. When hearts are close, we whisper. Lovers whisper. Enemies shout. It's hard for hearts to come together, because we are too judgemental. It's easy for hearts to split. It's difficult for hearts to be united.

Make them understand. In a time of crisis all you need is love. All you can have is love. All negative emotions will breed catastrophes. It will push man to extremes. He will regret this later. His life will eventually become too chaotic and he will become physically and mentally sick. Beware. Be aware.

Emotional pressure can be effectively handled by extreme physical action, such as sport. This is not a permanent solution. This is a harmless diversion. This vents the volcanic energy within, harmlessly. Let it be a heart-to-heart discussion from your side, and surrender all your actions at the feet of the Almighty. You are not the performer. He is the performer.

Indecisiveness

Indecisiveness has its root firmly placed in 'doership'. We feel we are the doer. We mean this body, mind, intellect, ego thing which we call with a name. We should understand one thing. In any given situation, at any given time, with the available faculties such as mind and intellect, as well as knowledge and experience, we are interpreting a matter or doing a thing. Ego is the reason why we fear failure. Success and failure are also relative terms. Sometimes, failure is better than success because it throws light on areas which might have been previously ignored. This helps a better positioning in the future. Success boosts ego and sometimes blinds us too. There are plusses and minuses in all situations. In absolute sense of the soul, there are only experiences. There is no good or bad. Only experiences. Good and bad are the problem of our conscious mind. When we sleep, even that is absent. So, we consider all aspects only during our waking hours. The rightness of our action could be interpreted as a historic blunder by the next generation. My friend, relax. Do not over emphasise on the right decision. Just understand that we have been given billions of sense objects, five senses to understand all of them, and one mind to feel them. We are so limited. Accept successes and failures with equanimity. Do not compare. We are what we are. Happiness is a state of mind. Some people always live their lives unhappily because their craving and comparisons never end. As the Upanishad says: "The food on your table today is the medicine for you." It may not be the food that you chose. You may not have got what you wanted. What you got is the right one for you. This is according to our invisible deserving level. Choose what is available and stand with your decision. Tell yourself that in the given circumstances, you could not have done any better. Never allow regrets to creep in and breed guilt. This is just a play of the mind. Never compare. Keep moving. Also understand that looking back and saying "I could have done better" is absolute nonsense. We could not have done any better with the then available time, space and intellect. We are constantly evolving. First of all, going back in time is impossible. Secondly, even if you go back in time, the current awareness that you hold will not be available, since you have progressed into this awareness level gradually. So please do not buy the idea if someone says: "Well, you could have done better." Just never allow others to put their trash on you. No one is perfect. The whole life works on a different symmetry, not according to what is in our finite minds. We need to remove our 'doership', then we will see the master play on the stage. We never wrote it. We never directed it. We are just playing our part.

Timely Decisions

Q: Often it is difficult to take a timely decision which results in lost opportunities. This creates regrets and often affects confidence and self-esteem too. How can I get out of this problem?

M: "There is a tragic flaw in every personality." I did not say this. This was said by Aristotle. This tragic flaw is well depicted in Shakespeare's plays. While Hamlet's tragedy is based on his complacency and delay in taking decisions, Othello's tragedy is caused by suspicion and his jealousy.

Likewise, each of us has some minuses, some deficiencies. Recently while travelling, I came across some very good people, but their minds were very closed. They were hiding behind their own minds. They were not open at all to even discussing subjects that mattered to them. Their deficiency is their closed mind. They fear changes. They fear evolution. They can never experience freedom and liberation as long as they hide behind their own fears.

If delay in decision is the problem that you need to address, you must learn to live in the NOW. Act now. Think now. Do everything now. How do we do it? Every person has a given time, place, body, mind and intellect and a given situation. Using these faculties, he/she has to take a decision. He/she takes a decision based on his/her available knowledge and understanding, as well as the emergency. This is the best one can do. Understand the limitations that one has and accept the result whatever it is. Never postpone a decision, mechanically. Postponement might cause lots of problems for you as well as for others. Discussion with others who are of reliable nature can also help you. If you cannot develop self-confidence, increase your faith in God. This will empower you.

Comparison based on the past or on someone else's action is of no use. Someone else has a different space, time and intelligence. Never compare. You are fine the way you are. And each situation, time and space will be different. It can never be the same. Please also understand that the world means variety. You can never duplicate anything 100% using your limited faculties. Infinite intelligence can duplicate anything. Man cannot.

So first of all, act in the given time space using your available resources. Then accept whatever the results of your actions are, and do not discriminate between good and bad as long as your intention was good. Never harm anybody through thoughts, words or action. Regrets are always related to a past action. When regrets arise, please make your own mind understand that you could not have done any better at that time, with your available faculties and ambitions. If you have many regrets, it will affect your self-esteem and confidence. Especially, if you have many regrets your self-confidence also will erode. Replace regrets with clear understanding. Nobody is perfect and nobody needs to be compared to anybody. Always be selfless and happy.

Lastly, the best trick for positive action is the mind being fully available when you take any decision. Any action of mechanical or automatic nature could create unwelcome results. Any action where mind is fully present and fully involved will have good results. That's the trick. Just as decisions based on emotions or anger will cause sorrows, decisions made with the intellect will have good results.

Enjoy life. Trash your regrets. Also trash your barriers. Be free from your own mind. Mind is suffering from conditionings. So, save yourself from the conditioned mind, and stay liberated.

On betrayal

Without prejudice, without sounding pessimistic, please let me state the basic nature of the world. It is selfishness. We all are selfish people. Everything is survival oriented. Every man and every animal. All are survival oriented. When someone asked Swami Ram Tirth, centuries ago, why are people so selfish? He humorously replied: "Why not? People must be selfish, because everyone is selfishly chasing the fulfilment of their own karma. How can one be unselfish and aid another one? Time is limited. Resources are limited. How can we compromise time, space and resources?" There is a big truth in those words. All our relationships are mostly—essentially—selfish even though on the outside it does not seem so.

One man had his pride hurt from early on when he could not date any good-looking female while at university. He sought to bridge that effectively by marrying a beautiful girl. He was not in love with her. He was only proving a point. He was proving to himself. It was all pretension. Earthly love is too conditional.

Another man worked hard for his rather large family and fell victim to his efforts and died early. His family was devastated. His wife started crying: "Oh, how can you leave so early? What will happen to me and your children? How will I educate them? Where will I get the money for your mother's medicine etc.?" They were only worried about their own sustenance. They were mourning the death of their milking cow, not the husband or father. They were not worried about the man who died. How conditional relationships are!!!

Society loves the materially rich. Their assessment is always two-dimensional. I have a friend who always used to dream about big and fancy cars. Eventually he acquired one, but he did not actually dream of the associated wealth and could not maintain his car, since his income was insufficient. When eligibility exists, then everything will fall in place. Otherwise karma pushes certain things forward and it creates anachronism (wrong timing). This is possible. We are all chasing vain glories.

Another man holds on to his status and position, and fears losing it. He does not gracefully step down. People ridicule him. His ego gets hurt. Not even for a moment does he think how shallow this whole game was. When new leaves appear, the old fall away. Life has to go on. Nature always explains deep truths of existence. All we need are eyes to see and understand. We create nothing. We take away nothing. We are only temporary custodians. We come because of two people (parents) and four people carry us to the graveyard, when we die. We are here on a picnic with a definite time span—between our birth and our death.

So if your children used you as a milking cow, understand two things: A. Expectation. B. Detachment. These are the lessons attached with this experience. You had expectations that your children will adore you when they are grown up, the same way they adored you in their childhood. When parents put a lot of pressure on children, the children tend to distance themselves from the parents at the first possible opportunity. This is human nature. We cannot take pressure for long. We try to escape from pressures as soon as we can. This is one aspect. The other aspect is what Swami Ram Tirth explained. Each person is essentially handling their own baggage (karma). Just imagine yourself in your last life as a relative who never cared about those souls that are now your children in this life. What we sow, we reap too.

Now, the other side of it all. When there is no comfort in relationships, when there is no comfort in material aspects, we turn to God. When material comforts are aplenty, who cares about God? Who cares about our own soul? Discomforts are given so that you get closer to the Almighty. Use this chance, understand God. Bless all. Never condemn anyone. Express love and eradicate hatred. The transit in the rest of your life, in this body, will be excellent. When we cry over spilled milk, we are wasting time, we'll never progress. Life moves on. Seasons change. Leaves come and fall. Men will take birth and die:

Punarapi Jananam Punarapi Maranam (Again birth, Again death)

Punarapi Janani Jatthare shayanam (Again in the womb of some mother)

Iha samsaare bahu dusthaare (This existence (cycle) is tedious, my (friend)

Kripayaa paare, Paahi Murarae (Attain Grace, get to the feet of the Lord-worship God)

Adi Shankaracharya said this.

Your time is right for speeding up your evolution. Do not shed even a teardrop for the past. Past is dead. Dead needs nothing. Past does not need anything, except perhaps gratitude. Future is unknown. Get to the feet of the Lord NOW. Nature has given you means for detachment in the form of relationship discomforts. We have to lose a lot to gain something. When man loses everything, even his ego, he reaches the realms of God. When a man attains detachment in aplenty, he also reaches God. The rest are all just glorified watchmen guarding their own wealth or relationships. They cannot sleep peacefully.

Keep evolving. God Loves You.

Handling Suffocating Situations

This is my message in reply to similar questions from three different people. The questions are based on suffocating realities and how to tackle them or what would be the right approach in any situation.

Take the following as a joke. It is one example of how different gratifications can stem from a similar action, for two different individuals. Or how two different purposes materialized from one job: Two soldiers were having a chat during their free time. First soldier: "Why did you join the army?" Second soldier: "I didn't have a wife and I loved war. So I joined. How about you? Why did you join the army?" First soldier: "I had a wife and I loved peace. So I joined the army!!"

There is a famous saying by Japanese author Yukio Mishima. It goes along these lines: "You should never go to the sea because you hate land. You should go to the sea because you love the sea. Someday, you will have to come back to the land."

Escaping from any situation is not the right action under any circumstances. It is always better to address each situation with patience and intelligence, and tackle it before we move on. Loose ends always tend to reappear as skeletons in the closet, many times in life. A job well completed will stay completed, unless improvements are required. That will still be manageable and will not turn out to be a nightmare. Loose ends will eventually become skeletons in the closet and essentially turn out to be nightmares in the future, unless you are lucky!!!

Let me repeat. Escapism is not the right way. Facing reality by using intellect instead of emotion is the right way. Never sympathize and procrastinate. Act. When roads are rough, drive with extreme caution.

Controlling

Q: I have always been in control of my life. I always used to think well and take decisions. Lately I seem to be losing confidence in myself.

I believe increasing age and the market situation are the reasons for it. Could you throw some light on this?

M: Be careful when you say that you have been in conscious control of your life. What factor of your existence have you actually controlled? Your heartbeat? Respiration? Circulation? Digestion? Muscular movements? Thoughts? Pulse? Sleep? Situations? What have we controlled till now? We do not know what we will think the next moment until the thought comes to pass. We know only on past-tense basis. All the vital functions of our body are under the control of our subconscious mind. Thank God!!! We are saved from some fatal 'forgetfulness'. Our conscious mind is not involved in any of the major functions of our body. Conscious mind recognizes a thought only after it has taken place. It does not have control on thoughts.

If we think that we are taking lots of decisions, then let's have a closer look. We have no control on the climate or the weather. We have no control on external situations. And to a great extent on our internal situations either, such as emotions and mood fluctuations, which often depend on other people's behaviour. So at a given space, at a given time, with the given intellect, with the given status of mind and body, we either think or talk or do certain things. Yet we consider ourselves as 'the doer'. This ownership over things or situations which are not at all ours, is the fundamental cause of many miseries in life.

Does this mean we have no responsibilities? We do. We have limited responsibilities, or perhaps we have grand responsibilities. First, we should understand who we actually are while we are alive. In order to understand who we are, we go through many situations and trials and errors. In most cases, it is only at the time of death that we understand who we actually are. We are essentially the soul. The next responsibility is to express our true nature. Our true nature is that of universal love, with perfect awareness that the whole universe is within us and we are part of the whole universe.

The third is to help others recognize the true nature of themselves. People have a 'herd instinct'. If one walks, everyone follows, not even considering the suitability of the destination. If you can responsibly detach another person to take strides on his own, and help him live with awareness, your life is worth it.

Otherwise at some point in time, we will lose this 'so-called control' and we will start feeling that there is something 'wrong' with us. The 'wrong' is not with us. It is with our understanding of ourselves and the realities of our existence. Please understand that this feeling of control that you had entertained was indeed not existing. The situations or circumstances made you feel that it did and you lived in that make-believe world for so long that you lost touch with the 'real' reality. That's all. Now, you are on the right track. You have recognized that there is something fundamentally wrong. This is the time for introspection. Now, you will understand that you controlled nothing and you will develop gratitude for existence itself. You will see the commonality amongst all beings. All that move on earth have the same soul running their bodies. You will recognize that soul inside all shapes. You will evolve higher.

Peter's Dilemma—Ours Too

Peter loved Jesus. He tried to be with Jesus wherever Jesus went. He often felt lost when he was away from Jesus. He carried out the tasks that Jesus entrusted him with, carefully and in great detail. He realized the power of Jesus and also realized how bright and radiant He was, compared to all others. He was strong and powerful, full of love and purity, truly divine. Peter could not recognize that radiance even in kings or nobility. Jesus expressed and created lightness, happiness, and brightness, wherever he went and everyone who came to see him experienced it and drank from it as much as they could. Some took their experiences home and remained blissful until the darkness of the surrounding interactions gradually eroded it. They came back for more and Jesus poured out purity and love to all beings—unconditionally. Peter trusted Jesus and would have given anything to be next to Jesus. He had seen and experienced the internal shift happening in hundreds of people who came to see him. That shift was the cleansing act that Jesus subtly performed in every being just to enable them for higher awareness. This was much more valuable than the diseases that he easily cured. Peter felt that people did not really understand this factor as much as he did. People only understood the tangible results. Deep within, Peter understood the task that Jesus carried on his rather fragile shoulders. He often wondered how he effortlessly carried such a huge task of transforming the hearts of the ignorant and often barbaric mankind into lightness and love. This was seemingly an impossible task. Even though Jesus never pretended any greatness in the work that he carried out, it was obvious from the way he handled his days, with no fear and no exhaustion as well as with firm conviction. Peter often wondered and feared how Jesus would penetrate the iron minds of traditional men and women. Jesus represented light. His whole being was radiating divine brightness. But his task was to penetrate the iron shields of utter darkness, barbaric, stoic ignorance. Peter often thought that those hardened people were like black holes. They had no capacity to give back love, let alone process it inside, when they received it in abundance from Jesus. They could never accept anything from a living Master. He often talked about his kingdom and that he was the son of the Almighty. These words were all unacceptable to the rigid religious people. They believed only in the words of scriptures and no other truths were acceptable. They also feared that God might punish them if they listened to any words of spirituality other than what was given in their old books. They closed their ears and mind to anything new, to anything unknown.

Then there was the dilemma of the age. Jesus, in the prime of his youth, sharing wisdom that even the much older had never possessed, was unacceptable and not even worth listening to, according to the religious heads and 'wise men'. It had to be blasphemy, triggered by the fire or adrenalin of being very young, or the ego of youth. Peter understood their thought processes almost through his sixth sense. He seriously contemplated strategies that they could possibly adopt if things got out of their hands. He also tried to share these strategies with Jesus, including that of retreating to another country, allowing the people to chew on the thoughts they had been given, and then come back when the people were more mature and ready. Jesus laughed them away as always, and continued to walk on a razor's edge, unperturbed.

Peter was sad and felt totally helpless. He was aware that the old would never accept a living Master, especially such a young one. They always wanted to follow the traditional. All those Masters were dead and gone, and would never come back to correct the interpretations of their teachings, which the current spiritual leaders had conveniently adopted and adapted.

Peter knew that Jesus was playing with fire. Often his fearless approach confused Peter, and there lurked within him a deep and subtle fear that the religious heads would take Jesus away from humankind one day. He hoped and wished that nothing bad would happen to Jesus, because he loved and cared for him and had tremendous faith in him. Peter knew that without Jesus, the whole group of ever-growing followers would be like rudderless boats. The earth for them would be like a sunless sky.

Days went by. Jesus started moving more dangerously closer to the clerics and religious fanatics, upsetting them tremendously. Jesus was not perturbed at all. He seemed unaffected and stayed focused on his mission. On one particular day, Peter realized that his fears were getting stronger. His heart was beating louder and a deep uncertainty was consistently overpowering him. Despite the Grace and presence of Jesus which calmed him to a great extent, he felt agitated. While having supper with Jesus, he could not refrain from expressing his thoughts to Him, who seemed to ignore everything around and seemed to be in a different world or different plane of existence. He also seemed to be too detached from his own body. There was a strange aloofness in him. Peter thought it strange, but then again he never claimed that he understood his Master too well.

Peter told Jesus: "Jesus, I cannot live without you. I love you so much that I would give anything just to be with you. I am even willing to kill or die for you. You are the only one that I care for on this earth."

Jesus looked at him. Smiled. And uttered in a controlled, detached way: "Not so fast Peter. Before the cock crows tomorrow, you would have disowned me thrice." Disowning Jesus thrice before tomorrow's daybreak? Impossible, Peter thought. Jesus must be joking.

Jesus was arrested that night. That was the last supper that Peter ever had with him!!!

Jesus was arrested and Peter felt completely lost and helpless. He was hopelessly drifting, his mind blank. On one side a deep helplessness and on the other side, an urge to save Jesus at any cost. He felt like an ant trying to move a mountain of opposition. It was a cold night. He felt cold and miserable. He could not locate the other companions of Jesus. All were scattered. Peter was recognized by one woman: "Hey, I have seen you with Jesus." Out of confusion and a strange urge to save himself, he said: "Woman I do not know what you are talking about. I do not know any Jesus." As soon as he uttered these words, something hit him deep within, a pang of the pain of guilt seeped through his spine. He went away from there. He felt more miserable by now. The cold wind was adding to his agony. He joined some people sitting around a campfire. As he slowly started feeling better, another one recognized him. The same words got repeated without Peter being fully aware of what he was saying. Again, he disowned Jesus and went away from there with guilt mounting further. The last time he disowned Jesus that night, the cock crew declaring the forthcoming sunrise. Jesus was being taken away by the soldiers and as Peter said for the third time: "I do not know any Jesus, what you are talking about, man?" Jesus turned and looked at him and smiled. Jesus kept his word. Peter felt more miserable than ever. He felt like killing himself then and there. He felt numb, exhausted and without any strength. He was as dead as he could be, with guilt and deep uncertainty torturing him.

Deep within, Peter understood that without a hard shock like his death at the cross, Jesus perhaps could not have woken up a sleeping generation. Though Jesus uttered thousands of words revealing the eternal truths, they were not quite reaching the hearts and souls of the humans who were clothed in absolute ignorance. Lack of awareness is ignorance and since they were not aware of their ignorance, they closed the windows of their minds to any light that could possibly take away their comfort zones—in other words, their ignorance. What's wrong with ignorance, if ignorance is not understood as ignorance? Jesus decided to spill his own blood in order to penetrate this ignorance.

Peter realized this later. He realized much later that this kind of suffering had been in Jesus' plan. He could have saved himself if he wished to. Why didn't he? Peter realized that he had never known Jesus well enough.

And Peter thought that it would have been better to die on the cross next to Jesus, rather than living in the guilt of disowning his own Guru. Peter would have very well killed himself, rather than suffer the guilt of disowning Jesus. He felt more miserable than ever. His instinct for survival had made him disown Jesus. Or on second thought, was this also a plan by Jesus to carry out his mission further, in his absence? Jesus had once said: "Peter, you are the rock on which I will build my empire." Masters can work through any bodies. They have that power. The words that Peter uttered were perhaps not his own. What if they were of Jesus? Peter realized that he needed much better eyes to see through the intricacies of the masterplan as well as his Master's plan. Both were same. Peter was an ordinary man. Jesus had made him a saint. A Master creates diamonds out of stones!!

We are all ordinary men. We constantly disown even our own brothers and sisters every day, if we feel that harm could befall us if we support them through thick and thin. We are often fair-weather friends. We offer others a seat only when we feel that they are comfortable by themselves and we will not be bothered any further. Can we accept another unconditionally at all? This is food for thought.

People keep disowning people still. People still keep accumulating guilt. People keep repeating and re-enacting the same scenes time and again, through generations. Maybe these words will help us think? Perhaps Peter's story is repeated every day? Maybe we are disowning some Jesus each day to save ourselves? This is food for thought indeed. My intention is only to facilitate the existence of more guilt-free minds on the earth.

HUMAN CONSTITUTIONS

Gunas

THE NATURE OF how we act depends on our gunas, our primary qualities and operating tendencies. The gunas are classified as sattva, rajas and tamas. Our character is based on the nature of our gunas—of which one is relatively more predominant than the others. A rajasic man will always be hyperactive and will also be subject to the swing of emotions. A sattvic man will automatically start his day between 3 and 6 am, at the time called Brahma Muhurtha, the subtlest of all times. A man of predominantly tamasic nature will tend to procrastinate and indulge in addictions of intoxicants. In everyone there is a mixture of gunas. Each cocktail has degree variations. The strength of ingredients, depending on which guna is predominant, determines the flavour of the man. Gunas subtly create bondages with the senses and aid our desire for sensory objects. Gunas exist in perfect balance and equanimity in the divine consciousness or enlightenment. This is a karma-less state. Imbalance of gunas induces karma.

Man behaves according to his constitution or gunas. We are a mixture of sattva, rajas and tamas. The predominance of any of these will be reflected in our character. We are born in a particular environment because that was necessary for the exhaustion of our prarabdha karmas—the core reason for the new birth. We often get relocated to different environments during our lifetime for the same reason. Vasanas or basic traits are formed out of karma. Thoughts are formed out of vasanas. Words are formed out of thoughts. Actions are formed out of words. This is the broad classification of the pattern of our existence. Or we can call this the chronology of action: vasana-thought-word-action.

There are billions of permutations and combinations possible in terrestrial existence. The parameters of do's and don'ts are also different. Demand and supply situations also exist in various combinations. Each constitution has its own demand. Usually it is said that a person who tortures others and spreads negativities will meet the same fate, either in this life or in the next. So we cannot assess one person based on just one life or current life. No action goes unseen. Nature records each action. Our own sub consciousness also records each action. It even records the actions that we witness without participating, including a harmless newspaper report. All of these are ingredients for our karmic future.

When I visited South East Asia recently, I saw that people ate snakes, rats, turtles, dolphins, dogs, monkey brains, insects and every other moving/movable objects, except perhaps tables and chairs. Dogs, cats and various animals are kept compressed in cages to be killed for their meat. Animals are tortured and killed for man's pleasure! People are grossly ignorant of the feelings of captive birds and animals. They have seen this lifestyle since birth, it was the karma that they chose. They feel nothing. Insensitiveness is also chosen. Everything is prarabdha. Sensitivity could happen in their path of evolution. Sometimes it never happens in a lifetime. A butcher will say that this is the only job he is used to, that he could not do anything else. Or the public demands the supply and he is obliging mechanically. Or even 'for the sake of his family', so on and so forth. Sensitiveness never happens in such cases. When we transcend from rajas towards sattva, the attitude of non-violence takes firm root. Then it is difficult to harm any beings.

So, prarabdha is written in stone. It happens as per plan. Addendums may or may not happen within one lifetime. Results of action could also be postponed to the next existence, which we cannot see now. The animals suffering violent deaths and confinement could also be the torturers of the past. We never know. According to our karma, we attain births. With great benevolent deeds we may be born into a pious family of saints and high beings. Likewise, beings who have just transcended from animals to man also display animalistic tendencies. They display insensitiveness. They also display selfishness. As they evolve through many lives, they slowly become more and more refined. It takes hundreds of lifetimes. Sometimes the spiritual evolution is so slow. So, we have to consider this in all aspects.

Q: Are gunas ego states?

M: Not quite, but close. In order to understand gunas easily, we could consider them as close to our ego states, such as child, adult and parent ego state. Indeed, gunas determine our response levels, just like ego states do.

Metamorphosis

Q: I was reading your answer on tamas (inertia). How can one overcome tamas? I am comparing tamas with laziness.

M: Tamas is laziness. And tendency to procrastinate and getting depressed, tendency to postpone things for no reason. Feeling tired without physiological reasons. Getting angry when disturbed. Interest in old food, which is food prepared last week and reheated a 100 times using a microwave and eating just to fill up the belly. Interest in tamasic food, which means any food that has no prana or aura (meat and alcohol for example). These are all tamasic qualities. When tamas is the problem, it should be countered by rajas. Rajas is action. Even action just for the sake of action. Go and play tennis or football. Go cycling or jogging. Beat inertia. This will help you overcome tamas. Lethargy should be countered by persistent and consistent action. It needs a hard kick. Otherwise, mind will tend to sulk and we will tend to switch on the TV and grab some aerated drink, popcorn and watch a soap opera which concludes nowhere. One must beat the mind with determination. It needs a strong will, then the results will be tremendous. Rajasic action will not only beat tamas, but will also energize your self-esteem and even the ego. Let it be, we will tackle it too.

Once you have beaten tamas and you are on a rajasic plane, which means hyper action, you will tend to swing between happiness and sorrow and the mind may tend to operate on unconscious mode. You will be egoistically target-oriented. You will care a lot about results and will not leave any stones unturned as far as achievements and results are concerned. You will move in social circles and will be carrying out your life on achievement basis. Applauses and accolades really matter to a rajasic person. Intellectual supremacy and 'proving' a point too. These are all rajasic traits. We will constantly go for new dresses, vehicles, ornaments, partners (just joking!) etc. We even change jobs to prove our supremacy to others or ourselves. When rajas becomes hyper, it creates disillusionment. That's the time to introvert and look into yourself. You will reach the sattva guna. This means, hyper inaction (tamas) leads to action, action leads to hyper action and hyper action (rajas) leads to relative inaction (satwa). I shall explain further.

Man is a combination of sattva, rajas and tamas as the basic ingredients of his constitution. There will be a predominance of one of them, in some ratio, all the time. It will keep fluctuating, it's never static.

When hyper action leads to a craving for shanti, the mind moves towards introversion and meditation. This usually happens when a person gets really fed up with the pendulum movements between happiness and sorrow—and deeply realizes his existence in the unconscious mode. The person cannot get any relief from external and essentially temporary happiness anymore, and will start to introvert, searching for the permanent happiness. This leads to contemplation. Contemplation is equally as important as meditation. Contemplation on one's actual form, one's self. This leads to meditation on one's actual form. Then 'doingness' stops and 'beingness' happens. There is nothing to prove anymore. There is only self-sufficiency within. This is inaction. But, this inaction is very different from tamasic procrastination. This inaction is with perfect awareness of one's own real stature and self. There is no tamas here. This is how the cycle works.

When a man becomes predominantly sattvic, he will start operating from sattvic time—in the morning, 3 am to 6 am. (Rajasic time is between 6 am till 4 pm and the rest is tamasic time 4 pm till 3 am.) This is why saints start their day between 3 am and 6 am and sleep early, thus reducing their actions during tamasic time. Tamasic time is also time for indulgences in an unconscious way—kind of a routine indulgence without thinking.

A predominantly sattvic man will seldom have personal agendas. He will exist for the welfare of the society more than his own welfare. He will be consuming more raw vegetables and only vegetables that have seen the sun, which means nothing from under the ground. He will not be able to consume any tamasic food which includes fish, meat or alcohol. The quantity of his consumption also becomes much less. He will only eat what is prepared for the time and does not store food for another time. Technically, stored food becomes poison and loses all its value over time. It becomes junk food. He will be ever ready to serve and he will always be existing in a plane of higher awareness and unconditional love. He will be in the being level and doing will reduce. When rajas converts predominantly to sattva guna, the person's whole character changes and becomes more self-sufficient.

In some cases, extreme action can also lead into induced procrastination such as addiction to alcohol or drugs. This is the negative angle. This leads to a further downslide, back into tamas. Then it's harder to climb up. So, whenever a vacuum is created due to a shift in gunas, it must be filled in with something higher, and definitely not lower. Then, evolution is certain. Otherwise, evolution will elude man. Be careful. In such cases, usually a Master of higher stature will come in handy. He could guide the man through uncertain terrains. In such cases, the man should trust the guide 100%. He should have faith in the guide, or else he will not reach his destination. Most people fail to reach it because when tests happen, their faith fails. When faith is lost, there is no journey ahead. Procrastination happens. Tamas sets in.

Hope you have understood the mechanism of how gunas work in human conditions.

Tamas

Tamas is darkness. Tamas wastes lives. We bring up so many excuses for not doing some things. Timeliness could be considered a sattvic quality. Being organised also is a sattvic quality. Being anxious is rajasic. Of all gunas (natures), beware of tamas or inertia, which is dangerous, as it pulls man down to inaction and lives get wasted.

Tamas is dense. Sattva is subtle. Tamas drives one to excessive craving for sensory pleasures. Sattva provides detachment in action, thoughts and words. Detachment is NOT non-commitment. Non-commitment is a tamasic quality. Detachment is the lack of expectation. This also means equanimity—a state where you have everything, but you are not dependent on anything. The denser the plane of your existence, the more lives you will need to take on denser planes before you can elevate further. Beware of tamas.

Just for your general awareness, let me put it all in a tangible format. Please remember that Sattva, Rajas and Tamas always comes mixed in individuals. So, always use your discretion. True faith is sattvic. Faithlessness is insecurity. Insecurity amounts to rajas. Rajas leads to action. This is above tamas. Tamas is indulgence. Tamas is procrastination. Tamas makes us dull. Tamas also breeds insensitiveness. Extreme insensitiveness. Tamas numbs feelings, rakes up emotions and destructive tendencies too. Beware of tamas.

Q: You had suggested to practice Surya Namaskar for my physical ailment. Thank you. There is tremendous improvement. This is to ask if it is necessary to practice every day or I can skip weekends? Everything becomes a bit erratic at the weekend.

M: The Sun does not ask this question. Irrespective of whether it's a weekend or a holiday, the sun performs its duty. The birds and animals also do not observe holidays. The plants and trees have not been taking 'days off' ever. Nature with all its flora and fauna has not been expressing inertia. Then why should we? So, do not drag your feet. Walk your strides, beating inertia. Trust you have understood my answer well.

Q: Is the occasional feeling of weakness and lethargy to do physical exercise also inertia (tamas)?

M: If you have no physical ailments, then it is inertia (tamas).

Dharma (Duty)

Turbulent minds search for discontentment. They search for some reason to complain. This is tamas. Conscious mind usually has a natural inclination towards negativities. Negativities are like weeds in the garden. Nobody nurtures them, they just appear and grow and parasites sometimes even destroy the mother plant. Our mind has a similarity with this aspect of nature. It destroys positive vibes and chooses negative ones. It creates walls and prefers to stay indoors. So, do not think that spirituality is always liberating. It can also be binding, depending on which practice you are up to.

In our times, spirituality often means escapism. People choose spirituality so that they can postpone or avoid their dharma. This is utterly anti-spiritual and anti-liberating. When there are hundreds of material matters to be accomplished on both the dharma and karma planes, how can we have solace in spirituality? By postponing our dharma, there will be no progress. There cannot be progress. Escapism is born out of tamas. Laziness is its sister. Pessimism is its cousin. Looking for opportunities for discontentment is its watchdog. We can see some people always choosing one negative point out of ten positive points. And negativity breeds further negativity. It produces itself in mass. The natural inclination would be to befriend tamasic company.

Prioritisation is important. Dharma should be prioritised. Work should be prioritised. Work is worship. Respecting work means respecting existence. If spirituality is your work, do it wholeheartedly. Swamis and Saints are doing that. This is absolutely fine. They have their role to play in society. A doctor cannot go chanting for the whole day, ignoring his patients. This is against his dharma. A warrior is supposed to be fighting or protecting the country. He has to do his dharma. Beware. Postponement is a sign of deep set tamas. It will eat you slowly, steadily and completely. Duty first. Duty also means the duty of parents to their children, children towards their parents, husband towards wife and vice versa, charity and selfless service etc. It's the same even between two lovers. When dharma is perfectly accomplished to 100%, spirituality will automatically set in. When duties are not completed, mind will remain unstable. When pending work bothers you, how can you concentrate? Your mind will be rotating around your unfinished tasks. Your tongue will be chanting and your eyes will be looking at the guru in front of you, but your mind will be far away. What is the benefit of such spirituality? Is that spirituality at all? What is it, if it's not escapism? Life gets wasted this way and we come back to complete the unfulfilled tasks, again and again. Why do we deliberately jump into a quagmire if we can help it? Wrong judgement and a corresponding mistake are far better than deliberate escapism. Remember that. Trust you have understood the basic reason for your discontentment. Unfinished duties are bothering you. You cannot keep all the skeletons in the closet. The closet will fall apart. Nor can you shove all your unfulfilled tasks under your carpet. You will stumble on your own carpet and fall flat on your face. Did I scare you? I am sorry. I only mean to awaken you. It's never too late. Perform your duties in style and confidence. Spirituality will happen. You will not miss any Gurus, if they are meant for you. Those whom you missed were not for you. Understand that.

Waking Up

Q: I have understood that anger is a base emotion, just like jealousy and frustration. When a person gets enlightened or when he goes beyond his gunas, will he still experience his base emotions?

M: It's true that genuine anger is a weakness, just like jealousy. All base emotions are weaknesses. An enlightened Master, established in the supreme consciousness, is not affected by base emotions. Yet, just like Shirdi Sai Baba used to do, he expresses anger. That is only in the external plane though. Just like the waves of the ocean exist only on its surface and only towards the shore, the anger of the true Master exists only on the surface, only for a certain purpose and only when he interacts with a certain crowd. Deep within, he is perfectly at peace. These expressions are meant only for the common man to understand certain aspects of existence or to ward off some unseen, yet impending danger. A Master like Shirdi Sai Baba also talks to unseen or body-less entities. So, the anger he used to express may not necessarily have been directed towards the person that he was probably looking at. All Masters work in their own way. There are no comparisons. There could be similarities. Shiva himself is supposed to be an angry deity, and at the same time, he is the Saint of all Saints, the Supreme Saint. This means, he is never truly angry.

When a man attains the consciousness of the Supreme through extreme penance, automatically, the need for base emotions drops away. There is no need to 'do' anything in order to get out of the clutches of silly emotions. It will happen automatically. Likewise, if at all after years of penance and achieving an exalted state, the person slips back into base emotions or gets actually angry and the anger causes an internal ripple, then he will have to climb back up again. This is a tedious process. There are many stories about how meditating saints were lured by celestial women (apsaras) and their penance was broken.

Expressing anger just for making others understand a point is your strength because you are not truly angry and thus not affected internally at all. On the other hand, genuine anger which causes an internal ripple is a weakness which will affect the man, whether he is a saint or an ordinary man.

When the body, mind and intellect are tuned into a certain practice, then man becomes one with that. This is the case with any habit. So when it is a high spiritual practice, it's even more serious. Body will react to any sudden change in our physical or mental constitution, because body and mind are well connected. We may not know why a particular disease has happened at a particular time. Here a symptomatic treatment will not work. If we dig deeper and find out the change in habits or thought processes that we have been "performing", consciously first and subconsciously later, the sudden change from that to another would have caused conflict within, and the external expression would usually be a bodily disease.

When higher chakras are well active through sadhana, the lower chakras take a back seat. This is why saints indulge in unconditional service. When you balance your sadhana with charity or unconditional service, you will stay elevated. All the chakras will be equally active and there will be perfect balance. Unconditional service also helps emotional purification. Sadhana or spiritual practice, and seva or service are a perfect combination. Amassing knowledge and developing ego on the other hand is anti-evolution. Ego isolates while seva or unconditional service unites. Ego is the nature of man while unconditionality is the nature of God. The closer you get to God, the more unconditional you will become. Knowledge should only be for understanding aspects of existence and not for debates. Debates and arguments are essentially ego-oriented. Ego is treacherous. You will not know where it exists until you step on it, slip, fall and break your bones. Understand that true Masters never waste time. They do not have inertia in them. They express anger at inertia, as it is anti-evolutionary. Tamas pulls people down. Masters throw stones at tamas and get the man back to higher planes. Masters beat tamas, sometimes even physically. On such occasions the anger is not directed to the man but towards the negativity in the man, which blocks his progress. Masters may also make fun of people in public to create the same effect. Both are meant to shake the man from his ignorance and slumber. Shaking the man to wakefulness. I hope this question is answered. Please let me know if I have only confused you more.

> Q: I am a bundle of complexes. I do not know what to give up in order to unburden me and how to keep my spirituality in progress. Can you please guide?

> M: Who is not a bundle of complexes? All humans are. So do not worry about that. Being aware of the complexes itself is a big step towards spiritual awakening. How can you give up anything? By giving up, there will be a vacuum. Hence giving up, deliberately, is not a good idea. Moving on to something of a higher, more sattvic nature is better. Then all you want to give up will drop off. This also applies to addictions. Forceful de-addictions without providing alternatives are not the right method. Diverting time towards more noble activities is the best way to move higher. When the lower automatically drops, it's usually for good, unless the vasana (inherent trait) for that particular activity has not yet died down completely. Be happy that you have acquired awareness. Be happy that you have recognized your own nature. Now, start walking the path. Never stop to ponder, walk with faith and determination. You will certainly reach your desired destination.

Evolving

Q: Mohanji, I am fed up of these routines. Where is the escape?

M: You cannot leave the land and go to the sea because you hate the land. Someday you will have to come back. You can leave for the sea because you love the sea. Escaping from anything which you have unconsciously chosen is not the solution. Escapism is not a solution. Evolving into something higher is the solution. The first step is to develop a positive outlook. Develop creativity through innovation. Develop hobbies which you can later convert into a profession. Slowly you could switch over. And it will be permanent too. When you love what you do, time and space will not tire you. Eternity will guide you.

MEDITATION & SATSANG

The Right Type of Meditation

MEDITATION HAS EVOLVED through generations. Thousands of teachers through thousands of terrains taught thousands of techniques that suited thousands of people. There is no one technique that suits all. So which is the right type of meditation for you? The answer is simple: the one that works for you. You are a unique being. There is none exactly like you, so innovate your own style. There is no harm. Once it works for you, just do not impose it on another person, thinking it the only method in the world which works. Respect the individuality of each other.

The best practice according to me, is being aware of your every thought, word and action. A constant alertness. Being in the present. If we make this awareness a habit, there will not be any anxiety or guilt, since the mind will not oscillate. Guilt is related to the past, and anxiety to the future. The movement of mind is between the past and the future, escaping the present as much as possible. Escapism is common. It is easy too. It is through escapism that our mind thrives. Through rudderless wandering, the mind establishes itself. We glorify the escapist quality of our mind as daydreaming or something like that. This is why I mentioned earlier that the only conquest that is worth the time is the conquest of our own mind. When you are a witness to your own thoughts, words and actions, you are in the present. You are being the soul. (Our soul is also a witness to every thought, word and deed as it never interferes in any of these and simply aids it without prejudice.) Awakening will dawn upon you automatically, just by being in the present consistently. When you are in the present, karmic accumulation through unconscious action will also cease to exist. The present is your real gift. The real gift of being in the present is awakening. Eligibility is essential for crossing over. Otherwise great damage can happen to the psychosomatic system, just like a five year old boy lifting 50 kilos of weight. It is bound to dislocate him. When you are established in the present through constant practice, you do not need to practice any other meditation technique.

Breath is the vehicle that can take you to great awareness levels. Breath brings in prana. Prana rejuvenates chakras. Chakras rejuvenate naadis. Naadis rejuvenate cells. This process is continuous. In a way, our system is using wind energy. When you travel with the prana through your naadis, you become closer to your own systems. When you become one with the flow as well as the path, you become close to the entity that runs the system. You not only achieve oneness with your physical systems, and through oneness control of your own system, you also attain proximity to the soul that runs the machinery. The usual activities that are controlled by the subconscious mind get transferred to your conscious mind, or in other words every activity of the subconscious mind is with conscious awareness. In that state you do not need any meditation. To attain that state you may need meditation. The lower the number of bodily functions that are controlled by the subconscious, the more you are in control of those functions. This is how saints control their circulation, heartbeat, digestion etc. There is no energy loss. You can function in perfect equanimity under any circumstances. It does not matter what you do, you will be a witness to every thought, word and action.

Meditation is the path. Teaching meditation is the method that I use to reach out and guide you. This is the path that helps me to reach out and elevate you. Your elevation will depend on your eligibility. Your elevation will depend on your faith and openness.

Faith is the key. Faithlessness is a kind of blockage. Comparisons are useless. How can we compare between methods? As I mentioned, there are thousands of methods. You are a free person. Choose what suits you. What suits your partner may not suit you. The difference is the karmic obesity or karmic bulk and individual constitution. Hence respect each other's choice.

Meditation is not a must. Do not force yourself. If you cannot meditate, take it easy. Just watch your breath consciously. Deliberately, till you slip back into doing it subconsciously. Again bring it back to the conscious mind. Like that, take control of your breath, by being the breath and not disturbing the natural rhythm of your breathing. Then follow the 360 degree meditation. It will have a tremendous effect. Do not force meditation on yourself even if your relatives are doing it and strongly recommend it. Forcing anything is bad. It will not work. How can we force meat on a vegetarian? A rajasic person, for example, will find it difficult to meditate.

Through meditation we are trying to reach a thoughtless state. Thoughtlessness is mindlessness. This means annihilation of the active mind. Nobody likes to die and the same goes for the mind. It will create all sorts of potential diversions. This is the cause of restlessness. Secondly, we sit for meditation with many agendas, lots of future programs, things to do. We are just finding time for meditation somehow. Do not meditate, if you are going through the motions mechanically. It will be absolutely useless. The best method for such people is witnessing themselves.

Life should be simple. Nature has a system and pattern. Everything works perfectly according to that pattern. We can neither speed up nor slow down. A thing can take place only at a particular place at a particular time. None can change it. Because of our ignorance, we feel we are the doer. We feel we did everything. We feel that our decisions change matters. This is false. We are only instruments. Just actors in the divine play. So do not take on ownership and stress related to that. Just be. Just accept the good and bad alike. Just do your thing with 100% dedication and with presence of mind. 99% will not do. Each thought, word and action should be 100%. When you do everything while the mind is unavailable, results will be catastrophic. Decide that you will not do anything unconsciously, except the movements in your sleep. May the Grace of the great Masters guide you.

Each person's inherent constitution is different from another. The first step is to shift from the gross to the relatively subtle till you reach the subtlest of all, your own atman or soul. Start with your breath. Be aware that you are breathing. Be aware that your breathing process shifts from left nostril to right and right to left, approximately every hour. Start observing that. There is no need to sit down and concentrate on breathing. If you are aware most of your waking hours that you are breathing, you are already on the right track. This is also a path to meditation. This is also perpetual meditation.

Some people are action oriented Karma Yogis, some people are devotion oriented, Bhakti Yogis. Some people are knowledge oriented, Jnana Yogis. We have to understand ourselves before we take up any kind of sadhana or spiritual practice. Once we know our inherent nature we can choose the practice that suits us. Until then we will do trial and error. Some people do this their whole life. A true Master can easily understand the nature of his students. Only then can he guide his students well.

When you start observing the breath consistently, you will start introverting automatically. It will lead to meditation. If you have further questions, please do ask. Our meditation can be downloaded from our website, www. mohanji.org and since it is guided, it should be helpful.

Bless All. Love All.

Why Meditation?

To get in touch with your soul. To go within ourselves. To go beyond the senses and use the same mind which usually travels with our senses into the external world. To travel within and find our origin, truth or soul, whichever way you want to address it. Peace exists there. Happiness exists there. When we find our own soul as the original entity that transcended time and space and assumed various forms and names over years, we will realise its origin too. Its origin is the supreme Soul. When we understand or experience its connection with the supreme Soul, we assume its state too.

Meditation is only a tool to go within. Meditation will strengthen your outlook and rejuvenate you tremendously if done properly. There are hundreds of types of meditation. You can choose what suits you. In fact, we must always try and test before following anything. Do not blindly choose something just because your best friend is doing it. Eat only what you can digest. Eat only what is palatable to you. Enjoy what you are doing. You are free to choose. Freedom of choice is one of the biggest gifts that humans possess. Also understand one thing: information or events will not reach you unless you are eligible for them.

The nature of the human mind is restlessness. Through meditation we are trying to bring the wandering conscious mind to calmness and eventual dissolution. If a person operates on the level of perpetual awareness, he does not need to meditate. That means, if he operates with perfect presence of mind or if his mind is available with every thought, word and action, he does not need to meditate. He is perpetually in a meditative mode. He exists in the present. Maximum energy loss happens when mind oscillates between the past and the future. Past is associated with nostalgia and guilt, and future is associated with anxiety. Both are unnecessary. Past is over and future is yet to be. We have to live in the present. If we create many anxieties, our future will be uncertain. If we walk with determination and purpose, with our minds steady, our future will be picture-perfect. Using meditation as an escapism from some unwanted situation is absolutely useless. Then a person is not meditating but just pretending. This is the same for ritualistic meditators. It will give them no effect. Just like some people say: "Oh, without my morning tea, my day is useless", this one will say: "Without the morning meditation I feel incomplete." This person has become a victim of that habit. Any habit that rules you is a hindrance to your spiritual progress. So we need to shift our consciousness to perpetual meditation.

Always be in the present. Always exist in the NOW.

Q: Best position for meditation?

M: Any posture where the spine is erect is good for our (Mohanji) meditations. The problem with lying down is that you could slip into sleep. Otherwise, even lying down on a hard surface is good enough for our meditation, as well as sitting in sukhasana (free cross legged posture), padmasana (lotus posture) or vajrasana (heel sitting posture).

Q: I cannot meditate. What should I do?

M: Do not meditate. Never force anything on yourself. You will start hating it sooner or later. You can start with being aware of your breathing. Breathe consciously. Eat consciously. Drink consciously. Do everything consciously. It will give you the same, or an even better effect than meditation.

Q: Chronology of meditation?

M: First is vasana (inherent interest to explore ourselves), second is knowledge (jnana—to satisfy mind and intellect), third is contemplation (manana—to satisfy the intellect), fourth is meditation (dhyana—to go beyond the mind and intellect and reach the soul). Then happens laya (merger), samadhi so on and so forth.

Q: Mantras and chakras?

M: Words have power. They have power to hurt and heal. We experience that in our everyday life. Some words hurt us deeply, especially if uttered by someone we love. Some words wound our ego. Some words heal us or expand our heart. Thus, words are powerful. Words if uttered in a certain way and style can create certain powerful vibrations within us as well in the external world. Mantras have the power to purify our inside and outside. They have the power to destroy negativities and accent positiveness. If repeated properly, they have the power to activate the nerve centres and chakras. Chanting mantras will create the right vibration (if chanted properly) and helps our energy flow and rejuvenates our system. This rejuvenation creates a shield of protection. The mind becomes stronger and immune to external wear and tear. Mantras are useful and chanting them will help you to concentrate also. Concentration is the key that locks our inner world. When the mind is at one point with concentration amazing powers get unleashed.

There are thousands of chakras in our system. The major seven chakras lay between the root of our spine and the top of our head: Mooladhaara Chakra (also called First Chakra or Root Chakra), followed by the Swadhishtana Chakra (Sacral Chakra), Manipura Chakra (Solar Plexus), Anahata Chakra (Heart Chakra), Vishuddhi Chakra (Throat Chakra), Agnya Chakra (Third Eye) and Sahasrara Chakra (thousand petalled Crown Chakra). Remember that they are not in our physical layer and hence invisible to our naked eyes. Just like we cannot see energy through naked eyes, we cannot see the channels of energy either.

Q: Pranayama before the meditation.

M: This is aimed at bringing tranquillity and equilibrium. We are all coming from various situations into the meditation hall. Some people are agitated, some are peaceful. We have to bring everybody to one vibratory level as much as possible. Hence, we practice a specific pattern of breathing to bring our attention to our breath and also to ourselves from the outside world. Mind will still be elsewhere. When we deliberately concentrate on breathing, mind is forced to come back. Then follows the meditation. Unless our mind comes back to ourselves we cannot meditate.

Mohanji Foundation Meditations

The Mohanji Foundation meditations 'Power of Purity' in different languages, and the '360 Degrees' (freely downloadable at www. mohanji.org—see appendix) were both given to me by Higher Masters during my communions with them.

Our meditation sessions started in Dubai in October 2007. Till date, people have experienced Mohanji Foundation's meditations in the UAE, in India, Qatar, UK, Germany, Serbia, Russia, USA, Africa, Oman and many other places. Also, there are many people around the world that are doing them individually. Our meditations are designed to bring you to yourself and all sessions are conducted with the spirit of service. The aim of Mohanji Foundation's meditations has always been to elevate as many people as we can to higher consciousness. Many people actually experienced the difference from where they began and where they are now.

Q: What is the source of your meditations?

M: Universe. Where else can you source anything from? Everything comes out of the universe and merges back into the universe. Nobody is apart from it and nothing can be created by man. We are only sourcing material for a purpose while existing in various levels of consciousness. Everything is downloaded from the universe. I own nothing. Nothing is original in that sense. While existing at a particular frequency we access particular information. We decode it and pass it on for the benefit of others. When we start owning it, the Grace element disappears. When we try to make a name, associating ego with it, the purity gets wiped out. Then the whole exercise becomes useless chaff without grains. God has left us the basic raw materials. Man is only trying to figure out which combinations of these raw materials give maximum happiness if combined. This meditation was not created by me. It happened to me. I delivered it in its purity and that's why you are getting the results. Grace happens when purity is at its optimum level. Who can patent God? Who can patent God's gifts? God's creation? It is foolishness to think that we are original and that all our thoughts are also original. These thoughts have occurred in many minds before. Some were clear and some were blurred. The more the clarity, the better will be the expression. The lower the clarity, the higher will be the confusion. So there is nothing to be proud of. There is nothing to be owned. We are all temporary custodians performing in the orchestra that God conducts. He does His job well. There are no mistakes anywhere, because He Himself created the world order, its symmetry and synchronicity. If we understand this aspect we will also play our part very well, without our mind getting stuck on the result of the show or the fruit of the effort. That's up to the conductor. He runs the show, not us. Once again, all meditations were given to me. I am delivering them with optimal purity.

Q: What is the purpose of the meditations offered by you on mohanji.org?

M: Offering the three meditations (Power of Purity, 360 Degrees and Blossoms of Love) is seva for me. I am performing my dharma or duty as a citizen of the universe. I am giving forth everything, unconditionally. I maintain my purity by controlling and nullifying my expectations. Through the meditations, I am trying to serve society, unconditionally. I sincerely hope it is working!!! All those who are associated with me are doing the same. They all are doing it unconditionally. Unfortunately, spirituality is bought and sold these days. The higher the price, the higher is the demand. In this scenario we are trying to give something truly precious to society, without any price tag. I believe that's the best one can do. I strongly believe that my spirituality is priceless. I am giving to you something that is priceless. This is why profound Grace flows in our meditations. Masters appear and bless everyone. The reason for the Grace is the lack of conditions and the supreme inner purity. Ever since we started conducting the meditation, we have touched many lives positively. I am deeply grateful to the Almighty for that.

Power of Purity

With every Power of Purity meditation inner cleansing is happening. But when you step into the world outside, contamination occurs again. If you want to maintain the purity achieved during our meditations, be aware of every thought-word-action. Whatever you take within should be pure. What is pure? Something which is not selfish, something which is selfless. No rituals can bring that purity. Selfless actions elevate man to the highest.

Presence of mind in every thought, word and action can eradicate karmas. It can liberate you. Rituals can bind you. Rituals are experiential in the beginning but soon become habits. You might start a ritual and have experiences, but later on when it becomes a habit you cannot live without it! Thus it binds you. Any habit whether extremely good or bad is ultimately a habit and binds you. How can liberation be possible when you are bound?

Purity of thought, word and action liberates man from everything. It strengthens his existence. Purity is power. Purity is truth. Truth is pure. The whole universe resonates with truth and purity. When we live truth, purity happens. When we live a life of purity by consistently expressing purity through every thought, word and action, we elevate ourselves to an existence of supreme consciousness. There are no barriers in the realm of purity. There is supreme strength in purity. The power of purity is tangible. The power of purity unburdens on various levels. The power of purity liberates. The power of purity immunizes from the rocks and shocks of daily existence. The power of purity radiates. Purity empowers. Purity strengthens. Purity liberates. It brings gratitude into existence. It quells the wandering mind to a thoughtless state. It quenches all questions. It brings contentment. It brings stability.

It makes our very existence a great experience. It fills our existence with life. It brings purpose. It fills life with faith and hope. It connects us to the Highest of consciousness. The Power of Purity is unfathomable. It is the nature of the Supreme.

360 Degrees Awareness

When we attain liberation, we shift from our limited senses to unlimited awareness. It is like a martial artist who says that his whole body serves as his eyes. This means we should be aware of everything around us. This is concentration and awareness.

Usually all of us are 'front-oriented', operating in 120 degrees. We do not see the remaining 240 degrees behind us. These remaining 240 degrees definitely exist, but we do not notice that. This is due to the limitation of our senses. When our sense barrier is broken and our awareness level spreads around us, we become centred in our spine. We become completely balanced. And we will operate from our higher awareness plane. The result? No anxiety, no fear, no guilt, witness consciousness, unconditional love, compassion, total equanimity. Being 'spine-oriented' is a big shift. This is why 360 degrees awareness is important. We automatically reach that level when the Shakti energy meets Shiva at our Sahasrara, the top of our head. Practicing to be on that level will help you to shift to that level easily and at will. Training yourself to have 360 degrees awareness will help your spiritual evolution. You will become barrier-less. Our '360 degrees meditation' can be downloaded for free from www.mohanji.org. If that meditation does not suit you, you are welcome to choose your own method. There is nothing binding you.

Cathartic Effect of Meditation

Q: I understand that if one meditates or is in contact with a Master, some karmas are burnt. One takes a physical body with some agenda and our Jivatma and Sutratma are pre-decided. My question: Is the algorithm of Jivatma and Sutratma re-adjusted when karmas are burnt with meditation or is it also pre-decided when one starts the journey of spirituality with meditation? Is the journey towards Parabrahma accelerated through meditation despite of the pre-decided algorithm?

M: Meditation if practiced consistently, is expected to bring our naturally floating mind to one's own self. Otherwise, the mind wanders all over the universe in the company of the senses. The senses also become useful only when the mind is present. Meditation has a cathartic effect. When the mind is still, vasanas are also still. Thoughts are still. This releases the push of prarabdha at least temporarily. As a general rule we can say that karmas need to be exhausted through corresponding action, the same way we gathered them. Higher Masters can burn some of the seeds of karma from the causal layer, because they can see the past, present and future of their subject. For this, the subject needs to have firm faith and total surrender to the Master. Chanting and selfless service reduce the effects of karma. Masters always guide their disciples to entertain presence of mind and accept life as it comes, because we chose those experiences, knowingly or unknowingly.

Karma is formed when emotions get attached to a thought, word or action. Emotion is the common factor—the glue that binds a thought, word or action to our subconscious. Then comes collective consciousness which could become individual karma. When we indiscriminately destroy the lives of many, even if the conscience of the destroyer is not affected, the collective agony of the victims will become his karma. This will affect his further lives. As I said earlier, karma can be effectively eradicated only through fulfilling the vasanas that are formed out of one's karma and through its systematic exhaustion. Then it is nullified forever. Suppression will never help. Whatever is suppressed will bounce back, sooner or later. When the mind stays in the present through meditations, creations of further karma is reduced substantially.

Q: I have seen bright golden and white light during meditation. It came suddenly as a flash, filled me, gave bliss and vanished. What is this? I know I should go beyond these experiences, but I am curious to know.

M: They are various energy bodies merging with your system. Colours signify certain levels of elevation too. It is true that we must drop the need for analysis. At the same time, being aware helps. Especially in the presence of Masters, each one gets what he/she needs. One's deficiencies get nullified. This is usually experienced in the form of coloured energy forms. Just accept them with gratitude and allow them to work.

(Non-) Doing During Meditation

Q: I had a beautiful and intense inner journey during the 360 Degrees meditation. I got clear pictures in total awareness. In that trance-like state I was given options of what to do in certain 'scenes' and I knew what to choose and what I needed to do in those instances. So I did something in that meditation BUT the doing happened through me. I cannot find words to describe it. Could you please explain this?

M: 'Doing' has different levels. Doing with conscious mind has karmic involvement. 'Doing' for the sake of nature has no karmic effect (like while we walk some creatures meet their death, we are killing them, for the sake of dharma—just like a tiger helps manage the deer population in the forest). This is part of the preservation of dharma. Nature is using us to maintain some kind of stability of existence, which we cannot understand.

In the 'doing' during meditation, even though you are the doer, the string is with higher consciousness or Masters. They make things happen through you. You never pre-planned it, nor did you control it. Your doership is surrendered to the larger existence. When this surrender happens, Grace happens. Grace takes over or divinity takes over. Divinity knows everything about us, all we need and what we do not need. Your deepest needs get addressed. The unwanted stuff blocking your progress in your transit towards the supreme Father, gets removed. Usually the blocking rocks are fears and conditionings, supported by individual ego. Along with the surrender, accented by faith, you are helping divinity to remove the blockages for yourself. Here too, there is doership. That means you are opening the door of your house for the cleaners to come and clean your house. You are not cleaning the house. If you do not open the doors of your house, the cleaners cannot clean. So you have a role to play, but you are not 'doing' what is needed. When you say you knew what to do, it is not the 'you' which is your conscious mind. It is the 'you' which is the substratum, and the knowledge is guidance from the divinity or Masters. Things are done through you, but not by you. The awareness of action is sure, because the command needs to be received in order to be executed. You will know what is needed for you to transit further because you have already subdued your ego through surrender and you are one with the higher consciousness which has no ego element in it. It tells you what you need for further transit and you come to know. It can see what you cannot see. Trust this is very clear.

My and Your Meditation

Some of you have sent mails apologising for not attending 'my meditation'. My dear friends, this is not 'my' meditation. My meditation would be the meditation that I practice for my own purpose, if at all. Even that would not be mine. Nothing is mine. Nothing is yours either. Everything comes out and merges back into the universe.

There is no need to apologise to anybody, let alone me. It's at your discretion. The meditation that is being conducted is absolutely free. Nobody binds anybody to anything. Binding is anti-spiritual.

If tamas is the reason for your not attending it, beware. If the reasons are personal, you are the best judge. Nobody else will judge you. Nobody should. Nobody can judge another, because each person is a unique karmic combination. So the meditation is not 'mine'. Just like words, once uttered don't belong to you; I would only say that the meditations originated in the supreme consciousness and that consciousness used the material that is called Mohan to convey it to the world. I became an instrument. It happened through me. I do not keep any ownership. I might keep a copyright to avoid others abusing it. But I never intended to sell spirituality nor will I ever do that. Consider it like a flowing river. You have the right to take a dip or stay away from it. Nobody is watching or judging. Be relaxed. I am just doing my job the way I can. I am not here to make any name or money from this. Thence, I have no expectations either. As you know, lack of expectation unleashes unlimited power. I am enjoying that.

Contemplation and Meditation

Q: Is contemplation equally or more important than meditation?

M: I appreciate this thought from a 14-year old. This shows your level of evolution. Contemplation on truth is very important. I mentioned this earlier. When you contemplate on what you are, the mano-buddhi-ahamkara-chitta (mind, intellect, ego, substratum) attachment will start diminishing. You will start realizing that the driving force is the soul and your soul is an offspring of the universal soul. Your whole thought process will change and your attachment will automatically get diverted to that soul. Thus contemplation leads you to the ultimate truth and from there, meditation begins. When you meditate on your own soul, the realization happens that "I am Shiva"—SHIVOHAM. Shiva, Vishnu, Jesus, Allah, Buddha—all are one. Please do understand that I am not referring to a finite entity called Shiva. I am referring to the infinite entity which you can call any name. So contemplation is very important. It is called 'manana' and this should lead to 'dhyana'. If you need further clarification, ask me again. I shall explain. One important thing—your thought process is correct. You are on the right track. You have every ingredient in you to reach the highest level of evolution. Keep climbing.

Presence of Masters

Q: Does the presence and proximity of a higher Master purify us?

M: Absolutely. It does. Tamas (inertia) will be non-existent in the presence of a higher Master. Just being in the presence of a higher Master will help the seeker to elevate. Ramana Maharshi used to sit silent, just like Ramakrishna Paramahamsa. No questions, no answers. Yet just with their sheer glance and presence they used to create internal shifts in those who came to them. First of all, unless you are eligible you cannot get to a higher Master. After achieving eligibility and if you are still not interested to reach higher Masters, it's your inertia.

Understand that higher Masters are most ordinary. They are unassuming. They will never pretend. This will confuse seekers. This is their style of filtering seekers. Those who have eyes will see. Others will go after flashy substance and pay huge amounts of money 'to get salvation'. This also might indirectly aid the cleansing of the seeker. Money and time lost could also mean lesser attachments. Eventually, the seeker becomes truly eligible and the Master appears. The seeker would be surprised to know that the ordinary person whom you meet every day, whom you take so lightly, might be the true Master. The true master will not stand to prove anything. They will just mirror your own self. They only guide you to yourself. Your self guides you to God.

During Satsang

Q: The moment you walked into the venue we felt tremendous power, masculine, Shaivic. We literally saw you becoming Shirdi Sai. Your eyes were sparkling and you looked older than you actually appear. This was so powerful that it shook us and elevated us. The meditation was unexplainably powerful. Much stronger than the meditations that we have experienced so far. We do not think that this was a meditation at all. It was a kind of trance state. We are glad we saw you as Baba. It was our deep wish. On the second occasion you were Babaji and many people actually saw you as Babaji. This confuses us. Please explain how this is possible.

M: I am an empty pot. I reflect my content selflessly. Content changes as per the situation. Ha! Ha! The first one was on a full moon day. The moon must have made a difference too. Plus the eclipse and its respective changes in the atmosphere. Meditation is only a realm or a platform where you can experience the Higher. Please do not get stuck with the word 'meditation'. Here I am working on you more than you do. Shaktipat is the key.

I was coming straight from Oman and after a five-hour journey I did not even get time to change my clothes or even wash my face. That's probably why I looked older. Ha! ha!

Anyway, your sensitivity is very high and hence you caught the subtle vibrations and changes. I am an empty pot. Any Master can fill in as per the need of the day. The power is definitely because of the presence of the higher Master. This cleansing is much more powerful than any of your spiritual practices. A touch from Shirdi Sai can remove enough karmas, which could eventually cut short many possible lives or rebirths. If you are sensitive enough, you can see the changes in my body too.

When a Dattatreya Master comes in, the changes are sudden

and visibly drastic. When Babaji comes in, it's gradual and more lasting. My physical form stayed in the altered state till about 4 a.m. the next day. The same happens during a communion with a Kriya Yoga Master. Biba could explain this as she has witnessed my communion with Babaji, which lasted for about 6 hours at a stretch. The communion is usually very long and the whole time, you cannot even move a finger. Completely paralysed. This is Babaji's style.

S. saw a purple light spreading and before that, M. caught my expansion and change. Biba could not make it to the meditation, yet she felt restlessness when I was expanding and shifting to higher awareness. This is natural. Physical proximity is immaterial. When you are connected, vibrations travel wherever you are. Physical proximity is only a mental need. Spirituality is beyond senses and mind anyway.

When S. saw the purple light spreading in the room, Babaji was already present. My body had already changed. I am glad some of you caught the change happening in me and even felt the change in my communication, words and the style of utterances. The nature of Babaji is silence. The nature of beingness is silence. And hence when His nature got transferred on us, nobody could talk anymore. Everyone fell into silence without me telling you to do so. There were fewer words and the meditation was also very short this time. Yet, it was very powerful. This was intense cleansing. Some of you actually saw Babaji sitting where I was sitting. Some felt the need to cry. Some were shaken. These are all signs that show where you stand spiritually. There was certainly an internal shift in all, for the better. Everything is fine. If the first one (where Baba was present) was expansion and being unlimited beyond earth, Babaji made everyone established or more stable and rooted. This is the difference in style.

Regarding your confusion as to why am I channelling different Masters, the answer is that I am not channelling. They are happening. I am an empty pot. Mohan does not exist. This is the 'I'ness. When the 'I'ness is gone, there is space for any Master to work. It's not in doing, that you achieve higher realms. It's in being. Second and most important fact is that all Masters are one. You could consider one as Baba and another as Babaji. I feel no difference except perhaps the difference in style and the immediate purpose. This depends on the crowd. What you need or deserve, you will get.

Now, you saw my physical changes and that is your ability to see. I am not doing anything special for anyone to achieve that. I never told anyone who will appear either. That was also immaterial. Jesus' presence was also there on the full moon day. The ability to see is directly related to your achieving further subtlety. The more subtle you become, the more you will see. The more you will use your third eye, the dependency on your physical senses will reduce.

Biba actually witnessed the physical changes that happened in my body. The skin became like that of a boy and my whole structure was boyish. As I mentioned earlier, Babaji's presence is gradual and it changes back gradually too. So, I remained in that form till about 4 a.m. Biba and some of you have also seen me physically changing (to Baba, Jesus etc.) before meditation and during Shaktipat. As I said, these are only natural external expressions of a deep internal truth.

The Mirror

Q: Sometimes during Satsangs your answers are rather sharp and pointed. I do feel that they could be hurting for some. Can I term this as arrogance? Do you get angry or are you pretending?

M: I am like a mirror. I only reflect back the constitution of the person who asks questions. Most of the time, I am only like a clean mirror. I do not impose my constitution on anybody. I sincerely keep reflecting the constitution of the person in front of me. Hence, responses vary. Responses will be given in a way that the other person understands. This is also a reminder to the listener about his own constitution. I do not get genuinely angry. Genuine anger is a weakness. I do not take in any emotions nor keep them. I do feel, I do enjoy, but I am not bound by emotions. Expression of anger is your strength, if you are genuinely not angry. This is used only to convey a strong message towards, or in response to some situation. During satsangs I am never angry. I will be in the expanded state which is beyond all human emotions. Mostly during satsangs you will feel the presence of higher entities. They are putting the words in my mouth or rather they are using my faculties. Then, expressions will depend on what they choose to say. When higher Masters are at work, each one gets exactly what they need and deserve. According to the listener's mental constitution he can discriminate those words as arrogance or kindness. The one who talks, stays neutral. When you are in love, every word that the lover utters will be music to your ears. You will crave for more. When you are married, it could be the other way around (just joking; only trying to prove a point!). Hence, what you hear is what your constitution is. What you choose to hear is what you called for or deserved, subconsciously. This is how it works. Trust I have not put that arrogantly!!! Ha-ha!

In the same context, just try to understand what is getting hurt. It's only the ego. Every Master works on the seeker's ego very severely. Often the barrier between the man and the truth is only the ego. So, it could be that Masters choose to bash the ego of the seeker. This could be termed as arrogance by the seeker who possesses the ego. One way or the other a Master will force the seeker to shed his ego and catch the higher truths. This is in the interest of the seeker, not the Master. A Master has neither wishes nor targets in this context.

About Sharing Experiences

I have been stressing the point of sharing experiences, mainly because of two matters. 1. To own your experience(s). 2. When you articulate it, it gets re-confirmed or clarified to yourself or your conscious mind. Owning one's own experience is very important to one's spiritual progress. How will articulation help? Simple. We are constantly bombarded with tons of information and many comparisons. Each person is unique. We cannot and should not compare the experiences of one another. But when you start owning your own experiences you will also develop a witness attitude (Saakshi Bhaav). You will start to observe yourselves more than listening to the words of others. When we read books and hear the opinions of other seekers, we may feel either inferior or superior. Both are harmful. We are ourselves. We are incomparable. We can only start walking from where we stand. So start walking and be happy with your own pace and growth. Never compare with another. We are all like planets rotating around the sun, existing in its realms. Each one of us has our own beginning, end and unique track. Be grateful to existence and keep walking. Divinity is definitely guiding you.

What brought you to spirituality? The innate craving of your own soul for liberation from the endless birth-death cycle. All the Gurus have echoed the same philosophy, in different words and times. The core is the same. It is love. Love without conditions. Love without boundaries.

If you are reluctant to share experiences, at least keep a spiritual diary. Note down your experiences with utmost gratitude. Your mind will need reconfirmations and affirmations at each step, because, we are not immune to the outside world's influence and opinions. At that point in time, when you will almost be ready to disown your own experiences because of other people's opinions, you can refer to the diary and take inspiration to move further. Disowning your own experiences is equal to blocking the divine Grace. Shyness to recognise and accept your own experiences could also mean that your ego is blocking total acceptance. Lack of acceptance is also lack of faith in yourself and your experiences. Without faith in your own thought, word and action levels, there is no progress. Not only spiritual progress, there will not even be material progress. Faith in yourself and in God is truly essential.

Now, your other question about why I have not shared much

of my own experiences during my own spiritual evolution. Well, because of two reasons. One is, I was too busy serving you and listening to all of you. I had no time to speak about my story. Secondly, each person is unique and grand. I did not want you to feel that my experiences are the agreeable benchmark in spiritual progress and disown yours. I want you to own yours and be happy with it. Anyway, I shall share a small incident which explains how Divinity uses various instruments to convey messages.

Some years ago, well before I started communicating with higher Masters and teaching meditations, I used to go through spiritual emptying myself. Those times were very tricky. I used to become totally blank and empty. I even sometimes forgot my name and signature. Please remember, at that time, I was working as the General Manager of a company in Dubai. Papers were sitting on my desk, while I figured out how to sign them. It became clear that divinity gives us a helping hand during such occasions and makes sure no mistakes happen. When we surrender our thoughts, words and actions at the feet of the divine, there is no question of mistakes happening. In spirituality we should be ready to accept anything that comes our way as a gift of God, not bothering to discriminate or compare with one another.

When you share your experiences, they get more clarified. Clarified butter is ghee. What is kept in the mind as a memory could vanish too soon. When uttered from thought level to the word level, the experience gets much more clarity. It becomes truly yours. All meditative experiences are unique.

The set of experiences is always different. It depends on your receptivity as well as faith. Faith is the key that opens your heart for the divine to work on. There are numerous thoughts, fewer words and still fewer actions. This is the chronology. So when you bring your experience to words it transcends one level.

There are two types of experiences possible during meditation. One is the projection of mind. People see deities or Masters. This usually happens when you are pressured for such experiences. The other is actual visions. This happens when you relax and let yourself go without keeping any agenda or expectations. How do we differentiate? The first one leaves no lasting impression. It never changes you from within. The second one changes you from within. You will never be the same again. Therefore beware of the projection of mind. Mind wants to stay occupied and entertain itself to stay alive. Meditation is a mindless state. Mind does not like that. It will occupy you with such projections. Do not lose heart. Do not lose hope. Counter it with faith. Stick to your soul. You will arrive for sure.

Masters do appear during meditations, if the levels of purity and sincerity of purpose is high. Everybody can feel that. Some are touch oriented and they feel the presence of higher entities through their skin. Some are vision oriented and they see, some are hearing oriented and they hear sounds. Thus, based on your constitution, you will experience. Experience is for sure.

What do I recommend? Share experiences. Write about them. When you share, it reinforces that which you shared in your mind. Owning one's own experiences is very important for spiritual evolution. I have seen people who could never meditate before, starting to meditate and achieving great progress. Then suddenly, someone gets scandalized, they believe it and leave everything. These people have fragile minds. They could not even own or acknowledge their own experience and hence got easily influenced by the words of others. Owning one's experience and uttering it will reinforce your faith in yourself, your experience and it will also encourage others to experience it. In other words, it is seva to yourself and others. So keep a spiritual diary. Share it if you like. Do not share it, if you are privacy oriented. Faith is absolutely necessary to grow spiritually and even materialistically. Faith in yourself, faith in the Masters and essentially faith in your own soul which is your personal Guru. A doubting mind never allows you to grow. It keeps negating all your experiences. You will always be at square one. If you fall prey to doubts and lose faith, you will stop evolving. All gurus are one. All souls are one. The master that appears in your life is the right one for you. Accept that. Don't resist.

Gratitude is associated with faith. When you have faith, usually you will be grateful too. Gratefulness reduces the intensity of ego. It helps evolution. Ego is a big burden. Some people cannot even walk freely because of its weight. How can they travel fast? When terrestrial needs reduce, we become light. When terrestrial needs increase, we keep coming back to earth.

Another note on sharing experiences. Our own experience is much more important than book knowledge or the words of others. And the mind, being sense-oriented, will always tend to deny our own experience and substitute it with the words of others or even compare our own precious experience with that of others. Time also erodes the intensity of our experiences. Gross life throws dirt on our subtleties. This is anti-evolution. We will tend to stagnate. We must cherish our own experiences and keep going ahead. This is because, in spirituality, all of us are walking our own paths.

Expressing your own experiences to receptive ears will re-establish those experiences in your own subconscious. Your subconscious will bring you to similar realities further. Thus you will evolve higher and higher.

Remaining Pure

Purity of body can be maintained through habituating proper hygiene and cleanliness. Mind can be kept pure through devotion and an attitude of gratitude. Purity of intellect can be maintained through entertaining selfless action plans. Spiritual purity is achieved when we stop comparisons and perform with detached attention. Purity will be established within by eliminating expectations slowly and steadily. This also means accepting everyday realities as your own unconscious creation and owning each experience whether good or bad as part of your whole life process. Being with the understanding that the food that comes to your table today is the medicine for you, even if that food is not what you probably would have voluntarily chosen. I am not saying that a vegetarian should eat non-vegetarian food if that's what is being served. You need not compromise on your vision and dharma. Resistance of any kind creates agony. Acceptance and adaptability to everyday situations will keep you soft, supple and peaceful. You can also remain pure by making sure every thought, word and action that takes birth in you is rooted in love and simplicity. Purity of thought, word and action happens quite automatically if our attitude is that of selflessness. Selflessness ensures purity. Purity ensures Grace. Purity is a state of mind that you automatically achieve when all your transactions are perfectly in tune with your conscience. Nevertheless, please remember that complacency and procrastination amount to tamas. This should not be entertained at all. Hence, do your very best, without ownership of or attachments to the results of action. This will keep you pure.

Signs of Evolution

Q: On the National Geographic Channel I happened to see hyenas in groups stalking and hunting baby deer. Afterwards I could not eat food or sleep properly. Is meditation making me more vulnerable or too sensitive?

M: When subtlety creeps in and gains strength, we cannot stand violence or aggression of any kind. Our personal constitution automatically adopts nonviolence. This is natural. This is a sign of evolution. Gradually you will start understanding and accepting the laws of nature through your higher awareness. Nature is perfect, if not tampered with by beings of lower consciousness. A wind or a storm is not out of place. A deer and a hyena are also playing their part in nature. Each animal has been given its duty, characteristics, method of behaviour and pattern. They live accordingly. Each has its dharma or duty or task. Each performs it perfectly well, without emotions, quite objectively. In the vast expanse of the forest they create their own territories and stick to them. They do not hunt for fun. They hunt only to appease hunger or kill for self-protection.

Man is the most cruel being on earth. He entertains sadistic pleasures. He tortures and kills. Eating monkey brain is an example, where they smash the skull of live and bound monkeys and eat their brains while they are alive. Man has also been cannibalistic. Most animals do not eat their own species. We skin animals alive for our comfort, and for our greed for money. We do not care about how the dying animals feel. Most or at least some of our delicacies have a history of violence and aggression. Some being has been killed to create those delicacies. We breed, torture, and kill. We manipulate nature. We care about money and selfishly go about making it. We never cared about our future generation and became surprised when nature retaliated periodically. We wanted the best for our children even at the cost of depriving sustenance for many other beings. We have always been grossly insensitive. We have always been grossly selfish.

It is good to feel and be sensitive. It is not good to resist the realities of life and nature. What you saw on TV is only a mark or pattern of nature and her rules. Nature, if left alone, maintains her own equilibrium. For nature, man is only another being occupying her space. No preferences. We acquire and distort. Nature sometimes may pinch our ears for being naughty. This is what we call natural disasters.

Practice non-violence in thoughts, words and actions. Help nature. Help other beings. Do not kill or torture. All beings will love you. Animals and birds will not leave you. They can feel more than we can. They can see, touch and smell purity of heart. We need many signs of proof and even if we have all the proof we will choose to follow the words of others, rather than our own tangible experience. This is man. Love man also, as we belong to that species. Also because, we are even torturing our own species. Love all. You will get lots of love back, many times over. God is nothing but love. All we need is love. All we can give sincerely is love. Understand you are on the right track.

Do not worry about being sensitive. Feel it and do something about it if you can. Compassion, when it wells in your heart, must be expressed. Then you will feel more complete and your existence will become worthwhile.

Spiritual Shopping Vs. Spiritual Evolution

The human mind tends to hold on to negative emotions and discard the positive ones as unreal. If someone humiliates us or hurts us in any way, that impression will be stored, energized (polished) and kept shining till we die and perhaps beyond. At the same time, good memories lose shine as the days pass by. Negative thoughts and words or negative feelings are spontaneous. There is no need to nurture them. They are like weeds in the garden and will grow by themselves. Positive thoughts, words and actions need to be nurtured, carefully pruned and well protected, like a sapling in the garden. If you ask someone how he/she is doing, depending on your familiarity with that person, he/she will mostly convey his/her sorrows, miseries from the past and what he/she is missing rather than what he/she is blessed with. This is human nature.

Writing down our own spiritual experiences is a must for all spiritualists and seekers, because that will serve as a reminder. They can also see their own evolution through that. Many Masters have recommended maintaining a spiritual diary. If your experiences can also inspire others through the telling or writing about them, then you are doing a great seva to society. You are evolving and at the same time you are also helping others to evolve. Many people exist at the borderline. They are so caught up in the tangible world that they tend to discard or not recognize subtle experiences (such as those experienced during meditation). They might also consider these experiences as unreal or just imagination. Then they will tend to choose the gross and tangible world or tangible reality over that of the relatively 'non-tangible' spiritual experiences.

People who enjoy profound subtle experiences during meditation do so because they are allowing it to happen and are not blocking the subtle experiences with thoughts, ego or analysis, e.g. intellect. In order for the Masters to work on you, you need to have unshakable faith and egolessness. We must allow the Masters to take us higher. By Masters, I mean the great Masters such as Babaji, Baba Jesus, Buddha, Adi Shankaracharya, Krishna etc.

Nurturing negative thoughts is human nature. Being positive requires hard work. Furthermore, many times our mind does not accept that we actually deserve the good thing that happened to us or will happen to us. If someone does something good for you or someone offers assistance, we automatically think: "This cannot be true. He/She has some ulterior motive." It is important to love everyone. It is also equally important to protect ourselves from treacherous people. Using the intellect more than emotions is the key. Respecting all individuals with the polite ability to say 'no' when you do not want a particular material or situation, along with a keen awareness, are the key points in safeguarding ourselves. We are vulnerable when we are emotional.

Coming back to the nature of the mind. The biggest change one can bring upon oneself is through changing one's patterns. Nurture kindness, nurture love, nurture the positive experiences you have had and replace the negative emotions that are already existing in your mind with positive ones. It is as simple as that! It is sure that negative experiences are stored and well-protected in everybody's mind. We must bring them up to our conscious awareness and shed them, like we clean up our closet. All the fears and guilt must be taken out of the closet (subconscious) and carefully discarded. You can do this. All of us can do it but to get there you must spend time at the 'being level' in order to make it happen. By 'doing' you cannot achieve this. This purification is what we are trying to achieve through our 'Power of Purity' meditation.

Meditation is not only 'doing nothing'; as some have said, it is 'doing everything through non-doing'. In other words, meditation is 'doing everything at the being level'. Doing nothing is only the physical aspect of it. By sitting still and doing nothing, one may not be meditating at all if the mind is 'doing something' because it cannot 'sit' idle. In that case, there is only a physical side to 'doing nothing'.

The body, mind and intellect as one, concentrating on one

point, completely united, ego eliminated, merging with your own soul, is called 'samadhi' in India. The soul is the Lord. When you are at the soul level, you are doing everything through non-doing. In other words, the Father or Parabrahma is within and 'without' everything. It exists in every moving and non-moving object. It is involved in all of the action of the whole universe. Yet, it is at one place. This omnipresence and this diverse action through non-action is what we too can achieve if we are firmly established at the soul level.

All in all, we need to be aware. Our senses, our mind and our intellect use up a lot of our energy. Sleep replenishes it. If meditation is done properly, we circulate the energy within ourselves and it rejuvenates our entire system and opens up the door for the Higher.

Once again, the scriptures have warned us to avoid falling into the traps of life by over-using the intellect.

Understand this clearly, the more intellectual we become, the more distant we become from the truth. Intellect and mind are connected to the body. We have to go beyond that to touch the higher realms of existence. We have to effectively use our intellect and slowly detach from our mind's pull. Unfortunately most of us are slaves of our mind. That is why even when the soul wants to use the most tranquil time of the day that is from 3 am to 6 am, for meditation or even just chanting or reading scriptures, we tend to sleep. This happens when we give in to our mind. Sleeping late is a tamasic quality. The more tamas we have, the more we tend to become emotional (which goes hand in hand with a tendency to smoke and drink alcohol or use tamasic products) and it prevents meditative states. On the other hand, if our subconscious has stored data which says that meditation is a part of your character, just like eating and sleeping is, you may do it mechanically, with no results. That's purely a waste of time. Nobody achieves anything like that. Just like our habits determine our character; our habits also determine our potential for evolution. Be careful of unconscious actions and unconscious living.

Navanath, a Powerful Tradition with its root in Krishna
Avatar of Maha Vishnu. Liberated Existence is the tradition
of the Navanaths. Simplicity in thought, word and action,
Faith and Purity are the visible signs of the tradition. Lord
Dattatreya is the Adi Guru (First Guru). The nine Nava
Narayanas incarnated as Navanaths for the preservation of
dharma on earth and to elevate the unconscious generations
to total liberation through supreme awareness.
(This sketch depicting Mohanji prostrating to Krishna, Lord
Dattatreya and Navanaths was specially drawn by Shanthy
Vaidya for this book)

Bhagwan Dattatreya

Shri Shripad Shrivallabha Swami

Shri Narasimha Saraswati

Shri Akkalkot Swâmi Maharaj

Shri Manik Prabhu Maharaj

Shri Sai Baba

Shri Gajanan Maharaj

Shri Satya Sai

Maha Avtaar Babaji

Bhagwan Ramana Maharishi

Bhagawan Nityananda

Lord Jesus Christ

The grand tradition of Lord Dattatreya and his various
avtaars; as well as the grand tradition of Kriya Yoga guides
us through time into eternity.

Parabrahma - the supreme consciousness

Unconditional love sees no boundaries and never
differentiates Bardinath during the deluge

Mohanji's satsang with soldiers of Indian armed forces at
Bardinath during the deluge

Unconditional love sees no boundaries and never
differentiates

Mohanji watches over the river Ganga during the Maha Kumbh at Allahabad, India

Mohanji at a satsang in the US

Guru's grace is like the flowing river.
It nurtures spiritual evolution

Do it today. Live it today. Enjoy it today. Who has seen tomorrow? People enjoying the nature walk during Mohanji Lifestyle Retreat at Serbia

All search ends when you find yourself

Satsang in progress at Mohanji Lifestyle Retreat
in South Africa

Mohanji enroute to sangam (confluence of three holy rivers)
for a dip during the Maha Kumb at Allahabad, India

Mohanji speaking at Life Positive Expo, Mumbai

The Guru who appeared in front of you is all Gurus. Look
no further. By ignoring what is in front of you and searching
for the intangible unknowns, you will reach nowhere

Beingness is being Natural

It is the union of consciousness that makes one "see"
the unity in beings

Lord Krishna

Lord Shiva

SHAKTIPAT

Shaktipat

THE CORE OF our meditations is Shaktipat—an energy transfer from the higher realms of consciousness. We usually give Shaktipat through the Sahasrara Chakra and sometimes the Ajna Chakra. Shaktipat aligns the system and reaches wherever it has to reach. The tradition of Shaktipat is to speed up the spiritual process. Shaktipat is sheer Grace. It is a rare, beautiful and divine gift. It is real and works wonderfully well.

The first ever Shaktipat happened with the first creation, when life entered matter and became a living being. That was a demonstration of Love and Shaktipat—which is life—was a gift of the Almighty. Love is the basis of creation. Life itself was the first of Shaktipats. Thenceforth, every Shaktipat that has happened from every Master who represents the Guru Principle or the Almighty has been transforming lives and bringing them, in awareness, to the level of the Almighty.

The one who gives Shaktipat is able to handle much higher energy than a receiver. The light bulb might only be of 20 watts but the electricity line carries much higher energy. The bulb is tuned to receive only 20 watts.

When energy is transferred you receive the quantity you can handle. So you are not burned! Shaktipat operates at the physical level because it has healing powers. It operates at the emotional level to heal emotions. It also operates at the intellectual level so that you think clearly and your awareness can grow. It shifts your consciousness to a plane of spiritual progress. Your awareness shifts, which you will know in the days to come after having received Shaktipat. Shaktipat energy works over a period of time. And it works in various ways (healing/cleansing). It also eases ego blockages. It works differently on each person, according to his/her constitution and needs.

As you are evolving your capacity will change. Then you will be given Shaktipat according to your capacity. Each time Shaktipat happens, a different set of blockage is removed.

The initial pranayam as that we practice are to create the platform for the meditation that follows. They are aimed at activating the chakras to receive and distribute energy evenly. The purpose of all these is cleansing and elevation.

Q: The originator of Shaktipat?

M: The original creator of the universe.

Q: How does Shaktipat change the physical and spiritual body?

M: It depends on the individual constitution. Change is for sure. Expectations are the main hindrance in experiencing the change. Changes can be physical, mental, intellectual and spiritual. It depends on where the blockage is. This is purely individualistic. Each one gets what they deserve. Each one gets their blockages removed, consistently as blockages appear at various stages of evolution. The effect, the lightness, is usually unmistakable. We need not even talk about it. Participants will feel it. The bliss cannot remain hidden.

Also any practice that meditators currently follow will give more results after the shaktipat. Our teachings are only complementing not contradicting other sadhanas. Our path is that of liberation, not binding.

No true Shaktipat is ever wasted. Every Shaktipat is transformative and life-changing. It is the expression of the Unconditional Love of the Almighty, the Soul and the Guru Tattva, which is one and the same. Our limited mind cannot understand the depth of the transformation that happens in the recipient.

Q: Which factors might reduce the effect of Shaktipat?

M: Meat, fish, animal products, alcohol will reduce the speed of elevation. If you want to have food soon after the meditation, please let it be raw vegetables, fruit, water and herbal tea. Please do not serve meat or fish or even cooked food for that matter soon after our meditation. The energy level will be very high after the meditation. It will get violated with the stomach suddenly charging into action. People can even sleep after meditation if they choose to. Then the transfer of energy will work even better.

Q: I loved your meditation and blessing. Afterwards though I underwent a fever and headache. And I felt confused.

M: This is the physical manifestation of the inner cleansing of Shaktipat. Just go through the process. Shaktipat cuts old unnecessary bindings. When these cords of impressions get cut, a gap between one's mind/intellect and one's spiritual evolution appears. In this gap it is normal to feel confusion or feel like crying etc. We have to understand that mind and intellect are repetitive, whereas spirituality is evolutionary. Trust that this gap will reduce in the course of time. However, a student has to have extreme patience. This gap could cause disillusionment; hence steadfastness to one path is essential. Total faith is essential until the journey is completed. The disillusionment can cause physical, emotional or intellectual agony. Invariably a spiritual student is supported by a Master suitable to his stature. There is nothing to worry. You will be fine soon.

Initiation in Shaktipat

To be capable of giving Shaktipat one needs initiation. Initiation into Shaktipat is NOT equal to receiving Shaktipat. One criterion for initiation is that the person should be operating from a high level of purity, not from the level of desire (desire to become a guru, desire to have money etc.). The initiated should be committed, selfless and pure.

Who will be initiated into giving Shaktipat is a choice of the Masters (I don't initiate anyone unless I have the permission of Higher Masters).

When the initiate is pure, the perfection of transfer happens. Receiver and giver are in perfect mode of receptivity and the receiver will get what he or she deserves. It would be like a software change for the better.

I cannot physically reach that many people. So through the initiates, I can reach more people at a time. No matter how many Mohanji meditations are conducted at various locations, the initiated Shaktipat givers are tuned into my consciousness, which means the field of my expanded awareness covers all of them.

Shaktipat is a big responsibility. Hence all those who are an instrument of giving Shaktipat maintain the sanctity and seriousness associated to this sacred task.

Further Clarifications on Shaktipat and Astral Shaktipat

Shaktipat is a great responsibility. Shaktipat is the power one acquires through Grace to transfer or transmit it benevolently to another. The basis is benevolence and unconditional love. In order to give Shaktipat, the Initiator (me) and the Initiated should become one. The Initiated is a channel. The connectivity is based on complete surrender and being like an empty bottle. The conduit is purity. When purity intensifies, Sushumna (the central canal in the subtle body) will become like steel and it can conduct much higher energy than individually possible. Recent proof is the experience in Chandigarh, where people who have never met me, saw me. This signifies the purity of the Initiate who conducted Shaktipat as a perfect instrument, completely surrendering to my consciousness.

Initiation into Shaktipat means big responsibility. The one who gives Shaktipat must maintain purity and most importantly, selflessness and egolessness. Just like Lord Krishna who always says: "Thus spake my Guru", nobody takes ownership here. No one says "I have done it". The Initiated simply allows the Grace to flow through them by nullifying their ego and surrendering completely at their Guru's feet. Shaktipat is closely linked with tradition. It is linked to the Gurus. The moment you detach mentally or consider yourself independent, you will lose this power and Grace. This is because Shaktipat is like a universal body. All the limbs should work in unison. It is a grand collaboration.

Astral Shaktipat is something else. For this, the entity should start operating in terrestrial plane and astral plane simultaneously and consistently. I have explained about astral plane in detail in the past, in a few of our satsangs. Astral existence is physical body-less existence. In order to give power to someone's gross body, the bodiless entity needs to be supremely powerful spiritually, completely detached, and also well supported by the tradition and his Guru. Otherwise, when the astral body moves out of one's physical body, other entities can come and occupy the physical body. It can happen fully or even partially. This will completely pull the person down in stature. This is quite a dangerous thing to experiment with. Astral Shaktipat is usually conducted only by high Masters who can extend their beingness in more than one plane simultaneously and operate with equal power both physically and astrally together. This needs a lot of nurturing from a powerful Guru. And the Guru will have to be with the disciple until he/she can do it alone. Otherwise, negative forces will completely ruin him/her. Please understand clearly, this is no joke. We call some saadhaks "Yoga Bhrashta" or fallen from the path. These are ambitious people who want to run before they can walk well. Some think this is easy, because they think it is like astral travel. Astral travel is easy, but not astral Shaktipat. You are doing a big job, astrally. Please do not confuse between astral travel and Shaktipat. Shaktipat is a serious matter. People can get burned with the intensity of this task, if proper purity and connectivity is not maintained.

So, once again, what is required is complete surrender, total faith in the Guru and the system, surrendering every thought, word and action at the Guru's feet—in this matter Guru represents the tradition, the principle, not a person. If you want to be a perfect channel, keep watching your own ego, which is prompting you to think that you are fine and individually powerful. This is dangerous. Negative forces will help enhance your ego, make you walk alone, in order to eventually pull you down. I have seen many examples. Many people have suffered such falls even in the Himalayas, in relative isolation. I remember an elderly person who came and met me in Delhi. He had done almost 40 years of severe practices, then started on his own and fell seriously. When he ventured out of his body, another spirit occupied it and was creating havoc. He came twice to meet me; the second time to thank me—this is one example.

Kundalini

Kundalini is supposed to be resting in the space between the anus and scrotum for men and the space between the anus and vagina for women. It is supposed to be a three and a half coiled energy in the shape of a serpent. It is also considered as Shakti energy which is of terrestrial nature. We can also say that liberation means liberating the kundalini energy or we can say that when we cease to be terrestrial, kundalini also leaves its usual position.

It usually lies dormant and unprovoked when we are immersed in terrestrial chores. It can only be fully liberated when it transits through the elements represented by the chakras. The elements are fundamentals of physical creation. When its journey towards Shiva, or the supreme consciousness begins, Kundalini energy breaks the Brahma granthi located before the Mooladhaar chakra.

The transit path is Sushumna naadi. A transit continues through the root chakra, Swaadhisthaana chakra and Manipura chakra, each representing the earth, water and fire elements respectively. After it gets purified in the fire element which means the Manipura chakra (purification by fire or Agni shuddhi), it becomes eligible to break the ties of Vishnu granthi and reaches the Anahata chakra. Through the Anahata, then the Vishuddhi chakra, it arrives and breaks the ties of Rudra granthi and reaches the Ajna chakra. From Ajna the transit is to Sahasrara and beyond.

When Shakti joins Shiva, awakening happens—enlightenment happens. The terrestrial binding ceases. It happens only when one's eligibility is absolutely right.

When kundalini energy transits through each chakra, it creates various feelings, delusions and illusions. We have to keep to our spine and sadhana to overcome these delusions. So many samskaras will be liberated; many matters which you thought were tremendously important for life on earth suddenly become unimportant. We may also lose interest in many aspects of terrestrial existence, including the urge for good food, sex or relationships. In certain people, it is the other way around. They could have extreme sexual urges, extreme hunger, feeling of floating or dissolving, feeling of involuntary movements, feelings of telepathy, so on and so forth. Just ignore everything and keep focused on your practice. Association with a Master is a great blessing during these times. He will understand what you are going through and will guide you further.

Q: Does Shaktipat activate Kundalini?

M: Kundalini activation is automatic when the path is clear. Usually there are energy clumps which block the free transit of kundalini. These clumps are not always stationary, they keep moving. What we are doing is intense cleansing and purification as well as activation of kundalini. We are preparing the path as well activating the kundalini through Shaktipat. If the path is blocked, kundalini will transit through wrong routes which could cause calamities. We are very careful about that. Kundalini activation and guidance certainly happens through our meditation.

Blessing

Bless All. It will make you serene and light. Blessing expands you. It makes you light. When we bless all the people we like and all the people we do not like, we truly become the perfect expression of the Almighty. His true expression is unconditional love. When we remove all the hatreds and fears from our mind, we become embodiments of love. Love expands. Love makes our life enjoyable. When we express sincere gratitude to all the objects and beings that helped our existence on earth, we become universal. Once we understand the true relevance of the food that we have consumed so far, the houses that sheltered us, the books that gave us knowledge, our parents and our teachers, and above all, the element of divinity that sustained us, we will be filled with humility and deep gratitude. Most of our vital functions including respiration, circulation, digestion, heartbeat and even sleep for that matter, are controlled by our subconscious mind. All these things are working in perfect synchronization because our conscious mind has nothing to do with it. We are given the time, space, intellect and situation to act out our inherent traits. What do we have in our control? Why do we blame others? Why do we entertain guilt at all? What is there to be afraid of? All experiences have been lessons. We could not have changed anything. So what else can we do except express unconditional love and compassion? What else can we do but bless everybody and everything? When we realize that we are not really the one who does everything, we will see our ego getting nullified and our doer-ship getting dissolved. We will then operate in perfect awareness and gratitude.

God is within us. God is to be loved not feared. The soul element that fuels our existence is the God within all of us. God, the one who Generates, Operates and Dissolves. Hence, all of us possess the same god element. None is inferior nor superior to anyone. Some evolved higher through rigorous practices, contemplation and meditation. Through lifetimes of efforts, they attained higher awareness. That's all. In principle, all are one and the same. The same soul element fuels the existence of all living beings, which includes plants and animals. Just like the same electricity is used to operate various equipment items, the same soul operates various bodies and some of them are human bodies.

All of us are temporary custodians of a body, of money and possessions. It is the same with relationships too. Everything is temporary. Everything has a definite longevity. There is no room for egocentric expressions, if we digest this truth. All we can do is forgive everything. Bless everything.

When we shift our consciousness to the spine and to 360 degrees, the impact, the wear and tear of the events we are exposed to, will be much less. Nothing will overwhelm us. You will maintain perfect equanimity and deep gratitude. Nothing happens by accident. Everything has a perfect reason. We often cannot understand the reason from our level of consciousness. That's all. Our inability should not be interpreted as cosmic deficiency. Cosmic perfection is infinite and incomparable.

My guided meditations have transformed many lives. Some people have stayed and evolved. Some came and left, perhaps choosing different paths. As always, each person responds according to his/her inherent consciousness and constitution. We did everything with the purest of intentions without any selfish motives. That's the best we could do.

All of us exist in various planes of consciousness. We carry the conditionings of our immediate past as well as other lives, without having clarity about it. We cannot usually figure out which conditioning provoked which response in us. But invariably we are victims of our conditionings. Hence, it is important to touch base with our own consciousness, our real Self. My guided meditations are designed to bring you to yourself.

We wish you great spiritual evolution in this life. We are one. We are one family and one consciousness. We will never be separate from one another.

The Fire

Fire is the eternal purifier. Water, earth or air can be contaminated, while fire cannot. All elements are prone to contamination, except fire. Fire burns everything and converts it into ashes. Cleansing by fire is considered to be much more powerful and effective than cleansing by water. This is why along with offerings of various materials to various deities—the effect of cleansing with fire through the aura was experienced by people who perform fire rituals, such as Agnihotra, Yajna or Yaaga.

Fire is the element that helps our digestion too. Fire is also associated as the cause for emotions such as anger, passion, greed etc.

Panchaagni literally means five fires. Cleansing through five fires, of which four fires are lit by us and the sun being the fifth. People used to do repentance (Praayaschittha), which means endurance and cleansing of the conscience.

Agni is the link between heaven and earth. The Mooladhara chakra, signifying earth, and the Sahasrara chakra, signifying heaven, are linked through Agni. Agni or fire always has its flames upwards. This is also the motion of the Kundalini energy. Kundalini energy, when it goes through the fire of Agni, gets elevated to Sahasrara. Agni burns everything that comes in its way, elevates, moves upwards and only ash remains on the earth. Ash represents the elements or the gross in this context.

Sita, the Shakti element, went through Agni Pariksha (test by fire) before she got united with Rama, the pure consciousness. Thus, Shakti or Sita, that was tested and tempted by the 10-headed Raavana (or by the 5 Jnanendriyas and 5 Karmendriyas = 5 senses of perception and 5 senses of action, thus the 10 heads of our daily temptation) had to cleanse herself in fire before she could reach Rama, the pure consciousness. Like that, the gross needs to be purified in fire to attain the pure energy. Kundalini rising up to Sahasrara and Sita attaining Rama mean the same in this context. Pure consciousness did not come down. Shakti had to go up and meet Rama. And heavy cleansing must occur before that meeting can happen.

The fundamental need for performing fire purification is faith. Faith is the key. Faith intensifies purification. Faith will create devotion. Unfailing devotion. This makes the transit easy for Sita to reach Rama. The elevation also means the elevation in gunas. Tamas goes through rajas and becomes sattva. Thus, elimination of tamas and attainment of sattva through an action which is rajas, can be compared to Raavana (the dark element or tamas), Sita (the seeker) and Rama (the sought) and fire as the vehicle. Sita got released from the clutches of Raavana (kundalini gets liberated through sadhana and moves up through Sushumna), fire purified Sita (and kundalini energy) and Rama (the guna-less) accepted Sita. Kundalini Shakti transcends gunas and attains Shiva, the pure consciousness. This means moksha, salvation. Thus 'Tamaso Ma Jyothirgamaya'—from darkness to brightness, or from bondage to liberation—is the same matter. Tamas is darkness or inertia. Light is liberation or sattva guna (or even the guna-less state). Elevation is the key.

The Manipura chakra is the seat of Agni tattva. This is why we say Agni is in the middle. This is the same Agni that aids digestion of food etc. When Kundalini Shakti moves up through Manipura, located at the stomach centre, its purification through Agni takes place. This is why we often do the intense humming or AUM chanting, based on the stomach centre, before our meditations.

This intensifies the Agni element in the seeker. This supports faster purification. Cleansing becomes more powerful. Kundalini has to break through the Agni and reach Sahasrara or go back to its old form.

Hanumanji burned the prestigious Lanka of Raavana. He in fact burned the ego of Raavana. When ego is hurt, the immediate reaction is violence. The mind becomes violent. When mind becomes violent, buddhi or viveka (intellect or wisdom) disappear. Ego and emotion destroy man. The same destroyed Raavana. Hanuman's power was unfailing devotion to pure consciousness, Rama. Sita was also craving to achieve Rama. Again, Agni played its role. We can even say that Hanumanji became the Agni here: the vehicle.

Ego torments a saint to some extent even in the savikalpa samadhi state. It keeps tormenting him till he attains the nirvikalpa samadhi state. Some saints opt for panchaagni meditation to overcome this aspect of terrestrial binding.

In the Kathopanishad, Yama attributes the three-fold fire to Nachiketas, in recognition of his sincere seeker-ship. They are dhyana (meditation), daana (charity) and tapas (austerity).

Panchaagni is four fires lit plus the fire from one sun. This is a test for purification. This is conducted either in Uttaraayana (Makar-Sankranti—mid January) or Dakshinaayana (Karka Sankranti—mid July). The panchaagni is used for cleaning five internal fires: passion, anger, greed, attachment and jealousy. The purpose is praayaschittha or repentance. This is also called Pashupati Vratha, dedicated to the supreme saint Shiva. The panchaagni during Uttaraayana triggers light and liberation for the soul. Dakshinaayana denotes rebirth and return to life on earth.

Uttaraayana helps the soul to leave the terrestrial clutches and hence the Great Bhishma of the Mahabharata chose his exit at that time.

PRAYER & VISUALISATION

The Best Prayer

THE BEST PRAYER is the prayer of gratitude. We are giving thanks for our existence, what we are enjoying now, like the fresh air, sunlight, unconditional love of nature, internal and external riches, experiences, relationships, everything that we have been given without any conditions. When we thank the Almighty wholeheartedly, it will decrease our ego and doership. The worst prayer is the prayer of asking for something. That way we are expressing the lack of something. We are expressing insufficiency. Thought is the first level of creation. Energy gets released there. Energy can never die. It stays and conglomerates with similar energies and creates your destiny. The nature or your subconscious takes things literally. When you say that you do not have something, your subconscious takes it literally and repeats: "You do not have that". That becomes your reality. While gratitude makes our heart rich, prayer of insufficiency makes our heart poor, helpless and dependent. So be careful. Your thoughts, words and actions create your destiny. Do not be fooled by yourself. Some people keep complaining: "I don't have this, I don't have that.", "If only I had this one thing . . . , then the other . . . and another." This only makes them poorer and poorer, inside first and outside later. On the spiritual path it is important to be happy with what we have been given and keep expressing sincere gratitude. This will make you grow spiritually higher and higher. Understand that the world can be compared to a mirror. It reflects what you are. A true Master also does the same. You will be given what you deserve and not what you desire. What you desire may not be what you are eligible for. Let's be clear about this.

Prayer is for our self. We are praying to our self. That's why we mostly close our eyes while we pray, even if we visualise another form apart from our physical form. When we close our eyes, we are essentially going within. We are getting in touch with ourselves.

Who is an external God or Guru? An extension of ourselves. There are no frames, gender demarcations for God. God has no sex, colour or shape. He is in every being. He attains the colour and shape of the bottle that carries him. So when he sits in Ram's body, he attains the form and characteristics of Ram. When he sits in Rahim's body, he attains the form and characteristics of Rahim. When he is in a flower, he expresses that. Likewise a bird, animal, plant, tree, soil, elements, space, you and I. We all are the expressions of the same God. So where and why is the discrimination? Discrimination happens in our own mind, because of our sense of duality. Through normal senses that we posses, duality must exist. Through the extrasensory vision, unity exists. The vehicle to reach unity is meditation and the path is inside ourselves. Through extroverted—ness we can only experience the sense objects. Through introversion, we can experience our self. Once we experience our Self, all external sense objects become separately insignificant. They become part of us.

Through prayer, we are re-affirming ourselves as to what we are. Even though the object of our prayer is an external deity, we are essentially praying to our self and re-assuring our own mind that there is a God. God does not need your prayer. God does not have any expectations. Therefore if we do something believing that God will be happy, it's utter ignorance. God is beyond duality, beyond gunas. Everything began from him and dissolves in him. God does not care for your prayer or abuse. Only you get exalted by your prayers. God can only be attained through sadhana and elimination of our samskaras through consistent exhaustion and avoidance of rebuilding them again. The method is being in the present all the time. Through prayers or worship we can only reaffirm to our own mind that God exists and he could be looking after us. God can be attained through internal exploration, meditation, elimination of vasanas (inherent traits and terrestrial bindings) and then, no prayers will be needed either. As we go beyond the need of external sense objects or minimise their requirement we get closer to the energy plane which is God. Gross plane is an extension of god. Gross is part of God. We are also part of God. When ego dissolves and oneness takes root, we grow beyond gunas, we become all knowledge, we become the greatest bliss, there is no duality, we become all religions or religion-less, we become one with all Gods, Gurus. We reach God. Then, usually our expression is overflowing compassion and love. Devotion to the soul element which overflows as Bhakti, songs and selfless service. Our personal needs become minimal and the need of the Universe along with its beings becomes predominant. We become one with God. One with the energy that Generates, Operates and Dissolves. GOD!

Limitation of Our Conscious Mind

When you express any need, this means there is something lacking. Nature will just echo this feeling. The subconscious will churn out that reality. Normal human beings believe that if we get what we lack, we will be happy. Terrestrial happiness is transitory though. Even if we get all that we desire, we will desire for more and will continue to desire. Desires run parallel to time. As time flows, desires are like waves, rising up and dropping back into the mind. Some get fulfilled, some are kept pending in our subconscious. The push of those pending desires will provoke more and more terrestrial lives.

Expressing the lack of anything will ensure the lack of that thing. Whether it is selfish or selfless. Hence, richness of our heart is even more important. Inner richness becomes external abundance. Love attracts. Love expands. When we love unconditionally, there will be no shortage of anything. If you base all your actions on love, without expectations, the result will be happiness without reasons. This is bliss. This is liberation. There are no expectations and the only expression is love. As I had mentioned earlier we should equally love our friends and enemies. Love all, serve all— the Dattatreya tradition is rooted in this principle.

So once again, the best prayer is the prayer of gratitude. Gratitude for all that we have and all that we do not have. A prayer that echoes in one's own self, as it is actually our own self that listens to our prayer. There is no one closer to us than our own self or soul. Every prayer is fuelled by the soul. Every prayer is heard by the soul. The one who prays and the one who listens to the prayer is one and the same. Where is an external entity? Who are we praying to? Krishna, Buddha, Jesus, Shiva, Vishnu are all our soul. Same soul that is expressed in different bodies or same family of souls. Same father. Just keep the conscious mind or ego, which created the duality in your mind and made you believe in your physical form and intellectual constitution, aside. You will understand what I am talking about. We are indeed lying in the lap of God every night. Our conscious mind is absent, and we sleep peacefully!!!

Suffering has a purpose. Usually sufferings are extreme cleansers. They clean us inside out. Suffering hits our ego big time. Suffering, especially if it is emotional or at the ego level, will push us towards spirituality in a big way. The more the suffering, the closer we get to God. God is always available. Our ego is the veil that separates and obscures God from us. When we express sincere thanks, love flows from our heart. There is nothing that God does not know. We need not tell Him anything, because He is inside every atom. He is our soul. What can He not know? It's our limited mind that makes us feel the duality and alienation. Take it away and pray, expressing gratitude. How do you take it away? By constantly being with every thought, word and action and not allowing the mind to oscillate between the past and the present. We will start appreciating every morsel of food that we eat, every sight in front of our eyes, every drop of rain, every sound around, the sun, the moon and the stars, the sound of music and the sound of silence too. We will float in everything. Everything becomes us. There will be no anxiety, no fear, no need, no complaint. We are at peace with ourselves. We need nothing else. Please understand that the reason for all calamities is the limitation of our conscious mind or the lack of higher awareness. When you are in the present, you will have razor sharp concentration. Rays transmitting through a focused lens can create fire. Likewise, a mind trained to be in the present can get you anywhere. And your subconscious will not be too crowded with junk data either. There is much more to it.

Prayers without Results

Q: I have been praying without results, why?

M: You have been praying conditionally, while God is always unconditional. You will get what you deserve. If you are a good devotee, you should be ready to accept whatever is given to you. It does not matter whether it is good or bad according to your understanding levels. What you may consider bad was probably good for you in the long run. We cannot see our past lives or the future ones. We have to accept the present as raw as it comes. No choice. Your present was demanded by you in your past, even past lives. Now, when you pray expecting tangible results, you will be disappointed and even disillusioned. You are a karmic being. You have created your own agenda consciously or unconsciously. You are continuously creating and building on it each day, even at the expense of not having time to clear your garbage or unburden yourself from the accumulated trash. No time. This means, we are passive towards ourselves. We are looking at someone else, maybe a Guru or an acharya to come forward and perform the role of cleaning your garbage. Unfortunately the Guru and acharya are only road signs. Road signs can only tell you where you could possibly go from where you stand now. They are not your garbage collectors. They could possibly show you where the garbage can is. It's up to you to use it to unburden yourself.

Understand that it is the quality of the sincere devotee to accept whatever God gives. Insecurity about the future and going to astrologers only states your level of faith. It is very weak. Faith is weak. When faith is weak, you will not have the power to endure realities. When faith is strong, you can move mountains. Faith is the key. Faith should be absolute. When you are constantly worried about the future, your present will go for a toss. You lose your present. When you lose your present, essentially, you will also lose your future. This is the law of nature. The more someone visits diviners, rest assured, the more insecure this person is. His faith is fragile. Lack of faith closes all the doors of our mind. It cannot accept Grace and blessings anymore.

Hence, the best prayer is the prayer of gratitude, for all that you have and all that you have been given. The best kind of richness is the richness of our mind, our internal richness. It is more durable and real. External richness changes. Money is money only when it flows from hand to hand. Otherwise it is just paper. Understand this clearly. Whether you are rich or poor, black or white, if you do not have a rich mind, you have to work hard towards creating one. A rich mind will be unconditional, filled with genuine love. Filled with compassion and care. It will not compare. It will have the courage to call a spade a spade. It will have no fear. Faith will be absolute. It will accept any realities that come its way. Its prayers will always be the prayer of gratitude. It will never energize fears and will systematically counter all fears with faith. Now do your own assessment. No need to prove anything to another person. It is only for your own sake. Ask the fundamental question: "Is my faith absolute? If yes, why am I fearing?" If there are fears, that means there should be more faith. "Why should there be insecurities when, with faith, I am willing to accept all realities?" Life is a mixture always. We will be given only what we deserve and not what we desire.

About Visualisation

Q: I need your help. I have been practicing the Kriya yoga technique of visualising the blue ball etc. Recently I attended another Kriya yoga class and they were totally against visualisation. Now I am confused. Please can you give clarity?

M: Visualisation is only a path in Kriya yoga. In the Kriya yoga tradition, this technique is used to bring our concentration closer towards our own body and into our self. Senses take our attention far and wide. Before we actually internalise our energies, we have to bring the attention to ourselves. Visualisation is one of the techniques and perhaps the most popular for that. Concentration is the key. Visualisation helps concentration. Concentration helps us to stay internalised and the more internalised we are, the higher will be our awareness level. If we are on the awareness plane, visualization drops automatically. Awareness eradicates or cancels the need for visualisation.

Each one of us is on a different stage of our spiritual evolution. Some need visualisation. Some meditate on the Ajna chakra or eyebrow centre, some meditate on Anahata chakra, heart centre, some are comfortable to stay at the tip of the nostrils, some in the spine, so on and so forth. Each person is unique and unlike any other. So, if visualisation suits your process, do that. There is no harm. Understanding the final destination is the most important thing. subconscious repetition of any practice will not help evolution. Patience is very important. Never compare your progress with another. Never try to imitate the spiritual sadhana or practice of another. Take only that which suits you.

Food is aplenty. But you can eat only what you can digest comfortably. If you overeat you will have indigestion. Avoid emotional eating. Trust you understood what I meant.

Every creative person does visualisation, constantly. An architect must visualise the end product before he touches his drawing board. If he does not visualise, what will he draw? Likewise, all of us are constantly visualizing whenever we enter into any discussion. We create mental pictures all the time. Visualisation should not be considered as the end product. It must be considered as the means towards achieving the end product. When the end product is achieved, the visualisation drops. So walk the path and understand that nothing is absolutely right or absolutely wrong in spirituality.

If a 10th class student throws his books away and declares them as utter waste and insignificant, after looking at the books of a graduate student, he will never get promoted. He has to walk the path and reach graduation, gradually. Some may do it faster. Then again, never compare yourself.

Visualisation techniques have been used by spiritual seekers, Masters and psychologists. Please discard the notion that it is wrong and create guilt around it. Even in pujas and tantric rituals there is a great amount of visualisation. It's all part of our existence on planet earth. As I said earlier, when awareness controls or spreads beyond your constitution, the requirement for visualisation will vanish by itself. Liberation removes all such requirements. Liberation sets you free. Till you reach that state use whichever method suits you.

COINCIDENCES, SIDDHIS & SUPERSTITIONS

Coincidences

There are no coincidences. Things happen only according to perfect symmetry with the universe. We may not understand how we are also an integral part of the universe. When we walk, breathe air and drink water, numerous organisms also perish and get shifted to another life. We have been used by nature for another re-cycling. Are we aware of that? Surrendering to the will of the universe is the best method. Just float on through all situations as a witness of yourself, detached and involved at the same time. You will see how nature brings propositions to you. You are not choosing. It was not always your conscious choice to bring forth any particular situation that you experienced. It was subconscious created realities that you are experiencing. Becoming beyond both conscious and subconscious is the realm of the Creator. That realm is achieved through being with your soul. Prana is more subtle than the gross body. Be with prana. Go through the inner organs and be in touch with your inside. Then use the mind to stay in the spine. Being in the spine will elevate you. And then you will reach the realm of pure energy. This is the soul. Soul can neither be created nor destroyed. Once you remain in that realm, everything will be fine. Everything will be at your will. You can be there. Do not be confused.

Siddhis

When we do sadhana we are bound to attain some siddhis. As all the usually dissipating energies (through our senses) are introverted, they work within us. Repeated meditation, chanting or selfless service to society could sharpen your otherwise dormant potential.

Just like animals, man also used to have a very active sixth sense. This aspect is still asleep in most of us. (At the time when the tsunami struck, all the free birds and animals had already relocated themselves. Only the bound animals and birds or domestic animals that were bound by men perished.)

The powers are natural. Sixth sense is natural. Just like you tune the antenna of your television to receive transmission of programs, our spiritual practices tune and sharpen our inherent antennas. This attains more and more perfection as we proceed further and further in our practice, if we do it consistently.

Man's greed for fame, recognition and money sometimes overtakes his actual need for using this life to attain the ultimate. Then he falls. Gravitational forces become more powerful than levitational forces within us. We become earth-bound.

For example, when the siddhi to know the past, present and future is obtained, if we use it to impress and amass disciples or money, it becomes a trap for the practitioner or the seeker. He stops right there. He also accumulates karma through his actions. Karma binds him to the earth. He slips and falls too.

Instead, if the seeker stays detached, but uses the powers he attained through sadhana to gently guide, without displaying the true inner potential so that he does not amass disciples, and at the same time he does his deed, he will remain relatively free and unattached. This helps his own progress. Spiritual practice and selfless service should be well-balanced.

Siddhis, when used discreetly and not aiming at power and glory, become your power. At the same time, when siddhis are used for our self-glorification, it is the beginning of our decay. Then it becomes your weakness. According to me, siddhis—if you have them—should be used only with utmost caution and also just for the sake of another being, without expecting anything in return. It is also very important not to use one's siddhis for one's own benefit. This is very dangerous for the seeker, or the saint.

Siddhis are a natural outcome for any sincere spiritual seeker as he transits in spirituality. Talking about them and glorifying them is dangerous as all these create traps into which the seeker himself falls. It is essential not to flaunt your powers and keep it as discreet as possible, because the powers can easily vanish too.

When the director of a company becomes the CEO due to his hard work, his perks change and he becomes richer. If he uses his new powers to do things selfishly, he can be de-promoted back to the position of director and lose the benefits that he gained as CEO. He can be expelled too. This is the way spirituality also works. It's a tightrope walk.

Patanjali keeps telling us to ignore siddhis and move forward. We should not even wait to check where we have reached. Just move with unshakable faith, eyes firmly fixed on the Supreme Father, Parabrahma. Name and fame are hindrances to a real seeker or a saint. Silent service is the best way, without expecting anything in return.

Siddhis are also tests. They tempt us and the lure of material success, along with this new tool, traps the soul back into the terrestrial quagmire, often eternally, over many lives. Once a seeker becomes established in the highest consciousness, the traps are removed.

Miracles

Q: Why are people getting addicted to miracles? I am referring to the miracles displayed by some spiritual people.

M: We are all essentially children. We get attracted to candies of life, whether it is physical (food and other objects of sensory gratification), emotional (music, arts, soap operas etc.), intellectual (science etc.) or spiritual.

Miracles are tools to attract people to the Master. Miracles become spontaneous when a person exists in the energy plane and attains power to conglomerate energy at will. Energy conglomerated is matter. Even our bodies are energy conglomerated. It could all disintegrate into energy at some point in time. When one evolves beyond his body, when he sheds his need and dependency on terrestrial matters, he exists in the energy plane. In that plane he is in tune with the Supreme Source. At that level, all materialisation is possible. These are siddhis. They use this to attract people to them. When people come to them, they can convey good messages and transform them. The first task is to get the attention of people. Miracles are a good tool for that. The second task is to convey the mission and message. The message is always the same, conveyed over generations. The key message from all Gurus, is unconditional love. The language might be different, expressions might be different though. This is because they are addressing different sets of people, different wavelengths, different mindsets.

Miracles, if any at all, are just to attract people. Do not be fooled by miracles. Miracles are possible for all. We attain that realm at various times when things happen at will. We are not constantly there because our samskaras or inherent traits pull us back. When we trash our samskaras through systematically exhausting them, we reach a plane where we have no thoughts generated out of vasanas. Thoughts will be generated as a reflection of the grand mind, the mind of the Supreme Father. I am using the term mind, just for your understanding. In fact there will be no mind and no thought. There will only be relevant action. Things just take place. Guidance will only be for relatively lower beings because their understanding levels are different.

Magic is different from miracles. So is teleportation. Magic and teleportation are skills. Materialisation is a status. Great Masters like Babaji even disintegrate and re-integrate their bodies at will. They can appear at various places at the same time.

Great Masters materialise objects only to serve a purpose. When the purpose is completed, that matter becomes useless or just vanishes.

Jesus used to heal people who had faith in him. Faith is absolutely necessary for conveying any miracle. It is not the power of the Master, but your level of receptivity that matters here. Masters are powerful, but if the seeker walks with filled up ego, he will have no advantage through the proximity of the Master. Jesus also taught one message: the message of love. Just love. He said: "Let your faith heal you." So the medium is faith. Faith opens our internal doors to receive Grace. Minus faith, Grace can never enter. Absolute faith can even move mountains. No doubt.

Our own mind, available books, and others, always try to tilt our belief systems and faith. True Masters also do the same to check the faith of their disciples. Masters behave in strange ways which tilt the disciple with expectation. Their axe falls at the root of our expectation. Ego also gets broken with that. Expectation is also a barrier between truth and us. Some will fall, some will stay. Those who stay are taken further. At every stage, there will be a filtering process. Those who consistently survive this will continue his journey. The Master will take him further. Those who get disillusioned, stay back and work their way up at their own pace. Both are fine. No true Master keeps any agenda. They allow their disciples to evolve over many lives. They allow their disciples natural growth. They do allow their disciples to engage and entertain themselves in trails that are errors. This is the path of unconditionality. True Love.

Masters who come with specific agendas use the appropriate technique to reach the people. Miracles could be one of them. Even Jesus said at one point in time: "I refuse to perform miracles." Even when he repeatedly performed astounding feats, people still doubted him. People were getting stuck with his miracles more than his teachings. This was upsetting the Master externally, and he expressed it in so many words. Internally he was the eternal deep calm ocean. Occasional waves were only external—just expressions for the sake of the seeker.

Hence, my friend, go deeper and feel the energy and love of a true Master. Do not be infatuated or disillusioned by miracles. Just understand that a true Master is well beyond his expressions. He has no needs. He is here for a purpose, a specific agenda. He is here only to guide you to higher realms, if you will allow him to. Masters are never born and will never die, in the absolute sense, just like your soul, which is imperishable too. Masters do not need miracles, people need them. A mother attracts her child to the nutritious meal by showing him a candy. We are all children. We get attracted to candies. Through this, the Master does his work.

Superstitions

Man's inherent fear is the reason for superstition. Almost everyone entertains at least one superstition. The question is whether it is good or bad. It depends on what your aim is in this life. If material success or well being is your aim, entertain superstitions because they also add to the comfort factor. If total liberation is your aim then shed superstitions because they also are part of your eternal bindings. How to shed superstitions? It's possible only through higher awareness. And most importantly: dare.

According to the cycle of time, tamasic time (3pm till 3am) is the time of indulgences and procrastination. Elders used to advise sleeping early, so that we sleep through the tamasic time. Sattvic time, the most auspicious time of the day, begins at 3am. People used to wake up early, around 3-4am, and start their day with prayers and pranayamas during the calm and serene time of the day. Scriptures say: "A person who starts the day at the Brahma muhurtha (sattvic time) can never be defeated." So early waking was well recommended, through time and traditions.

Superstitions are bondage. They are also habits. They are born out of fear. Eradicate fear through higher awareness and superstitions will vanish.

Guidance

Man is always interested in the supernatural. Normal human beings get shaken to altered realities when they witness miracles. Some get addicted and expect more and more. Some evolve beyond miracles to the realms where everything is fine. Jesus has been explicit about miracles and Christianity has acknowledged the fact that it is possible. This is not wrong. In fact nothing is absolutely right or nothing is absolutely wrong. Man's quest to know himself, know God and identify oneself with God has always created many situations. It has even created events. Some are miracles. When faith overflowed and obscured reasoning, miracles happened.

There are vast differences in the awareness levels of individuals. People are never too identical. The awareness levels of a society, just like the morality aspect, are usually based on regular intellect, not spirituality. The justice system, law and order etc. are all based on logic and intellect. Basically intellect is the seat of logic. Criterions are also formed out of it. When the awareness of a human being shifts from intellect to spiritual consciousness, the whole benchmark changes. Miracles won't have that fascination anymore, because everything is natural in that plane of existence.

Miracles are like fireworks that light up the sky. They fascinate and attract. When the fireworks die down, we are left with the mundane realities or bare necessities of life.

In Christianity, sainthood is not connected with miracles, per se. It is more an extra—ordinary or exemplary display of compassion or love, beyond the boundaries of regular human peripherals that can be called miraculous. When man sheds his ego and expresses compassion to the highest degrees, just like Jesus, he is considered a saint. It is not always materialisation or miracle cures that make saints. Miracle cures are possible by just maintaining extreme purity in thought, word and action.

I met a 32 year old Dutch girl in a hospital in Himalayas. This place is only for lepers and aids patients. She has an old mother in the Netherlands, whom she visits once every year. She is fully devoted to the treatment of aids patients and leprosy patients. She lives in this centre. When I met her, I saw purity and a powerful aura of sheer determination. She herself was cleaning and treating the patients. I saw extraordinary compassion in her. She had stopped meeting general visitors because she was fed up of sympathies and non-action from visitors. I thought she was just like Mother Teresa. A European girl leaving the world behind and deciding to take care of the people who are rejected by society! Such people become saints. People cannot ignore their service to our society. Talking is one thing. Physically expressing compassion without talking is another matter. Selflessness pushes up our spiritual evolution.

We meet higher souls for guidance. This is fine. Nothing is right or wrong. Our need for knowing our own future essentially reflects our own insecurity. When we are self-sufficient inside, that means, when we have accepted our own self as our personal Guru, all the searches will come to an end. We will be fine in the beingness. Cures are possible when we are eligible to get them. Then a Master appears and miracles happen. Other guidance such as in business, marital relationships, education etc. can be provided by an intellectual, an astrologer or even a saint. It needs no miracles.

Grace oils existence. It makes life smoother. Grace flows from purity and purity attracts Grace.

GOD, MASTERS, TEACHERS & RELIGION

The Real Form of God

God is formless. We attribute forms to God according to the style we can identify with. God is like water. It can fill any container. The major difference is that God does not get contaminated like water does, if poured into a dirty container. The God element stays pure, irrespective of the container that encompasses it. Just like the soul does not get contaminated ever, irrespective of the karma of man.

Man has been trying to understand the supreme force since his birth or in other words, since mankind began. He saw God's hand in destruction more than benevolence. Then later men shifted their focus from external to internal. Thus the Upanishads formed. These are thesis works based on man's inner journey and identification with the supreme. This leads man to understand infinity—by being infinity. To understand infinity, intellect is not enough. Trying to understand infinity using the intellect is like understanding that you slept or dreamt after you wake up. The understanding is never complete. Infinity is only a theory for the intellect. Man has to go to the being level. Thus, theory slowly became experience. Once experience began, man started dropping the necessity and dependency on external materials for his gratification. He started becoming complete within. The more self-sufficiency he achieved, the more selfless he became. And the more universal he became. His only expression became unconditional love. Love without any expectation. Thus basic man formed out of elements became a Master. The God man.

Once man became the Master he could easily control all things within and essentially all things external. Nothing affected him anymore. The limitedness dissolved into unlimitedness. He started expressing the nature of the Supreme Being.

God is formless and assumes any form that we attribute to him. Understand that He is not any form. He is beyond forms. Essentially you are the God element that you can touch and feel, if you insist on a form. You need to go within to understand that the God element within you. Mind is the vehicle, contemplation (manana) and meditation (dhyana) are the paths respectively. The primary destination is your own self. The self leads to God, man's final destination.

Q: How can we experience God?

M: We can experience God, when we develop subtlety. This may take lifetimes. We have to transcend sheath by sheath, within ourselves, until we unite with our own soul, the source of our existence. We can call it enlightenment. Enlightenment also gives only a micro glimpse of the God experience. When we have to continue operating in the body level, we keep shifting between the micro and the macro. Maya (illusion) lurks around each corner. It constantly attacks. Delusion is easy. It takes extreme vigilance to stay connected to the soul. From soul, through extreme devotion, by shifting all the actions to dharmic mode, we can start to taste God. This is easier said than done. We have fallen so deeply in consciousness. Fortunately, we do not know how deep we have fallen. In this way, Ignorance is bliss. Since we do not know the depth of our fall, we can keep our hopes up and keep climbing. Well, it is a deep subject. One can write volumes about it.

Q: I have always been a God-fearing woman. Lately, I started feeling disillusioned. Can you help?

M: Why are you fearing God? Does God look like a monster? My dear friend, God is kindness. God is love. Take any religion in this world. God is not a terrorist. Man who cannot understand God, fears God. Understand that you are carrying a part of God yourself. That is your soul element. Do you fear your soul? I know that you fear death because of your identification with your body, mind and intellect and all other attachments. Soul is silent and faithful. We are not even aware of the existence of a soul within, until the time of our death. Isn't this interesting? The whole life is spent in ignorance of our true nature, fighting frustrations. The soul silently watches the show. We fail to recognise and what we do not understand, we fear.

The fundamental shift should be from 'God fearing' to 'God loving'. Then half the journey is done. Do not look at God as a greedy priest who needs money to take you to salvation. The priest is a human who needs money. God needs nothing from you. What can you actually offer to God? Can you show me one thing, including yourself, which does not belong to God? The disillusionment is due to the wrong path. Once you correct your path, there will be no confusion. You are God. You are self-sufficient. Self is sufficient for you to worship.

Before we start any journey, the destination should be clear. If the destination is sensory gratification through pujas, rituals or offerings etc., do that. But you may still get disillusioned, because rituals are usually done with expectations of some favour and as a transaction between man and God. God does not need it. You are creating your own destiny through your own thoughts, words and action. If the path is achieving God, then ego is the biggest blockage. Doingness must be reduced to beingness. I know many people who follow many sadhanas and are still the same. You need to do contemplation on the Almighty which should lead to meditation on the Almighty. You could call the Almighty also Father, Jesus, Allah or Parabrahma. It does not matter. God is formless and beyond names. Form leads to formless. Use any form and go beyond the form, eventually. Take time. Do not be in a hurry. Understand clearly that God does not need your offerings. Offer kindness and love to the world as your offering to God. You will see yourself shining, glowing and becoming God.

So, do not fear God. Start communicating more with the God within. Start expressing love unconditionally, despite the responses that you might receive from society. Do not be affected by other people's behaviour. People are different, so is their behaviour. If your life depends on other people's actions or words, mental suffering will be permanent. If you start expressing love without expectations and stay rooted in yourself, all your external problems will be solved. All your confusions also will be solved. End of the day, love always wins.

Gods

Q: There are many Gods in the Hindu system. Around 330 million? Whom to worship? I am confused.

M: Nobody can worship every deity for sure. When you become enlightened all entities become part of you. Then you will become one with all deities, all individuals, all beings. I shall explain. There are 33 crore (1 crore = 10 million) deities in Hindu tradition. Do not be confused. They are all representing one father. The same Parabrahma. Secondly, each person is distinct. There are no two people exactly alike. I am not talking about physical resemblance. I am talking about their total constitution. So each person can recognize and accept only a deity that suits their constitution. He/she can worship only that deity, even though he/she might be able to appreciate many other deities. Just like we invite our realities, we also have an element of the deity or Master that suits us in our constitution. The deeper imprint of every reality is within us also.

People are made out of elements and character is made out of gunas or traits. The soul is the power that runs the systems and makes it functional. You will only follow a path that suits your constitution. You will vibe with a Master who complements your constitution. So in that way, you have already carried an element of that aspect, which the master or deity represents, in you. You will just express that and attract that to you. You get attracted to that system or God. This is why the tradition allowed worshipping multiple kinds of deities, so that each person is comfortable that way. In effect, each person is worshipping the predominant element of his own constitution.

In short, thirty-three crore deities exist because there are thirty-three crore types of individuals. Each individual can choose a deity with whom they can comfortably identify. Various deities represent one supreme Soul. Almost all deities are addressed as 'Lord'. All are Lords. Lord Krishna, Lord Buddha, Lord Jesus . . . There is only one God. That God is omnipresent and all encompassing, beyond time, space and limitations. All Lords represent the God. All Lords lead to the God. All Lords will merge into the God in the absolute sense. There is no duality. There is only oneness.

All limited beings are representations of the limitless. Finite represents the infinite. So understand that all finite matter will disintegrate and dissolve into the infinite, including me and you, sooner or later. Worshipping any finite forms should always lead to our transit to the infinite. Finite should lead to the infinite. This is the purpose. Infinite is difficult to comprehend until you expand to that state, hence we need the finite. Otherwise infinity would remain as a theory in your mind. You will not feel or experience infinity at all. Jesus said that the way to the father is through me. Same principle. Finite to infinite.

We also see many people trying to impose their deity or truths onto others, thinking that the other person will have the same effect or experience. This is stupidity. We must consider the uniqueness of each individual. Nothing can be forced onto anyone. Nothing forced will become forceful. So thirty three crore deities represent the human race on the face of earth. Perhaps we could say that they represent the embodied beings on the face of earth, hence the diverse systems and traditions. For each a deity according to their capacity and stature, according to their need and constitution. We need all the Masters available and we need all the Gods. Then all the people can identify with one or the other. Comparisons and arguments as to which one is better or which is worse, is the worst stupidity possible. We have to coexist. Allow everything to exist. Each person is identifying and enjoying individual realities and this can never be compared or compromised. One person's food could be another's poison. How can we generalise which is good or which is bad? We need to appreciate other people's belief systems. We need to appreciate other people. There is nothing for you or me to prove, because nothing is permanent. Realities change constantly. People appear and disappear. Life and death are part of our existence. Systems change. Change is the essence of terrestrial existence. So live and let live. Serve unconditionally. Never compare and condemn. Intentions need to be pure and truly unselfish.

Worship your own personal deity. Your own soul. It is also part of the thirty-three crore deities of the world.

Saints

I have met many unassuming and powerful saints during my trips to the Himalayas. I like to believe that they have all helped me one way or the other, helped my spiritual evolution. The contribution of each is difficult to assess. Many bricks come together to make buildings. The same with our current reality. Many events made us, our personal constitution. They date back centuries. Our character has transcended over generations. We have met many saints in our past lives as well. A visit, a meeting, some information, some transformation, a companionship, an event or even an experience is not coincidental. They are all part of the larger symmetry. Nobody meets anybody by accident, even though it may often seem so.

Writing about my experiences in the Himalayas would run into pages. A saint, who never consumed food and possessed the capacity to disintegrate food into molecular level at will as it crossed his throat chakra, fascinated me and made me aware of the possibilities of existence without dependency on elements like food and water. A very old saint who meditated above the Narayana Mountain in a small hut ashram, almost 13,000 feet high in the Himalayas blessed me with his presence. I just expressed my wish to meet him and two days later he appeared. He clasped my hand firmly for a few seconds and vanished. I could still feel the way he clasped my hand. I wanted to touch his feet but it was impossible because of the crowd.

One very old saint who was standing near the Vasishta Cave, gazing at the Ganges flowing majestically, caught my attention. He had white hair and a white beard. He looked at me and asked me what I was doing? When I explained about my maritime job, he asked me questions about the currents colliding near the Cape of Good Hope in Southern Africa. He asked: "Are these currents still destroying ships?" I said we had grown beyond such mishaps. I became curious as to why a saint meditating in the Himalayas was worried about hot and cold ocean currents colliding near Africa which twist and curl ships!!! He said calmly: "I used to own ships." He explained that he once was a ship-owner, a very rich man. He had his own fleets and staff. He visited the Himalayas a few years ago and never went back. He has remained a wandering monk ever since. I was curious to know what happened to his ships and his companies. He said: "My children should be running them. Who cares? I never checked." Zero regrets or longings. I saw complete detachment in him. There was a deep satisfaction, a divine glow in his eyes. He never even bothered to check the well-being of his family that he left behind. A millionaire hermit!!! He swapped his concrete terrestrial riches for intangible spiritual riches.

He asked me if I wanted to have lunch with him. I joined him for lunch. He had made some chapathis (bread) and a curry from locally farmed vegetables and curd/yoghurt. The love with which he shared his food with me added to the taste. I never saw this saint ever again, even though I did wander in the same region many times later.

When I see many un-evolved people using spirituality as good business to make money, I think about this millionaire saint, who forsake everything and chose spirituality. Many of the modern gurus never give up anything. They only add to their riches. They like to be pampered and taken care of. Saffron has great effects. Seekers of evolution can easily be misled by dresses and appearances. Those who knew everything, seldom spoke. Those who knew things partially, spoke a lot. This is the tragedy of our existence. We have to be careful as to what we listen to. If guilt and fear underlies any teaching of any modern guru, trash it unceremoniously. If he says you are not running fast enough, tell him, everyone has their own pace. If a guru pretends, trash him. Experiences should be tangible and real. Theories become a burden if they remain unprocessed into experiences. Do not over-burden yourself.

A man with a terrible, failed business track record became a saint to escape from the people to whom he owed money. Heavy pretensions. He paid money and arranged for people to sing his glories and created a halo. He started earning money, created empires and many ashrams. If you ask him, why he left his business? He will say: "Pull from divinity." or "Call of spirituality". This is utter nonsense. He could not succeed there and escaped into saffron. Pretensions can sell well. The more you pretend, the more you are revered. Great Masters like Baba, Babaji etc. will never be found through such fakes.

What's the Game?

Everything is part of the divine play. Births, death, events. Without the soul element, there is no life in our existence and we call it dead. Without energy, there is no matter. Energy conglomerated is matter. Matter disintegrated becomes raw energy too. Behind every thought, word and deed there is an energy element, unseen but inevitable. So behind the curtain is the GOD (the energy that Generates, Operates and Dissolves). The actors are temporary, the show is time-bound. The master planner hides behind the stage, invisible, yet effective. Go beyond the skin of every action, develop macro vision, you will see the true Master at work.

Conversations with Master

Disciple: Who is a true Master?

M: The true Master, as far as an individual is concerned, is his own self. The soul is the true Master for the individual. He must listen to the advice of the soul. There will be no guidance more apt for him than his soul's guidance. It is very important to listen to one's soul.

D: Then why are there other Masters on earth?

M: One needs to transcend through physical existence, emotional existence, intellectual existence etc. to get in touch with one's own soul. We can theoretically understand that soul exists in our body as the fuel that runs our body-mind-intellect system. But it takes a lot of shedding and hard work to understand and get in touch with one's own soul, even though it's at hand's reach. The soul can be accessed only when one achieves a mindless state. A seeker will often need an external Master to keep guiding him/her to one's own soul. The soul is the only permanent entity in our temporary terrestrial existence.

Masters are guides. They exist not only on earth. They exist in every plane. Their sole aim is to guide individuals to their own soul. This means liberation. True Masters are liberated beings. They exist to liberate others. They have no purpose of their own, apart from that. They do not create lots of disciples, they create more Masters. So the true Master is the one who creates more Masters, not the one who teaches well.

D: Master, we often fail to practice what you teach. How can we overcome our lethargy?

M: Failure to practice that which would help your evolution has two major reasons:

1. The tamas or inertia in you is preventing you, or

2. You do not need it.

The first aspect is the most likely aspect. First of all, information does not reach you unless you are eligible. Even if the information reaches you, you cannot use it, unless you develop an understanding. The textbooks of postgraduate level are of no use to a high school student. Even if he gets it, it will not help him. This is one aspect which we can call premature knowledge. This is quite fine. The other aspect is when the student is eligible and is actually in need of the textbook, but is too lazy to learn. This is the major obstacle called tamas or inertia. This is anti-evolution. In most cases, mind blocks activities that take the student beyond the senses and the mind. Ego also plays an important role. Ego says: "You knew that." or "That's nothing new, it's a repetition of what the other master has taught or you read in that particular book."

Or: "You are far too evolved for this low level information or activity." This is all mind's play. Unless the student realizes the importance of the teachings and develops a strong will to practice it, against all odds, he will not succeed. Mind will certainly produce thousands of excuses. The student must stay afloat and use his life and the time given to him for higher evolution.

The last aspect is that of the student being evolved beyond the Master. This is possible. Jagadguru Adi Shankara was already well-evolved before he met his guru at the age of eight. When his guru Govindapaada asked who he was, he replied: "Mano Buddhi, ahamkara Chittani naaham . . . Chidananda roopa Shivoham Shivoham." ("I am not the mind, the intellect, ego or the substratum . . . I am the ever blissful Shiva. Shankara is Shiva.") This is the state of complete god-realization. If an 8-year old boy has this understanding he needs no further education. He is already beyond all education. This is very rare. Maybe one in a million can obtain this status.

> D2: Master, when we are near you as well as when we are in the ashram, we feel so closely connected to you. We feel deep love towards you. We feel as if we will be empty without you. I have never experienced this kind of deep love in my life. Can you explain why this is happening?

> M: First of all, all emotions are temporary. Do not give your emotions more value than they deserve. Love is natural. Love is our true nature. The true 'nature of Nature' with its entire flora and fauna is love. This is unemotional and unconditional love. Whether you offer the sun some water to quench its thirst or not, it will certainly appear at the appointed time tomorrow morning. The wind and the rain, the blossoms or the fruits, they all exist unconditionally. Such is the love of a true Master. The Master loves his disciples irrespective of whether the student is rich or poor, good or bad, lucky or unlucky, beautiful or ugly, lean or fat. It does not matter. The Master stands as the signpost guiding all those who need guidance.

When the Master's love flows unconditionally, relentlessly, it transforms the hearts of the disciples. They respond to that love effortlessly. Lack of conditions truly liberates the disciple. There are neither fears nor guilt in him. All that remains is love. Only love. The love towards the source of this abundance is natural. And the reflection of this love on others is natural too. This feeling will not be found in the stark external world of conditional love. That's why you feel the soothing difference between the ashram and the outside world. In the ashram you are free and natural. In the outside world you mainly have to pretend and become unnatural. This is the subtle gist of this matter.

> D2: Will we feel the same love towards you wherever we are, irrespective of time and space?

M: There is no guarantee. Relationships are usually temporary or in other words, there is a definite duration to all relationships. However, the soul-to-soul connection stays. The mind often dilutes feelings or enhances feeling. Time also erodes feelings. And many times you will need to come back to the same place to feel the same feelings. There is no guarantee for that either. If you maintain the same love even after the person whom you considered very dear to you leaves you for many years, or you leave for many years, then your love for that person is real. If it erodes in time and gets replaced with other matters, then understand that the value was temporary. Usually the connection between the higher Masters and their disciples stays on, irrespective of time and space. This connection is for higher purposes, which only time can reveal.

D2: What is the will of a higher Master?

M: Higher Masters are not controlled by mind. They remain in a perpetual state of mindlessness. Their will is the will of the universal Father. They work in union with the universal Father. They are like good mirrors which reflect your own nature. They show you who you are and guide you to your own liberation. The same teaching may not work for all here.

True Masters are pure representations of the immaculate Almighty. This is why, even though Masters assume many shapes or forms, they are all essentially one. They work for one cause. The cause is that of liberation. They lead stranded beings from darkness to light. This is also why, in their mindless state, their wish is nature's command. They have power over nature. Whatever they say is bound to happen. They talk from the absolute level. This is the level of the Almighty. Guru is both macrocosm as well as microcosm. The same principle that governs all existence is Guru and Guru is God. Again, when I say this, do not think of a Guru or restrict him into a physical form. I am talking about the

Guru Tattva or the Guru principle. A true Guru is well beyond his physical form. Physical form is usually too binding for him and he keeps it only to serve his higher purpose of guiding his disciples.

Higher Masters are embodiments of detachment. They will explicitly display detachment on all levels of existence—total detachment to their name, their form, material wealth, spiritual wealth and everything else. They do not conform themselves to any frames that society creates. They live in a liberated state always. What you usually see is not their actual stature. What you see and what you hear could be quite different from what they really are. They are not after applauses or approvals. They do not care about your respect or disrespect. They do their duty on earth as un-karmically as they can and exit their physical form, when they have to, with as much detachment as they had while existing in form.

D3: How does one evolve to become a Master?

M: The potential to become a Master is in everyone. When the karmic attachment to material stuff diminishes and attraction towards subtle gets stronger, detachment towards worldly stuff takes root. While travelling through this path of detachment, one encounters various obstacles, various tests. These are tests of endurance. Those who are weak or non-resilient will fall. Those who have the karmic push, an iron will, those will continue, despite tragedies in life. They do not consider the setbacks of material existence as tragedies. They treat everything as part of their spiritual evolution. They consider severe hardships as part of their cleansing process. They pursue the path to a level at which total liberation takes place. First of all, such experience happens in one's life only after they have undergone lives of cleansing. They would have experienced lives and lives of purification and higher understanding. When such trashing has happened in previous lives, through lives of purification, they reach the level of purity where they are able to raise themselves up, to higher realms. Thus, when mastery of sense and mind happens, one becomes a Master.

When a person gets established in a perpetual state of God awareness, he becomes a higher Master. True mastery is the mastery over one's own mind, ego, expectations and all other such attachments. When one is truly in pursuit of this path, the whole nature aids him/her. Masters appear in their life to guide them. They reappear over lifetimes. They will be protected and delivered home by the Divinity. This is the truth and promise of the Divine.

Competency of Spiritual Masters

Who wants to compare? Whom are you comparing? Me? And whom are you comparing with? Why? From which level are you comparing? Can a 5th class student understand the awareness level of a graduate student? Why do we compare at all? These are all wasted exercises. Utter waste. Instead, chant the name of God. Surrender to him. Understand that all of God's creations are unique and never identical. Nobody can compare anything with anybody. Live that uniqueness. Express it. The competency of your guru will be equal to your receptivity. Understand that clearly. You will not get the tutor of the 10th class while you are still in 5th class. Grow up. You will become eligible for higher Masters. At that point in time, you will realize that all Masters were one. All have the same expressions. All are children of the same father and there is no difference between the guru and you. Then you'll win the test of life and touch the realms of non-dual reality.

Endorsement

Listening to one's own soul is the right and sure way to liberate oneself. Great Masters act as road signs. All they do is take yourself to Your Self. When your Self is Parabrahma, why should I endorse another? I am endorsing you.

Our world is filled with gimmicks and pretensions. The blind leads the blind. This is why I stated in my class that if my image is the hindrance for your spiritual growth, remove me, ignore me.

Greed breeds cult. Once we are in the cult, there is no escape. We are forced to endorse the guru and whatever he does. Sometimes our own conscience will say: "He is wrong." Still, since we have herd instinct, we follow the other cows. We adjust and adapt our thought process to that of others. Then we also make justifications. This is equal to cheating ourselves. We make lots of compromises to make sure that our Guru is depicted in the right light and bright colours. We attribute many qualities to the Guru, even though we know very well that it is all fake and pretentious. This act is more out of our necessity than a social need. First of all, we have a dire need to convince ourselves that we are right. None of us are ready to accept a mistake, let alone a failure. Our ego never permits that. All of us are cowards in that respect. We cannot call a spade a spade, on most occasions. I have always encouraged people to do so and to maintain their self-esteem. Cultism is based on man's inherent insecurity and fear. Fear is used to control people. We are afraid to leave the cult. We fear victimisation. We feel the 'known devil is better than the unknown angel'. We pretend everything— happiness, bliss, divinity and everything else. We will also carry call signs or identifications, like a ship's call sign, such as 'Jai ...' or 'Om ...' this is our identification. This tells most importantly us and everyone else that we belong to this group. Thus we brand ourselves. This is our comfort zone. We prefer living a lie than searching for the real hidden truth. Searching has uncertainty. "Known lie is better than the unknown truth." Like one man said: "Light is sorrow, my child, darkness is bliss." This means, living and dying in ignorance is better than exposing ourselves to shaky truth or knowledge. This is human nature. Those who create this mentality in passive humans, can I endorse them? To most of us, it also becomes a feather in the cap if we say; we know this guru or we are part of this group. When selfless service is misinterpreted as bringing a few more people into the cult, how can I endorse them?

Selflessness is to be experienced as a part of our character, our constitution. When cult influences even that, we are slaves. Just helpless slaves. I cannot endorse that.

I believe in liberating people. Unbinding them. Enhancing

them. Liberating them totally and completely. In that aspect, I feel pity for people who exist in the make-believe world of cultish mentality and blindly follow the man who leads them, blindly believing all that he says. Their life gets wasted that way.

Then again, there is a matter of eligibility. We should be eligible to reach Babaji or Sai Baba or Paramahamsa Sri Ramakrishna or Ramana Maharshi. We should have walked the whole path to arrive at the feet of a Vivekananda. Most of us are comfort-oriented. Living room philosophy is the best thing for us. We are satisfied with what has been door delivered, even if the food is not that tasty and perhaps even stale. Our inherent tamas or inertia does not permit us to go all the way to the restaurant which is just about 100 feet away. Some of us do not have a choice. The cult leader exploits our helplessness, choicelessness, fear, ego, lethargy and money. Thus they grow and we fall. I cannot endorse them.

Trust I have answered your questions on my non-endorsing any Masters. It's not because there are no gems amongst the stones. It's because you will automatically reach the gems once you are eligible. Till then, keep searching, keep seeking. It's worth it because it also purifies and smoothens our sharper edges, especially our EGO.

Q: Who is your Guru?

M: I have many Gurus. I am guided by both the Dattatreya tradition and the Kriya Yoga tradition of Masters. I am one with all of them. That is why many people have seen different Masters working through me. I am an empty pot that gets filled in by any Master who is relevant and appropriate for that situation. This mind and intellect stays in surrender to the Maha Guru, our very existence. Appropriate knowledge flows at the appropriate time. Shirdi Sai speaks to me. Mahaavatar Babaji has spoken to me. It is not like me speaking to another person. It is like me speaking to myself. They are all within my consciousness. When we speak to an external entity, there is duality. Here, I do not exist and my consciousness contains all Gurus. The wisdom is the same. The information is the same. Those who are connected to me also experience my consciousness. All those whom I have touched are also within my consciousness. They are one with me and in that way, one with all the Gurus of the universe. We all are one. There cannot be any duality. Guru is a principle and that principle does its dharma without fail. It operates through many mouths. All mouths represent the same principle. All are one. Hence, in that context, my existence is in service to the Guru Principle. I am THAT. I am Everything and I am Nothing. I am like a mirror. I mirror the people or the Masters who come in contact with me. I do not have any particular identity. What you see is unreal. I do not exist. The techniques that we are using have not been taught by any physical Master. It came to me. It happened to me. I am linked to many embodied and astral Masters.

Connecting to a Master

Q: I am not able to connect to any Masters. Why?

M: Doubting mind closes the doors. This is the blocking factor. Faith is the key. All Masters are one. Just connect to the Master with whom you can connect effortlessly. Shed your "I"-ness, the ego. You will get connected automatically.

Q: I am pretty disillusioned with the so-called Masters. You keep talking about 'Masters', I am not able to comprehend, why do we need them?

M: Masters are road signs. They just aid your journey. When you are travelling in unknown terrains, especially when you know your destination, a road sign will come in handy. If we are travelling, not knowing our destination or any destination, then we need no road signs. You would be comfortable without them. The same way with Masters. If evolution is the aim, Masters can be of assistance. If the aim is just passing time and 'testing the waters' or 'tasting another dish', Masters are a botheration.

Why do we get disillusioned with Masters? Because we develop expectations. (By Master I mean a person who is of a higher spiritual stature and is able to convey original thoughts and wisdom, not an acharya who is basically a teacher, teaching others' ideas. Do not be confused on this point. Acharyas or teachers are aplenty. True Masters are rare.)

When we first meet a Master, the first few days go by in analysis (intellectual), trying to understand what he/she is and which type, path or method of spirituality he/she belongs to. We are eager to categorize him/her into some slot. Defined slots exist within everyone and all of us, because we all are conditioned beings. We try to categorize a Master according to our understanding or conditioning, and if he does not fit into that we discard him. This is quite fine because we may not have evolved to understand the realm of certain Masters. After this analysis, we start evaluating the behaviour of the Master or content of his speech. We start comparing it with other Masters whom we have met or heard of before. If something tallies, we may tend to accept the new one. In short, it is all in our mind. Each Master caters to different individuals. All Masters have definite roles in their own realms.

Then again, Masters also behave in strange ways. Some smoke, some drink intoxicants and some behave like mad people to distract unworthy disciples. A doubting seeker will get disturbed by these bizarre mannerisms and will eventually quit. A true Master wants only true seekers, not random shoppers. So do not judge a Master by his behaviour. There will be a purpose behind every action. A higher purpose. A point is proven by each action.

1. Do not try to put any true Master into a frame because this will be your limitation, not the Master's.

2. Do not try to judge any true Master using your limited understanding capacity, because you will be missing the key points.

3. Accept a Master's teachings only if it suits you and

do not try to eat more than you can digest. This would not help evolution.

4. A true Master is like a flowing river of unconditionally nourishing nature. You can draw as much water as you want. Allow the river to flow and others to draw water, too. The river neither belongs to you, nor to others. You must remain unconditional to gain true benefits from a high Master.

5. Do not have conditional faith when you want to evolve. Many people only accept what they want and not what they need for evolution. The difference is like nutrition vs. taste. Most go for tasty food, instead of nutritious. A true Master can see what is essential for us. They give only that, whether we like it or not. Whenever we doubt the true Master, we block his energy. While faith opens us to receive, doubt closes the lid. People often despise a Master because they did not get what they expected (often materialistically, not spiritually). This is not correct. Be open and receptive. You have lots to gain. Use your intellect and senses, so that you will not fall into traps. Understand that there is only one true Master in the whole universe the Father, Parabrahma or Allah. All others are representations and all others are signboards to take you to the one Master. The representation of that one Master is your own soul, which resides in your body. Worship that soul. Take care of that soul. Through that you will meet your Master.

Q: Whom can we choose to guide us?

M: Sadgurus or those Masters who are selfless, the ones who have appeared in your life need nothing from you. Understand that any Master with lots of needs is insecure himself. He will only exploit your state of insecurity. A sadguru, who needs nothing from you and is filled only with love for all beings, will never exploit you. He will take you to higher awareness and thus help eradicate your insecurity. Insecurity will automatically vanish when you are in deep sleep state. Insecurity exists in both waking state predominantly, and in dream state, to some extent. In deep sleep state and turiya state it does not exist. The best way to get away from insecurities is to get to the higher states of existence, which is also karmically safer.

The chronology of action: many thoughts, fewer words and still fewer actions—means that insecurity is hidden at every level. This is because all thoughts, words and actions have a definite duration and are temporary in nature. Body is temporary. Emotions are temporary. Any kind of emptiness can breed insecurity.

At the subconscious level, when indiscriminate impressions are fed in and confused results are churned out as your realities, insecurity is the result for the conscious mind. When a man is pressured for pleasure, stress is built up. This means, he deliberately engages in various 'recreational' activities without any ability to enjoy them and that will breed even more stress. This is why often after the holidays we see more tired people than refreshed people. They tired themselves out and encountered physical, financial and mental fatigue during the holidays. Thus, lifestyle breeds insecurity. Ego breeds insecurity too. Especially when we have to constantly prove better, it is definite stress and the end result of consistent stress is insecurity.

How do we tackle it?

1. Do not worry about what others think about you. As long as you are honest to your own conscience, just take it easy and stop 'proving' yourself by default.

2. Do not worry too much about others and keep comparing yourself with others. Understand that

everyone born here is acting out his/her karma. Just allow them to. Do not disturb them.

3. Do not run after sensory objects indiscriminately. When senses pull the mind, bring them to the level of intellect. Thus, if you don't allow emotions to rule your actions, stress will lessen and suffering will be less too.

4. As soon as you see an ad, do not be fascinated. Just allow the intellect to analyze and decide whether you actually need that material at that point in time. In other words, don't fall prey to borrowed desires. New models should not be your criteria for a purchase. It should be utility value.

5. Do selfless service. Understand other people's issues/problems/sufferings and try to be of help to the society and the country that you are in. If you can be helpful to the whole world, be that. That will give you higher vision and better clarity on how the world functions, which will take you to higher awareness. Temporariness will stop affecting you. Selfless service is one of the best ways to eradicate depression due to insecurities of existence. Selfless service must be done by oneself, and not by proxy or through others. You must feel the action.

Wish you great evolution.

Q: Where to look for spiritual solace?

M: Within Yourself.

Q: What is the use of Masters if the destination lies within oneself?

M: True Masters guide you to yourself. Your SELF.

Q: What is the minimum requirement for the seeker while approaching Master?

M: Faith and openness. Without these, do not waste your time or his.

Q: Do we always meet Masters because of past connections?

M: And also because of your eligibility to receive the Master and his teachings. It's not always a past connection. It's more about your new eligibility based on spiritual evolution.

Q: Prostration—lying face down at the Master's feet—why?

M: We have learned to prostrate at the feet of the Gurus. Our elders used to do so. We gracefully inherited this habit. It made us feel better and lighter. Sure. But do we know why we are doing that? We were told that it shows reverence. We are assuming that the Guru whom we prostrate to, is well established in the supreme truth, which means he is God realized. We assume that his feet are resting on the ultimate truth, the supreme truth. We are prostrating at that stature of the master, not exactly at the physical image. The stature of being established in the ultimate truth. We aspire to be in that state too. We aspire to be God realized. When we prostrate at the feet of the Master, we put our head and heart in one line, which nullifies our ego and intellect, and we express total surrender to the divinity that the Guru is representing or is established in. We cleanse ourselves inside out this way. When the Guru's Grace flows as blessings, we burn some of our terrestrial traits effortlessly. Grace is essential for everything including our complete spiritual evolution.

The right Guru

Q: Who is the right guru for me?

M: The one who is available to you. The one who appeared at your doorstep. The one who appeared in your life and spoke to you. If you miss him and look outside for the guru of your dream, you will miss him and this one too. You will get a guru or teacher according to your eligibility. A 3rd class student will not get a professor of higher class to guide him. When he reaches the higher class, he will get the teacher that suits his stature of that time.

Q: You mentioned that a Master is only a road sign or a mirror. How long do we need the support of a Master?

M: Only as long as you travel. As long as you are a traveller or seeker. Once you reach your destination you do not need any road signs. The delay in reaching your destination is because of your deliberate detours. An external person needs an external guide. This means, if you are essentially sense oriented and you tend to look outside for happiness and guidance, you will need an external Master or Guru. The moment you are self-reliant through your meditation or spiritual practices you will be guided by your own soul. That's your personal Guru. So, the need for a Master depends on where you stand and on your spiritual status.

Mad Masters

Q: Some sages behaved like mad men. History has many examples, some walked naked etc. Did enlightenment tilt their equilibrium?

M: No. Lack of enlightenment tilted our equilibrium. Ha! ha! They exist/existed in higher realms beyond our levels of understanding. When they became one with the reality, they dropped many social formalities, including the agreed pattern of behaviour and even clothing. The rest of us less-enlightened beings considered this as madness. As you said, if lack of proper clothing is considered to be a sign of madness, Gandhiji might have been truly mad? Do you agree? If the father of our nation was mad, all its children could also be mad. Who is really mad? We need to think about it and ponder on it.

Liberation actually liberates you from pretensions too. You will become completely free to call a spade a spade. Sages were like children. What do small children care about nakedness? Simplicity and childlike innocence are signs of enlightenment. And they always lived in the present. They never stored anything. They lived in perfect abandon, in absolute peace. Unlike us, they never were watchmen of their own possessions. They stayed liberated from all terrestrial bindings, including clothes.

Habits of Masters

Let me reiterate, for general understanding's sake. Follow the teachings, not the habits of gurus. Shirdi Sai Baba smoked chillum. Vivekananda smoked. Nisargadatta Maharaj smoked. Shirdi Sai Baba ate meat. Various saints including Ved Vyas impregnated women. Can a saint have sex? So what? Understand that the stature matters here. Higher Masters do various things for higher purpose. This is not out of lust. This is not even out of the kind of selfish love—of binding and owning—that we understand and are familiar with. Adi Sankaracharya had to experience a woman before he reached the pinnacle. They do everything to satisfy a higher purpose. Do not imitate that. It is like a kid smoking or consuming alcohol, because its father does that. I am not saying smoking or drinking is right or wrong. It is all up to you to judge, if you like. If you imitate great Masters who have crossed the barriers and live in higher realms of consciousness, you will get caught up in addictions. You will never evolve. They are doing it because of a certain purpose, not because of a karmic push. You are doing it because of a karmic push. That's the difference. The opportunity to dilute your karmic push is at hands reach. If you justify your action, blaming it on a Master, will there be any progress? There will only be doom. Please understand this very clearly, do not imitate Masters. Leave them alone. They do things for a certain purpose. I cannot dilute my words. I have to give you the truth as it is. You are free to accept it or reject it. Please understand that I will not be affected the least. I am beyond expectations.

Copy-and-paste gurus

I would like to share with you a part of the discussion that I was having with R. He is matter of fact and does not have a problem to call a spade a spade. He does not get excited with miracles or esoteric stuff. He is simple and likes to remain so. He always shares his thoughts with me and thus we share a mutual respect. The discussion has been about the mushrooming 'copy-paste gurus' in our society.

My reply was as follows:

If you think about it, apart from the Parabrahma himself or let's say for convenience's sake, Shiva himself, whom can we call original? All else are copy-paste gurus. They all adapted the available knowledge to their living conditions and rendered it in the language that the then society understood. So who is not a copy-paste guru? This is one way to look at it.

We always confuse a guru and an acharya. A guru is an enlightened being. He is self-sufficient and does not need any external support to fulfil his mission. He attracts people to himself by his sheer will and energy. You can see Adi Shankara, Dattatreya, Bhoganathar, Babaji, Akkalkot Maharaj, Mata Amrithananda Mayi, Shirdi Sai Baba, Parthi Sai Baba etc. who fall into this category. They never create fear to control. They only impart love.

The other type is an acharya. We often do not know the difference between these two. One who observes the rites is an acharya. He does not need to be enlightened. Just like the priest of a temple, he does his teachings to earn his daily bread. Pardon him. He is just doing his job. He needs to copy-paste. He is compiling data from many sources and making them into packages for money or to earn a living. There is competition amongst acharyas. True gurus only complement each other. The acharyas who compile data do not have anything original in them. They are only echoing others' words and thoughts as well as imitating others' actions. They constantly 'learn' to teach. People call them guru because they also clear the ignorance of some.

My opinion is that we need them all. Just like we needed specific teachers in each class during our school days, we need all these acharyas and gurus. I do not buy the idea that when an acharya visits a house, prosperity blooms there. Maybe prosperity blooms in the acharya's house, not the house that he visits. Ha! ha!

The world is busy. It does not need more intellectual stuff. That's why the feel good stuff sells like hot cakes. Who has time and patience to wait till the rice finally boils? All are going to fast food joints, right?

There are many modern day acharyas, who play with words to attract attention. I feel that the world needs them too. Someone is enjoying some of these. Why should we waste time judging which is good and which is bad? Every human being has the same capacity to judge what is good for them. None is inferior to another. Why do we worry? The problem happens only when we impose our views on others, forcefully. That should not happen. Allow people to be free and free to choose. Let them have their own experiences, not borrowed ones. The only word of caution that probably might be useful is to beware of 'huge amounts of money linked to gurus with tall claims'. One friend recently attended a program in Dubai which ensured enlightenment. They said the kundalini will rise. Later I asked him whether it actually rose. He said he waited and waited; finally he rose, went home and slept peacefully. Tall claims! Ignorant people fall for them. Once fallen, they refuse to accept their folly and pull many others into it. Thus life works on chains. Accepting mistakes and rectifying it is against one's ego. People seldom do it. Then they fall again and again.

There needs to be a time-space-junction point for anything to take place. None can increase or decrease its speed. If someone walks up to you and says that he will cleanse all your karmas and give you enlightenment, first of all, make sure that man himself has attained enlightenment. Secondly, check if he is doing this out of love for you or out of the need for money? Some do it because they have a strong need for recognition, name and fame. They crave popularity. Thus, there are many types.

We have seen many acharyas picking up bits and pieces from everywhere and putting them together as programs and giving them fantastic names so that it sells. This is why the feel good self-help programs run so successfully in the West. One of my friends attended a program called 'Reiki in business', the fee was USD 2500. I asked him if it had helped him. He replied: "Half of the things they told us, I have forgotten. I remember about half. I still do not know how to put it into practice." This is the truth. We cannot remember that many things. We waste our time and money by going to buffet dinners and eating well beyond our capacities. Later on, we spend sleepless nights nursing an aching stomach filled with sundry stuff. We are emotional beings. We try to achieve the impossible by paying money. Life is not like that. Life gives us only what we deserve. We should not take 10 tablets at a time with the belief that it will cure us faster, instead of taking the pills at the prescribed interval. Such actions will only lead to lack of self-esteem.

I shall conclude this with a quote from Adi Sankaracharya. This is a rough translation, please pardon.

"Some walk with matted hair, some shaven heads, some keep a switch at the back of their head and shave the rest of the hair, some wear saffron, some dress themselves up, some walk naked, such a variety of existence. Please do not be fooled by all these. The fundamental reason for all this is survival, existence, food, and nothing else. They are doing all these to survive and have their daily bread."

R., tolerance is essential in today's world. This is often lacking. God Bless All

Disillusion

Q: I had a strange experience. I have been following the instructions of one guru considering him as enlightened over the last two years. I really believed that I was progressing quite well. I was never able to meet him, even though I tried many times. Recently, I met him and I was shocked. He was not at all what I thought he was. Now, I am unable to perform the practices what he was suggesting, because of the new impression that I got of him. Can you please help me?

M: This is natural. A true Master is well beyond his body. We can feel his presence, if we have the ability, patience and dedication. What we feel is so real. When we actually see him, our senses takes over and the usual judgment pattern of our conscious mind categorizes him in our own native system using the conditionings that we harbour in our conscious mind. This has nothing to do with the stature of the Master.

There is a poem by Keats: "Heard melodies are sweet. Those unheard are sweeter." Often our perception or imagination creates images. Large images. Larger than life images. And when we physically witness the cause for that image, we may tend to become disillusioned. What we see may not conform to what we imagined. A Master's energy is well beyond his physical frame. Shirdi Sai Baba also used to disillusion people the same way. People came with great expectations and Baba behaved more ordinarily than any ordinary person. People will get confused, disillusioned. This is also a method the Masters use to segregate the truly devoted and the random seeker. Random seekers are aplenty. They often do not have eyes to see the Master in a man. They operate from the ego plane. They try to match-make between their perception and the immediate reality. If it matches they stay. When it fails to match they leave. There is neither patience nor ability to perceive the intangible.

Senses have limitations. Conscious mind has limitations too. In order to connect to a Master we have to go well beyond our limited senses and our conscious mind. As I said earlier, a true Master is just a true mirror. He will reflect your own image. True image. If you do not like what you see, do not blame the mirror. Change whatever could be changed inside and outside yourself and look again. We tend to blame the external for our internal chaos. It is actually just the opposite. Our internal chaos gets reflected in our external world. Masters just hold the mirror in front of you. Have a look. Go beyond the mirror. You will see yourself better. Masters never impose their own image over you. They just allow you to see for yourself. The moment you see your real image, you will also see the Master's image and the image of the Master in you.

Once again, do not judge a man or a Master by what your senses tell you or do not give up because your mental picture does not match the physical picture. Do the necessary correction inside and be steadfast with your spiritual practices.

One important thing is: it does not matter who your guru is. If you increase your spiritual eligibility through strict practices and shedding of tamasic vasanas, you will attain the Highest. You will gain the eligibility to evolve higher than the Master who might have triggered your spiritual life. So you need not be disillusioned about the image of a man or Master. Do not take that as an excuse to drop your spiritual practices. Trash all mental images and reach the shapeless. You will see yourself. Your SELF. You will attain the highest.

Astrology and Astrologers

Astrology is science. I respect it. But please don't send your astrologers to me to check my horoscope. Be satisfied with yours. I do not know why you felt that I might be interested in astrologers or palmists or face readers!!! Did you feel that I am too insecure? Friends, I am not eager to know my future. If they say that my future is great and bright, the maximum that I would do is smile. If they say that my future is very bleak, still I will smile. So please do me a favour, do not send them to me. I do not have much insecurity, by the Grace of the Lord Almighty. I am ready to accept whatever He wants me to endure. I have endured a lot—much more than you can imagine—in the past. I am not scared to face my future, head on. I have observed that most of these astrologers are not doing astrology as a passion. For many it is a profession. First, they will tell you what you like to hear—some bright story about your future. When you are thus pleased, they put some fear in you about some inevitable catastrophe ahead in your life. Then they will propose remedies such as pujas, gems or stones. Thus they bleed you of your money and possessions. Your otherwise secure future will become insecure when you have lost all the money. And many people carry a lot of stones and metals on their body, just to feel 'future secure'. Anyway, I am only living in the present and the future does not give me any fear. Once again, I am not against astrology. I am only against those who create fear in you. Our path is that of fearlessness and liberation. Avoid all those who put junk in your mind. Thank you for your kind understanding. May your future be as bright as the ever-benevolent sun.

So many religions?

This is because of man's quest for the truth and his interpretations based on his levels of awareness. Mind has limitations, intellect has limitations and body has limitations. Hence man had to transcend all limitations and go beyond to peep at the brightness. Some were blinded. Some came forth and said to forget the gross. Some were considered irreconcilably mad because their realities did not make any sense to their particular world also consisting of others. Some were killed and made silent. After they attained silence, they were honoured and made gods because we cannot tolerate talking gods! We like to listen to ourselves more than others. We are well aware that we are always right and others are usually wrong. Ha! ha! Thus, many religions were born. They divided people. We failed to see men beyond the colours of religion. We failed to see unity and love. Thus, bloodshed began in the name of religion. While compassion and love are the basic qualities of the Almighty and the basis of all creation, annihilation of opposition became the requirement of terrestrial religion mongers for the sake of power and control. Religions divided men. Religions created wars. Those whose wisdom created religions were well established in love and compassion. Since we destroyed them first, we could interpret their teachings our way or the way we liked. This was convenient for future leaders. When selfish interests got rolled out, religion often became the best tool for cleansing opposition. Men forgot men. God escaped and devil got himself established, if there is one. Trust you could take these words as proving a point. Do not waste your time debating on degrees of god and devil in each one of us.

Remember, love is God. God is love.

God Bless All

Love All Serve All

Q: Do you believe in religions? Do we need them?

M: I do not believe in religions in the context that you are asking this question. Religion as an opinion is fine. If it binds man to rituals, it's wrong. If religions create misunderstandings and wars, I am not at all interested. Religions are formed out of the teachings by great personalities. They existed at certain places at certain times. They talked to their contemporary people. They were understood partially and misunderstood mostly. Most of these Masters were ahead of their time. They were usually never understood by their contemporaries. After they left their bodies, they were interpreted according to the society's intellectual capacities. Just like many sects were formed out of Jesus' teachings, many interpretations of most Masters also happened. People believed in their own or borrowed concepts. Interpretations were often not even remotely related to the original teachings. But since the Master is inside the frame on the wall, the interpreters were free to do their deed. None questioned. Everyone believed.

No true Master will ever say: "I am the only path." No true Master will bind any of their disciples to themselves. Masters appeared to liberate ignorant masses from the terrestrial turmoil. Yet the religions built around them bound people to ritualistic worships, even certain idol worships. While true Masters always stayed beyond forms, later generations believed in forms.

We attributed all our interpretations to the Masters. Even contextual or subjective teachings of Masters suited only for a particular time in which they existed, were stretched beyond time to a totally different era and implemented as religious necessity. This made many crazy and many dependent. This was the kind of binding the true Master stood against.

Unfortunately, he rests on the wall in frames and he could not reply to anybody in person.

If you study any religion deeply, you will reach the Master who originated it. If you study the Master deeply you will know that he appeared to liberate mankind from eternal births and deaths. And you will know that the basis of all religion is LOVE. If you are able to go beyond religions and stay at the realms of Love, you don't need any religion. If you have insecurities and need the cloak of a religion to present yourself in society, then you better have a religion. The need for a religion will depend on where you stand. Passivity of people is good for religion mongers. People fall easily into ritualistic existence and religions thrive on it.

A Master who appeared on earth to liberate masses can never create fear and control in the hearts of the people. This is anti-liberation. We can very well understand that using the Master teaching, interpreting it wrongly, the later interpreters bound people to themselves through spreading fear in order to control. This was only an expression of their insecurity, not the Master's will.

Just like the soul does not interfere in your decisions, a true Master allows the people to experience their realities and walk the path. They never block anything.

So, if religion helps your elevation, thank the Master. If religion binds you to a ritualistic belief system with zero evolution into higher awareness, get out of it. You don't need that. Your own soul is your God and guide. All you need to be close to, is your own soul.

God Bless All.

NATURE & NOURISHMENT

The Five Elements and Man's Rituals

MAN HAS ALWAYS been curious about how life works. If you look back, all the rituals, customs and traditions are formed based on man's perception of his own existence. The ancient man worshipped nature and all its elements, because they all had some effect on his existence. Slowly, he learned to take care of himself and protect himself from the raw elements. He even dared to venture into unsafe zones, such as the ocean and the poles where extreme and irregular conditions and elements prevailed. Man worshipped them, thanked them, and kept his superiority complex under control. His thinking mind started creating hierarchies. He found that one element surpasses every other element and has the capacity to burn to ashes anything that comes its way. FIRE! He found that this element can be used as a good vehicle to transport offerings to other deities. The prayers are to appease various deities and the offerings are placed into the fire with a request of safe delivery to the end recipient. Thus, rituals (Homas) formed. Man found that the water element can control agni (fire) but it gets contaminated in the bargain. Agni is the only element that survives any kind of contamination, irrespective of whatever it digests.

Later on, man went beyond rituals and started seeing more depth in his existence. He found that something else works through all these elements, unites them and makes them function. He found ether. Subtler than the air, fire or water, ether is intangible but highly relevant. This way he started meditating on the unseen.

In short, man's rituals and customs are the outcome of his quest to know the secrets of his own existence. They are based on his interpretation of reality and his effort to build bridges between himself and the creator. For a long time, God was an external entity and man worshipped external gods including fire and air. Various manifestations were created based on man's understanding of this entity. Then man started creating specific mantras for specific idols. It was established that, when chanted in a particular way, the mantras created healing vibrations. Man was slowly understanding the secrets of creation. Soon people's concentration started falling unto themselves. They started looking into themselves and the changes happening in themselves with the mantras, chanting, offerings and all kinds of rituals. This led to contemplation and meditation. With regular practice, the seekers slowly became the sought. A saadhak became a Master.

The men who lived during Vedic times were in tune with the subtleties of nature. They understood the nature with its seasons, flora and fauna. They also identified what kills and what cures. They co-existed with nature and all other beings. They learned to respect nature and even sought permission from a tree before it was cut. And they never cut a young tree. They identified old and about-to-perish trees that had lived long lives and would appease them through certain rituals before cutting. They did not destroy life indiscriminately. (There have also been barbaric tribes in many parts of the world who performed extreme forms of 'appeasement' through human sacrifice. I am only touching upon the topic, making the point that co-existence with nature took care of most of the ailments of man.)

Once man started understanding the subtleties of existence, he realized the one unifying factor behind all life. He started contemplating upon that unifying factor, its nature and intrinsic characteristics. Thus theories evolved. Many different understandings took root. Some were very high and some very low. In India the Vedanta happened. The Upanishads talked about even subtler aspects. Seekers who became masters contributed significantly to the evolving generation. They identified themselves and helped the masses to understand themselves. They identified the faculty beyond the body, the mind and intellect. They also identified ego. Finally, they reached the soul. Through the soul, they understood the nature of the supreme soul, the creator. Then they tried to understand creation. Great Masters who have seen and established themselves in higher realms explained.

"There is only one Paramatma, the supreme Father. All dualities originated from Him. He is genderless, formless and colourless. He is sheer brightness. Out of him, ether formed. That's the subtlest of all formations. Out of ether, air formed. Out of air fire happened. Water came out of fire in contact with air and from water, earth formed. These five elements were the basis for creation. These five elements will go back to the Lord when the body perishes. When a man dies, first the ether leaves, then breath or air, then fire leaves, water dries up and body shrinks and finally the earth element which is the gross body also disintegrates and goes back to mother earth. Parabrahma was overjoyed. The base is created and with this base, billions of options for creation became possible. Thus, relativity began as the basis. The basis of everything was akasha, vayu, agni, jal and prithvi (space, air, fire, water and earth).

Awareness brought man immense wisdom. He started seeing the difference between real and unreal. He started seeing the drama or divine play behind individual existence. Progress was inevitable.

Animal and Mankind

Q: Animals usually live a prescribed existence in a specific way. How is mankind different?

M: Who said mankind is different? Most of us also live in a prescribed or formatted way. Birth, education, job, marriage, children, old age, death. This is the way life goes. If we fall off this line of existence, we are considered freaks. If this is the way we live, what else are we doing? I am talking about the gross mankind. There are a few who choose to be different. They talk about alien matters. As early as we can, we kill them, so that we can live peacefully without hindrance. We also love to glorify the dead as they will stay peacefully within the frames that we have created for them, decorating the wall of our living room. They also add to our personal flavour as a hint of our level of evolution. We criticise and ridicule the living who gave us all he got without any expectations just out of love and compassion. This is also human nature. Thanklessness is human nature. Animals are usually thankful. They express gratitude the way they can. We kick anyone we can to achieve a personal glory. So, who is better than whom? What is our superior intellect for?

In the forest there are predators and preys. In our society also, there are predators and preys. Those who are weak and cannot run fast, fall prey to the predators. In society the confused are devoured by the intelligent. In nature there is both shallow glamour and deep truths. It exists in society also. We are all essentially the same. The only difference is the superior intellect and the ability to express emotions. We are probably better actors than the animals, while animals do not have pretensions. That's all.

The real difference happens only when a man rises above all others and shows light to many others to reach higher realms. This means, the real difference happens only when a man attains Godhood by developing and nurturing the God in himself. Everybody has this potential. Otherwise, it is only a question of degree variation of intellect and expressions, just like various species in the forest.

Human beings have the same pattern of existence as animals. In animals it is very visible. They take birth, eat, drink, migrate if necessary, live in groups, support each other, have children, become weak and die. Men also do the same but in a more sophisticated way. The major difference between an animal birth and human birth is the possibility of enlightenment available for humans. Animals are not worried about knowledge, contemplation or meditation. They just follow the pattern that nature has set for them. Man also is actually helpless. He is also under the illusion of ownership of action. He constantly feels and says: "I did that.", "Without me, it would not have happened." etc. Ownership becomes ego. Ego becomes a burden and a reason for re-birth.

What's wrong with terrestrial existence? Nothing is wrong. This is another plane of existence. This is denser. The denser plane is always illusory and because of that man is caught up in duality all the time. He moves like a pendulum between happiness and sorrow. He is never at peace. He travels to other places in search of peace. The same man in a different location, no peace, only more stress. Migration does not help, addiction does not help, relationships do not help. Some turn to meditation. The mind chatters all the time and meditation does not help either. Some go to gurus or masters for a quick remedy. True Masters tell them to listen to their own soul, instead of others. Others take their money and leave them even more miserable. This is our existence. The only difference is that we are more sophisticated than animals. They do not have as many worries as we have. Man binds them, tortures them and kills them. Man gives them worries. Leave them alone, nature looks after them.

Vegetarian Food

Q: It is scientifically proven that plants also suffer pain. They also respond to love and care. So is vegetarian food in a way destruction of life?

M: Not quite. The fruit of a plant, whether it is tomato or brinjal or mango, is the reproductive mechanism of the plant. These are produced by the plant to keep the species alive. Just like millions of flowers bloom and only about 30% become fruit, all the seeds inside a tomato do not become plants. When you pluck a tomato the plant is not in agony of destruction. It is somewhat like cutting your nails. The nail is a dead cell and it does not hurt you when it is cut. Likewise, almost all the fruits and vegetables which face the sun or which exist above the ground, are the seeds of the plant. There is sufficient and even excess of such seeds on each plant. Nature will not allow all the seeds to sprout, just like nature controls the deer population through carnivorous animals as a natural control system. There is sufficient. The cow eats grass. It does not destroy the grass forever. It just crops the top. The grass sprouts again. Rains fall to help its growth. Sun gives it energy. The cycle goes like that. If you destroy a plant just so you could eat one of its fruits, then we can say that it's similar to the destruction of an animal's life. We could anticipate similar pain and suffering for both. If you pluck a few leaves or a few fruits, it does not really affect the plant.

Q: If all became vegetarians would there be sufficient food to eat?

M: If we do collective farming and proper distribution, there will be sufficient food. Countries are hoarding grain. People are greedy. Many cultivation areas are used up to create animal feeds, to grow grass and that kind of stuff. If there is a will, there is a way. In the Indian tradition, the sattvic food habits were based on the philosophy of Ahimsa (nonviolence). Those who followed these principles, never ate dead organisms. They only ate vegetables which were exposed to the sun, grew without fertilizers or chemicals. They cooked food only for the time they needed it and never ate yesterday's food, which was considered as poison. Even if we cut a vegetable, it still has its aura. It never loses its aura. A dead animal loses its aura as soon as the soul leaves its body. So in order to answer the Q: Yes, there can be sufficient food for all, provided we do a bit of revamping of our current system.

Q: Are you a vegetarian?

M: Yes. I am.

Q: What about plants?

M: In our tradition, eating roots like carrot or beet root was considered as mediocre, because it destroys the plant. We used to consume only the fruit and vegetables that have seen the sun. They are alive, for sure. Plucking a fruit does not kill the plant. The plant is not in agony as the fruit eventually has to fall off the tree and it enjoys its selfless service. Trees are also called 'sages in meditation'. They give shelter and shade to both a weary traveler and a wood cutter, who comes to chop its branches, alike. It stays completely neutral. All embodied souls need nourishment. If that nourishment is achieved without destroying the right to live of another being, we will not add to our karma. You are what you eat. Your nature will change accordingly.

In order to gain sattvic nature, we must eat sattvic food. That's the highest guna possible for a normal occupant of the earth. Once we are in perpetual turiya state, we could probably live on sunlight too!

Q: You mentioned in one of your earlier blogs that animals can feel like we do. You had also suggested that we must see everything as part of ourselves. I am not able to do that. How do we go about it?

M: Nothing can be forced. Only through increased awareness can you recognize the commonality of all beings. Animals, humans, plants and trees, creatures living on land and those that live in the water, all of them have come out of the same father. That father is the universal Father. The supreme God. God is energy. Pure energy. Divine, intelligent energy. All the beings on the earth or on all possible places are part of his body. If you eat an animal, you are eating your own brother or sister. In order to understand our existence and the co-existence of other creatures, we must understand the nature of God. In order to understand the nature of God, we must understand the nature of our own soul. Just like a drop of sea water has all the qualities of the entire sea, this unit of soul that exists in our body has all the qualities of the supreme Soul, the Father, Allah or Parabrahma. The same soul exists in all creatures. Same drop of water that exists in the sea. What is the difference between us and them? Only outward appearance. That is because the water is filling a mug, a bucket, a bottle, a tank or a vessel. The water is the same in all these containers. The shape and size of the vessel is different. Character is different. Equipment is different, while the electricity that runs the equipments the same. Understand that all creatures undergo fear and pain while dying. The fear and pain creates certain secretions in a creature's body. That goes into its blood, nerves and flesh. When we eat that meat, we will tend to digest those negative feelings. We become more and more base and elementary.

Q: Animals undergo immense fear before they are slaughtered. How does that affect the meat?

M: Every living being fears death. Especially animals, as their sixth sense is much stronger and more powerful than human beings. For example, before the Tsunami hit various shores and killed thousands of people and domestic animals, many free animals including rodents and snakes escaped to safer areas, away from the seashore. I have read many articles about this phenomenon. It does not surprise me as their warning bells never fail, while we have stopped using such facilities that are within us, for many generations. Animals know when they will be killed. Terrible fear grips them. They cry and try to escape. But they cannot as they are bound. They cannot go anywhere. Fear automatically changes the inner rhythm of the animal.

Just try to recollect your own experience when you were under tremendous fear. It shrinks you. Your intellect stops working and emotions take over. We will try to do any crazy thing to escape the fear. Heavy anxiety builds up. Sometimes, unable to withstand extreme fear, people even commit suicide. Even relatively small fears such as fear of the unknown, fear of exams, fear of flying, fear of losing a relationship, fear of losing a job etc. make a difference in our breathing, heartbeat and thinking process. While love expands us, fear shrinks us. The fear of death is the highest fear of all. This fear is universal, it's the same for animals as well as human beings. Once a person has conquered the fear of death (it is, in a way, also fear of the unknown), this person can be called liberated.

Animals know their impending death. They suffer terrible fear. Fear creates toxins in their body or activates the toxins of their body. This also affects their nervous system and definitely muscles (meat). There is a saying that fear even stops the circulation of blood. Literally, the animals experience this. Before they actually die, they smell death. They see death. When they understand that they cannot escape from death, they mentally resign or surrender to their own fate. It is a kind of semi-conscious insensitivity. And as soul leaves their body, in this confused state of pain and fear, it is also very likely that the soul could be earthbound for some time. As we consume the meat of this animal that has undergone tremendous pain and fear, we also absorb the same effects into our system. This is because our body is made of cells and each cell is a unit which is alive. Each cell represents the bigger you. Meat consists of dead cells, because the prana or the soul element has gone out of the body of the dead animal. The last emotion while the soul exited was confusion based on fear and pain. This gets imprinted in the cells of the meat. This is what we consume.

Hence, it gets transferred into our system too. People say: "You are what you eat".

The animal that was programmed to live is put to death. It does not know why it is dying. The worse is the case of lambs that await slaughter in butcher shops, dogs that are tortured before slaughter in Korea 'to soften their meat', chicken awaiting death en masse in front of the chicken stalls etc. They know very well why they are kept there.

I am sure some of you have read 'Autobiography of a goat' which I had posted in this group earlier. The goat (in fact a lamb) was a human and a voracious lamb eater in its past life. Suddenly it saw itself reborn as a lamb in the new life after leaving the human body. The lamb's soul saw its own meat cooked and served to its children of the previous life, when he was a human. So, in a way, his own children consumed their father's meat!!! This is an example of how karma works.

Q: I have effectively cut down on my consumption of animal products as you had suggested and it is indeed giving me tremendous lightness and peace. But those I try to convey the same message to, do not accept it. What is your technique that makes people try what you suggest?

M: I practice what I preach. That is the secret. I try to lead by example as much as I can. Yet, when I am suggesting certain things by observing the aura of the person who is asking the question, those will be pertaining to that individual only and that I cannot practice. So on the one hand I live by what I preach, on the other hand I become a perfect mirror to the seeker. He can see himself clearly in that mirror and if he chooses, correct himself. He need not look at the backside of the mirror, which is my personality.

He should be satisfied with what he sees in the mirror, as that is the only reality that is applicable to him.

Regarding consumption of animal products, I have no objection if someone consumes animal products with perfect awareness.

This means, your job is just to put the thought in the mind of the consumer. Whether they choose to follow the path or not is none of our business. By awareness, I mean that the animal that died to appease your appetite was alive a few hours ago. It suffered tremendous pain and agony at death. It was bound and helpless. It was killed against its will. It craved for freedom and life. We denied them all that. It may have been denied even sunlight, food and water. Thus, it was killed for the sake of our appetite. If you watch the 'PETA' videos or 'Meet your meat' and 'Earthlings' on YouTube, you will know what I am talking about. Our insensitiveness and cruelty towards animals and birds also gets translated into our very own existence. We become cruel to our own brethren. We wage wars at home and outside. We learn to play with blood and fire, killing and war, destruction of life and environment. Anarchy breeds anarchy. Our food sheath inherits the vibrations of what we consume.

Now, what I am saying is, let people eat meat with perfect awareness, if it is part of their karmic agenda. Do not suppress your desires. By increasing awareness, if the desire dies out by itself, let it happen. If you suppress desires, they will bounce back sometime. Some people are proud of being meat eaters!!! I only sympathise with their folly or ignorance. Meat means dead animal. Anything dead has no prana or universal life force. If you take a picture of meat with a Kirlian camera you will not see any aura. If you take a picture of vegetables cut into pieces, it still has an aura. This is the difference. Consumption of meat only induces tamas or inertia. It also slows down spiritual evolution. When a man evolves further and further, he automatically drops his craving for tamasic food, including alcohol and meat. Because sattvic stature and tamasic food habits cannot coexist.

Do not worry. You can only choose your own habits. Tell others. If they understand, well and good. If they do not, it's still alright. Lead by example, not by words.

Prana and Light

Q: I am interested in sun gazing and sun energy. Can we cross the barrier of dependency on food with sun energy? Kindly enlighten.

M: Sun is the key source of sustenance for all life on earth. Earth cannot exist without the sun. Sun exists in the Father (Parabrahma) and the Father is the source of all energies of the universe. It is possible to source energy from the sun and disentangles oneself from the need for gross food. Sun's energy is Father's energy. So essentially you are using the father's energy, and food is the gross form of the same energy. Food and our body are essentially gross. Both are made out of atoms. Microcosm is the same. Macrocosm or the universal energy that runs everything is the same too.

Soul is the energy. Energy is present everywhere and in everything. If we can tune into the subtle and adapt our body to the subtle, we can process sun's rays and be self-sufficient. Human capacities are tremendous. If it's not done as per the guidance of a proper Master, lack of food can cause hyperacidity and ulcer. I strongly recommend your contacting a thorough and evolved practitioner of sun yoga and do not rely on books.

Food and Shaktipat

Q: Which factors reduce the effect of Shaktipat and which food slows the spiritual process down?

M: Meat, fish, any animal products, alcohol and food from under the water and under the ground will reduce the speed of elevation. Please do not be rigid. People cannot change overnight. Physical expression of love and compassion will definitely help anahata to expand further and further. Gratitude is essential for growth. Gratitude towards all beings on earth and beyond.

Smoking Masters

Q: Some Masters have been smokers, such as Shirdi Sai Baba. Some have used other intoxicants. Does it not misguide a disciple? Isn't it a wrong precedence?

M: A Master and disciple exist in distinctly different levels of evolution or awareness, or else they would not be Master and disciple. The awareness level of a 5th standard teacher and the students sitting in her class should never be compared. If the student starts to imitate the teacher in all aspects, it will not work. Likewise, an enlightened Master struggles to stay put in his body because of his expanded state. They may use intoxicants to bring back body awareness or dull their systems to interact with this world. If the unenlightened disciple does the same, he will only get deviated from his spiritual sadhana. He will not get enlightened. Hence, the disciple should follow the instructions of the Master, which would be apt for him and never imitate the Master, who exists in an entirely different plane of evolution. Someone said that a great Master is dying his hair black. I asked him: "So what? Does this affect his commitment to society? Is it affecting his thought process? Is it affecting his teachings?" We should only take the good messages from the Master. This is why the ancients say that we must never get too close to a Master. We will start taking him as ordinary. An enlightened Master's characteristics or mannerisms might be erratic. This could confuse an elementary level disciple. Nisargadatta Maharaj used to smoke bidis. Some of his disciples told him: "Swamiji, many important people are coming to see you. Why don't you smoke cigarettes?" Maharaj laughed and said: "I am not interested in smoking. I am beyond that. It is a requirement of this body. I am allowing it. I do not want to take another body just to smoke." Social bindings do not affect an enlightened Master. Akkalkot Maharaj, another great Master, once urinated in front of everybody, in front of a house. Society will call it madness. There is always a larger purpose for every action of a Master. No thought, word or action gets generated out of a Master for nothing. This is the truth.

Hence, do not worry about how the Master behaves in society, just follow his instructions carefully for your own benefit.

Q: I have read about the controversy that you created with your statement that 'wine and women are fine'. Do you still maintain this view at your current level?

M: I believe this is easily the hundredth time that I have answered this question. That statement was manipulated. For record's sake, let me make this very clear. The question that the journalist asked me was whether I approve of alcohol and prostitution. I had explained the karma related to those aspects, which was not printed at all. Let's analyze. Chronology of action is thought, word, action. On these three levels, energy is released. We do not control our thoughts as we do not know what our next thought will be. There is a substratum from where thoughts arise. These are called vasanas. Vasanas are the basic inherent traits. If a person has no vasana for alcohol, he will not have an urge for it, hence neither thoughts nor action towards it. If the need for alcohol is part of his inherent prarabdha, he will have the vasana, which develops the thought, eventual words and further action too. Environment also will get automatically created. He will do everything possible to get it done. If alcohol is not available in one location he will migrate to another location where it is available. A person brings forth the power (fuel) to complete his karmic journey along with his prarabdha. Thus, all prarabdha vasanas get exhausted. One cannot suppress karma and proceed in life. It's like a metallic spring. The moment you release your hand, it will bounce back. If it remains suppressed for a life-time, that soul will come back taking another body for predominantly this purpose. This being the situation, can we control anything at all? Can any government control anything? If society needs to be clean, there should not be many frustrated people. Frustration happens because of karmic non-fulfilment. This is why I said, everything is fine. I cannot see any good or bad in anything. All are creations of the same supreme power. Good and bad are aspects of the same mind. In order to shed the lower, we have to get to the higher. When each thought, word and action is done with perfect awareness, most of the negative traits of our existence will automatically get discarded as unwanted. This is the remedy. So, I was neither recommending wine nor women. In the same context, someone asked Swami Sivananda, whether his giving Sannyas to anyone who asked for it would diminish the value of sannyas at all. He replied jokingly: "Let them live with me here as sannyasis. They will be harmless here. Imagine what the state of our society would be, if they were all in the society as an integral part of it!"

Dharma of Existence

In a world where everyone talks and no one listens, I hate to add more sound. I always feel and am sure that I can do much more through my silence and being-ness rather than through movement, external articulation and doing-ness. People who can touch and feel silence deeply, from deep within their heart, can be elevated to the highest this way. The gross minds with terrestrial and more physically tangible expectations will be terribly disappointed. Vomiting emotions indiscriminately and clinging on to habits and conditionings, they expect us to do miracles and liberate them.

Who will buy the intangible, even if it is the real? We can wake up those who are sleeping. Can we wake up those who pretend to be asleep? People cannot stop accumulating garbage. Yet they expect us to do the cleansing part. This is the way the world goes. Pretensions. Gross pretensions and unjustified expectations.

Images, words, sounds, all proclaiming something sensory and tangible or 'value for money' and people run after them. People sell people, their intellect and emotions. They cheat and kill. What can silence and subtlety do in a world of gross sounds and human-induced bitter agonies? When people refuse to give up, how can we give in? When people like to choose emotions rather than liberation, who visits our store? This being the truth, religiously, we open the shop every day, irrespective of whether anyone comes to buy or not. Some come out of curiosity and do not invest. They peep from outside and disappear. Some taste a little, never buy and leave after some time. Some stay for some time and leave without even tasting. Very few make a purchase. Still, some do not use what they bought. Some abuse. Some, discard. Out of a million of such window shoppers, perhaps only one strikes the deal. If the shopkeeper lives with expectations, he will die a sad man. If he stays without expectations, he will not be affected. Anyway, that is not the story here. If you have the time, please read on . . . .

We have already spoken about the eternal Sanatana Dharma or basic ground rules of existence. What follows are messages from the soul of our beloved Mother Earth. Let us spend a few minutes in introspection into our own conscience and see what we have done so far and what more we can do, to deliver a few more drops of fresh air into the parched lungs of the Mother. The Mother speaks . . .

"My beloved children, you have been busy. Too busy to remember me. I know that. No complaints. I appreciate that you are busy. I see you emotional and always under tremendous stress. Your Father, the eternal Almighty, never wanted you to burn out like this. Remember, He, who is the creator and maintainer of the whole universe, is not as busy as you are!!! Please think about it. Why have you brought all these burdens onto yourself? Why are you killing your own kind? Why are you so angry? Remember, my children, all I gave you is nourishment and love. Had you been connected with my spirit, you would have never become so helplessly stressed out. You still have time. Connect to my spirit, which is your spirit too, and see the same spirit in everything. They are all your brothers and sisters."

"My beloved children, my whole body consists of rivers, oceans, mountains and many expressions of life. There is a spirit in everything. Do not think that the tree outside your house is separate from you. The tree inhales what you exhale. And what the tree exhales is what you inhale. Can you see this subtle collaboration and deep love? You are inseparably connected, with the trees, plants, flowers and nature. You are existentially connected to all of them. Why do you isolate yourself from them? Why do you destroy trees? They are part of your own existence. What will you inhale if you break this eternal bond? What will your children inhale? You are breaking the cycle of existence, my beloved children, please do not do that."

"My children, your life is full of glory. You look exactly like your father. He is brilliance. He is the Almighty. He is always truly majestic and never subject to any kind of weaknesses. You are the same. He created the whole universe based on Dharma. Dharma of existence. Just like the trees collaborate with you for providing fresh air, and the lions help maintain the deer population, all beings contribute towards the smooth running of dharma. Dharma should not be disrupted. It should flow eternally. Dharma is eternal."

"Dharma is the expression of your father. We all exist in that. We have no life apart from that. Have you seen any lion killing for pleasure? Have you seen any bird sitting in the nest, lazy and procrastinating, when the day breaks? Have you seen the sun taking leave even for a day, over centuries? Have you seen any change in the system of life and death? Everything born must die. Killing to satisfy senses, anger, hatred or lust. This is against dharma. This will bring your downfall. When you inflict pain on others, similar pain will haunt your existence too. This is also part of dharma. Your own people explained the theory of relativity. This is also an aspect of that. May your minds obsessed with science understand it that way. My children, beware, science should not make you insensitive. I have reasons to believe that it does. How many beings are you torturing and killing in your laboratories!!! It's a shame, my children. Torture and killing of any other being amounts to accumulation of agonizing karma. Karma is the chain that makes you take physical bodies again and again. This will make you suffer similar pains and agony. Your sufferings of this life have roots in similar acts by you, on others, in other lives. But, if nature used you to carry out its dharma, you will not suffer karma due to that. That means, when you walk, without your knowledge, if some ants die, it is part of their destiny and not your conscious doing. It will then be a different equation, if you add guilt to your thoughtless action or unmindful action. Then, you will suffer karmic undoing through suffering. If nature makes you an instrument, which it often does, you are only doing your dharma and never karma. So, do not worry about that. Karma is not punishment oriented. It is accountability oriented. You are accountable for all your deeds, including all thoughts, words and actions."

"My beloveds, a major portion of your body contains water. Water is sacred. All elements are sacred, because they have formed out of your father, the Lord Almighty. Everything is made out of pure spirit. You need to connect to the spirit behind all materials. So, respect water. Save water. Preserve water. Be sensitive towards water. You need good water to stay healthy. Your ancestors were able to drink water from any river and stay healthy. River water was so healthy at one time. Can you do the same? You have contaminated the rivers of the world. You can contaminate the oceans too. You will fall sick if you drink water from your neighbouring river. My beloved children, your unconscious living has brought much harm onto yourselves. You are existentially connected to water and those rivers. You are deeply related. Why did you poison them? You are deeply related to the flowing rivers. Your life is also flowing. Time is flowing, existence is flowing. Look at the river sand learn to flow without attachments, unconditionally. Rivers have lots to teach you, the most important of all is its very nature of being unconditional, the very nature of your father."

"My children, you are only visitors here. You will depart one day. You cannot own anything here. There is only one owner—the Lord Almighty. Everything belongs to Him. Everything is formed out of Him and everything will dissolve back to Him. He could withdraw this whole drama anytime he feels like. By the way, why are you agitated? Why are you resisting everything? Since you do not know the whole story of any existence, let alone yours, why are you so determined to change things? What can you change, when you do not know the reason of any event in your life? If you feel you are all-powerful, tell me—can you change your heartbeat? Can you change your blood circulation—or maybe reverse it for a change? Can you stop breathing? Can you stop eating? Drinking water? What can you change? Only one thing— your inner world. You can choose to fill your inner world with goodness instead of venom. That will also make your outside world look more beautiful and positive. This is the least you can do for yourself."

"Understand that your father gave you the power to understand your true nature and also to understand Him. No other being walking on my body has that capacity. Why are you then behaving like the lesser beings? You should be behaving like your father, the kindness incarnate. You should be expressing His nature, complete love and compassion, without discrimination. He is wholesome. He is ever complete. You divided and made things look seemingly micro. He is absolute and infinite. You made yourself look, seem and feel finite. Your father is always surprised at your choosing limitedness. He never interferes, you see. He leaves you to live your life. He has faith in you and believes that one day, you will reassume your unlimitedness and come back to Him. He is waiting. He is happy and thrilled when you express. His nature of selfless compassion and unconditional love. He is sad when you express negativity, anger, hatred and the silly emotions of an average terrestrial being. Keep Him happy, express love. You will see the difference happening in yourself."

"My children, we have a common destiny. My destiny is linked with yours and yours with mine. We are not separate from each other. When you contaminate the same source that you came from, reactions are inevitable. This is not my choice. This is my destiny. Yours too. This is natural with my sickness. All the calamities that you see on my surface are inevitable, because I am tired. I am sick. Your mother has become seriously ill. My body is reacting to the poisons that have been pumped into me for years. Your advancement has been at the cost of my health. Do you know that? When I sigh or pant in pain, storms and floods are your experience. How can I help it? I am helpless, my children. You are born out of me. You are myself. I have given birth to millions of bodies over millions of years. Now, I am tired. It is time for me to be re-born. Those of you who will connect to my spirit, which is the spirit of existence, will survive the change. Those of you still immersed in senses, mind and intellect, will wake up to uneasy realities sooner or later. Never tell me that I did not warn you. Save yourself while you can."

"Changes are not negative. They are inevitable. Changes mean evolution. Nothing ever stays the same in your father's creation. Dynamism is the core of creation. It never stayed the same in the past and will never stay the same in the future too. Otherwise, you would not be here. You would not be here without the evolution and change."

"My children, treat all things as spirit. All are made out of that. Realize that all are one spirit. Me—the earth, plants and trees, water, air, the sun, moon and the stars, birds and animals, you—all came out of one spirit. All one spirit. Do not worry about death. Death is not the end. There is no end. Life is an evolution. Constant evolution. It never stops. There is no need to worry. So, my children, be kind to yourself, and to others around you. My blessings are always with you. I love you and have always loved you, even when you never understood and felt my spirit. I have always been waiting for you to know and understand. I do not have much life left now. Before I withdraw, I had to tell you this. I Love all my children alike. I have no favourites. Your father also loves all His creations alike. Close your eyes and feel us. You will understand this truth. I love YOU."

UNCONDITIONAL LOVE

Love

Q: We are using and abusing the word love. According to you, what is the meaning of love?

M : According to me, love cannot have another meaning. If you insist on a meaning, it means life. Life is formed, sustained and dissolved out of love and nothing else. Human beings during waking hours make it conditional. Otherwise love is unconditional. Be aware, love heals and love expands. So, all we need is LOVE. 'Love is Life.'

The Real Strength

A man becomes superior only when he expresses sincere benevolence. When a man expresses lower emotions, he can never be called superior to other species. Superior intellect, if used for destruction and controlling others, cannot be called superior. Barbarism cannot be called superiority. Kindness, love and compassion make a man superior. Unconditional love makes a man superior. A dog also expresses unconditional love towards its owner. That is its nature. Man is different. He can express god and devil. Both are within his capacity. He can express unconditional love at will. This makes man superior.

The will and the choice though, if not used properly, cannot make a man better than other species on earth. Mundane routine existence, excuses for staying confined to the pattern of existence, work patterns, own mind blocks, escapism from own duty, destructive tendencies, anger, greed, anxiety etc. will not give man the status that he claims to have.

When a man understands himself fully and completely, a deep silence takes place. A silence of fullness. Fullness in emptiness. Needs disappear, requirements vanish. Contentment settles in. Comparisons cease to exist. All actions attain Grace. The need for terrestrial glory dies away. Pretensions vanish. Words become spontaneous. Actions become offerings. When deep contentment in his own emptiness takes root, the only emotion that springs out and overflows from his own being is devotion. Devotion beyond all limitations. Devotion to the supreme self, the creator. Devotion to the supreme self is devotion to one's own self, which essentially is only a reflection of the creator.

Rama meditates on Shiva. Rama is Shiva. Rama meditates on Himself. Rama dissolves into himself. Rama dissolves into Shiva. Shiva and Rama are one. The consumer and the consumed become one when digestion is completed. Man becomes devotion. Spontaneous expressions of devotion without any need takes birth. (This is not the ritualistic puja or worship that we are used to. This has nothing to do with any rituals. This is beyond all rituals.)

There is no need for any more knowledge. Knowledge also binds. All books are burned in the mind. Ashes of all that is smeared on existence. Ashes of detachment. Perfect renunciation. The only feeling and its expression that flows forth, in tune with the rhythm of the infinity, is love. Unconditional Love. The expression of unconditional love is devotion. Bhakti. Bhakti towards oneself and the reflection of one's self on all. The devotion towards all beings as part of the universal father. In emptiness, there are no more images. Only awareness. Awareness expresses itself as compassion and love. Devotion overflows.

Equanimity first takes birth in one's mind, in the form of deep love for all creations. All creations are himself. We cannot kill or bind any creature. We can only liberate all creatures and allow their natural karmic evolution. We cannot disrupt the flow of karma.

Nature maintains its equilibrium guided by the divine father. Nature's laws are justified. The weak perish and the strong rule. When the strong amass the wealth of their strong ego, the pride of their strength, a stronger one defeats them and crushes their ego. Once ego is lost, death awaits. Death is reawakening. Death is the shifting over. The remnants of the ego get carried forth. The cycle continues.

In human existence, we develop various types of ego every day. Our youth is full of pride. Old age is full of anxiety and agony. The ego is the string that links both. Old age usually takes the beating of the nature. Physical weakness makes man emotionally weak and that reduces ego. Ego is the barrier between man and God. The more it is reduced, the closer we are to the God.

So, according to me, man becomes truly a superior being—a hero—when kindness, compassion, unconditional love, overflows from himself and merges with the whole society. When deep love envelopes the whole world, it is truly greatness. Showing strength, destroying, conquering, torturing etc. does not make man superior at all. No way. It will only make man equal to an animal. An animal that has evolved a bit more maybe physically or intellectually, definitely not spiritually. A true hero is one who protects all beings on earth, with equanimity. He cannot even discriminate between species. If we cannot be benefactors, life is not worth it. All the knowledge that you have accumulated only becomes a burden for you and others (because of your ego attached to your knowledge). If knowledge does not translate into wisdom, then the time is wasted. If wisdom does not breed compassion, there is still a long way to go. If compassion is not expressed, it is only a theory in your mind. So, be aware that if you want to express superiority and experience superiority, express unconditional love. Live it. A conquest of your own senses and mind is the only conquest that is worth the effort.

Unconditional Love

Unconditional love is the shade that a tree on the side of the road gives to a woodcutter, who arrived to cut its branches. This is unfortunately not too visible in human beings, but very much present in the nature. If you are one with nature, you will know that every heartbeat of yours is encased in love. And the love rebounds manifold and reflects back through many beings. I shall tell you an example of this aspect.

Two days ago, while I was strolling through an island garden near Thailand with a companion, he pointed out to me that an elephant, about 100 feet away was staring at us. I stopped, looked at him and understood that it was crying inside. It was so sad and lonely. I blessed him, conveyed energy and love and moved on. Through its eyes, the elephant thanked me. And it turned towards us, wherever we went. Even stopped moving its ears and was observing me, till I departed. And even when I got into a boat to return from the island, the elephant was looking at us. Also, a wandering horse, followed me towards the boat. I had nothing in my hand. My expression of love, was reciprocated by nature through animals. All I had to give them was love. All they needed was love.

Human beings are different. They have five senses and usually no active sixth sense. They cannot understand another being totally, and they love only conditionally. Society has set standards for human existence. If we conform to that, we are loved. If not, we are rejected. So, the remedy is to start expressing love, without expectations to every plant, tree and animal around. It will come back manifold.

Unconditional love cannot be experienced until you start expressing it. This means social service. Serve unconditionally and you will attract like-minded individuals into your life. You cannot go out and search for a soul mate. He has to come to you. For that, you have to be visible. Visible in kindness and love. And then, you will attract a soul that suits you. This is the only way to have stable relationship, which is both meaningful and independent.

He Loves Me, He Loves Me Not

Q: I am deeply in love with my neighbour's son. We are of different castes. Do you think our marriage will take place?

M: Aha . . . , you want a prediction!!! Well, I do not know. What do you think?

Spreading Love

Q: There is so much hatred in this world. How can we spread love?

M: By being ourselves. By expressing our innate true nature. By not pretending. If you have the guts to express love in all situations, you will never see hatred. You will only see love. Love is the mightiest weapon in the whole universe. Love conquers. Love heals. Express love anyway. Love is light. Hatred is darkness. Darkness is a state where love does not exist. Bring love and hatred will vanish. Have patience. Have faith in love. Love is the nature of the Almighty.

Charity

By doing selfless service we cleanse ourselves tremendously. Compassion is our innate nature. The nature of the soul. It is because of this nature that the soul is accompanying our trash of karmas life after life, while it craves for liberation at each moment. The soul is suffering by being in our body. Embodiment is not its nature or its wish. It is like a house arrest for the soul. When we start expressing compassion towards all beings around us, it enhances our aura tremendously. We will glow and start shining bright. Life becomes more meaningful and worthwhile. We start expressing the nature of our soul and the supreme father. The more we become selfless, the more liberated we become. Being liberated, while in the body is the greatest gift one can achieve in one's life. Our selflessness will touch and soothe many, whom we do not even know. It also enhances their spirituality and faith in divine intervention. One does not get more than what one deserves. This is the law of the nature. When we become the instruments of nature, we become natural, we become contented. We will be satisfied with what we have. Book knowledge is often a burden. It boosts ego. Selfless service is liberation. Selfless service is not always shelling out money. It is getting someone educated, giving tuition (conducting free classes or guidance for poor students) for free, guiding one to higher levels in physical, emotional, intellectual or spiritual planes, teaching skills, providing medicines etc. It's up to you. There is no need to be a member of an organisation either. Just be natural and help all. Love all and serve all. Like Jesus said: "Unless you develop the capacity to love those whom you hate most, you cannot reach my realms." Our life should be used to bless everyone. Love everyone. The attitude of charity flowing from your heart, will cleanse you tremendously. Love will overflow from your heart and overflow into you too. Do not just give money. Please be deeply involved in the charity activity. You should feel what you do. Then it becomes your character.

Charity should be pure and selfless with zero expectations from the side of the giver. The receiver also should never feel bound or guilty. Purity is essential in all our actions. True acts of charity should always be liberating to the giver and the receiver. It should never be binding and obligatory.

Higher Souls

Souls from higher realms do take birth on earth. This is not because of their karmic push. This is because of sheer compassion. They arrive and live to elevate people to higher understanding and awareness. They exit when the deed is done. Non-attachment will be their sign. They sometimes get bound to terrestrial relationships and get caught up. This is rare, but possible. You can differentiate them from others by watching the way they operate, with perfect equanimity and non-attachment. They always operate on the basis of unconditional love.

On Man's Virtue

If you are powerful, your expression should be unconditional love. This is the real virtue. This is the real strength. Unfortunately, our novels, movies, TV serials and soap operas depict greed, anger and intolerance as the nature of our society. This might give the impression to the reader and viewer that it is acceptable. A man becomes truly powerful when his expression becomes unconditional love and kindness, against all odds. Greed, anger and all such kinds of negativity are our weakness. Jealousy also blocks one's progress in spirituality. The lower emotions prevent man from elevating himself or taking himself higher. Even if you hate one person, that will bind you to earth. You will have to come back again and nullify that. We must be aware of that all the time. This is why we are placing so much emphasis on purification in our meditation. Internal bathing is as important as external bathing. Usually, we only bathe externally and most people do not know how to trash the internal garbage. For those who remain confused, the best method is seva—unconditional service. Serve and save animals and human beings with kindness and love. Let kindness flow from your heart, unconditionally. You will slowly, but steadily wash away all the internal trash that you have carried over many lifetimes.

I do not believe in the middle class morality, which is neither applicable to the rich nor to the poor. Morality is subjective. I do not consider a man who drinks alcohol as an immoral person. We must understand that he will be necessarily drawn towards weakness if that is part of his karmic agenda. Nobody can do anything about it, unless he exhausts it himself. Exhausting also cannot be suppression of the desire. It should be substituting of a base desire through higher awareness and with something of a higher nature, perhaps spiritual nature. One cannot leave a vacuum and move on. Whenever one leaves a vacuum after any addiction, he tends to go back and fill the vacuum with the same addiction with more intensity, if it is left unfilled with something higher and better.

A man's real strength lies in his ability to express love in all conditions. The ability and will to give the helpless and suffering a helping hand unconditionally makes one strong and powerful. Self-esteem will flourish. Doing sadhana for one's own benefit has its advantages. Yet, when the tranquility attained through sincere and selfless spiritual practices flows from your heart (spiritual heart) to all the beings of the universe you become more powerful. The Masters will start working through you. Your barriers will lay broken and liberation will happen automatically. You will see your own reflection in all the eyes around you. Serving unconditionally will enhance the spiritual power of the seeker, because internal cleansing happens without his knowledge through purity of selfless action. This enhances the benefits of his sadhana. Expecting name and fame for selfless service will completely destroy the benefits of one's efforts. It clearly nullifies the effort.

A ruler can rule his country in two ways. Through creating fear or through expressing sincere love for his people. Management through unconditional love is much more effective than managing through fear or infliction of pain. The rigid tree is always ready for the axe. The supple tree is difficult to cut. A spiritualist should always remain supple, yet firm. The more rigid his character, the harder his shell becomes. The shell is formed by sheaths of ego and habits. He will automatically cut himself from the supreme and will stay married to his ritual. Non-conformity to any habit or ritual keeps a man subtle, firm and in the present. This is good for evolution.

Fear is very powerful. Love is more permanent. When fear leaves, love can still be seen in the background. Love always exists. Fear comes and goes, like waves of the ocean.

Love exists just like the sun. The sun is always available. We may not be able to see it due to the clouds in the actual sky or the sky of our own mind or because of our particular location which obscures our view. But the sun is never affected by the clouds, which are much lower than the sun. We are affected because we cannot see the sun, because of the clouds. Clouds happen on their own in our minds because we entertain fear or anxiety. When we stay with the sun or supreme, fears cannot exist. When we grow beyond the clouds of our mind, there is always sunshine up there. The head, the intellect, should always stay beyond the clouds of emotions lurking in our heart region. The head should always see the sun, even if the heart or emotion cannot see it.

So understand that the real strength of man is in his expression of kindness. Love is the strongest of all medicines. Love heals. Love creates harmony. Love expands hearts. Expressing love unconditionally is the biggest virtue any man can possess. Morality, as far as I am concerned, is subjective. We must be aware of one's karmic agenda to be able to judge the action of a person. This is difficult. This does not mean that one can do anything he likes, ignoring the sentiments of others. I am only referring to harmless indulgences, pushed by one's karma. And detaching from these vices should be permanent and done by creating a better alternative through higher awareness.

Keep loving. Keep living. Always appreciate and express the beauty and brightness of your own soul. Mind does not understand the soul. Soul understands the mind, as well as all the minds that it activated through all your lives. Soul also understands the residue of experiences that you carried from all those minds. This data is stored in your subconscious or primitive conscious or whatever you want to call it. Conscious mind cannot understand the past lives because it is limited to your current system. The electricity that comes to your house has only enough power to run your household gadgets. It does not have the capacity to run a factory or a city. But the source where this electricity was generated is much more powerful and has the capacity to run the entire city. Our mind has limitations. Our soul does not have limitations. Our mind cannot understand why a particular thing has happened. Our soul has seen it all, because over many, many lifetimes it has been witnessing this karmic play. It has been fuelling our lives and witnessing our role-play in each life. We have taken many lives, had many minds, the soul has been the only connecting thread between all those lives. The thread of the garland. So have faith in the thread. Be one with the thread. This is higher awareness. One will never express any kind of immorality!

BEINGNESS

Be Yourself

MANY YEARS AGO an old saint said: "My son, be always aware of who you are. In the world that we exist in, you will see many masks, many unreal faces. Sometimes the unreal faces will make us confused. Sometimes, we may even believe that the unreal is the actual real and we could be unreal. This is how Maya plays. At all times, be aware of who you are!!! Always be aware!!! That will be your strength. You will stay well beyond the play of Maya. This is the real freedom. Existing in the unreal, being fully conscious of the real at all times, is liberation."

Time passed. Years of wandering. Many places, many houses, sometimes, just on sustenance level. The conscious mind refused to accept changes and it pitched up conflicts within. This happens to everyone. Especially in the current times of recession, this will happen to many. Many people may get confused. With all their qualifications, experience, talent, why are they laid off? The feeling of redundancy is destroying. It damages the self-esteem of individuals. I can see this all around now. These are signs of the times. We must always be aware of our real nature, who we are, and stay with that permanent factor within us, our soul.

I have experienced a tremendous lack of continuity all my life. In my childhood, almost every third year, I was in a different place. My father used to be a government servant, a medical practitioner, and was transferred to a new location every three years. My whole set up used to change. House, friends, school, environment, everything. Apart from parents, everything else changed every third year!!! It was difficult to find uniformity in continuous changes. Changes became a part of existence. As an adult, there were constant turbulences at the job front and relationship front. Constant changes in location, in employment etc. Slowly one thing became clear to me. Changes are given to eliminate the comfort factors of terrestrial existence. When we fall back into our comfort zones, we fail to evolve. When comforts are often removed, we are forced to leave our procrastination and get on our feet and walk. Nature arranges this scenario. We may try our best to resist. Our weak resistance cannot help the situation at all. We are forced to take steps.

One of the major challenges that everyone will face is the lack of understanding from their dependants and relatives. The relatives may not accept one's realities and will add oil to the fire by blaming and accusing. This could drive the individual crazy. What is happening here? Understand that this is ego-bashing as well as karmic cleansing. When people blame and criticise you, your ego is severely affected. Sometimes you feel terribly helpless. Helplessness is the opposite of ego. Secondly, you will understand, sometimes the hard way, that most people, including relatives, are just fair weather friends. It helps your efforts in detachment. This will destroy your expectations from the root. It will take some time to accept realities. It is not easy. I fully understand and appreciate that point. But essentially inside your own conscious mind you will see changes, deep changes. This helps to control your expectations about others and will also teach you detachment. Henceforth you will do your duty (dharma) perfectly well, minus attachment and thus keep yourself away from building up karmas. Thus, negative times are usually great times for learning and evolution.

Seekers used to wander without money to eradicate tamas or procrastination, as well as to come in terms with the deepest of their fears, and attain the Self. They move from one place to another by feet and by means of simple transportation. They never stay in one place for more than three nights. They do not store food or money. They beg for their living. They beg and eat their daily food. (This is why in India it is sacred to feed a wandering monk.) They sleep in one place for only three nights. They also tackle fears and loneliness this way. They learn to live only in the present. Thus, they constantly nullify their comfort zones and establish themselves in their soul. Wandering monks do not cook food, because while cooking, thousands of germs get killed. They avoid any conscious destruction. When a householder cooks the effect is the same. Yet, when they feed the saint, the saint blesses them and the bad effects of cooking get nullified. This is the collaboration between a saint and the society or a householder. Feeding anybody who is hungry is truly sacred, whether it be a saint or a sinner.

In a way, my wandering started very early and it still continues. People who have not moved so many times will never understand the trick of this constant movement. With constant movement a person is forced to base himself in his own soul. Everything else changes. How can we base anything on shifting realities?

Shifting realities are the truth of our everyday existence. Conflicts will happen within. This is also related to our ego, name, fame and position. These also need annihilation to reach the soul. All these are creating walls. Hence, emotional approach will not help in changing times. An approach firmly rooted in the Self will help. This will help your evolution and even if the situations change outside, you will remain calm.

This is my reply to about 12 mails with relatively similar questions.

Beyond Pretensions

A small boy is looking at the wide universe in awe and wonder. The body of the infinity stretches beyond what mind can comprehend. The boy needs to shed his gross and become light in order to know the magnificence. Becoming light is dissolving in light. Being one with the light. There are no identities and identifications anymore. There are no dualities. In non-duality it's only the awareness of being light. There is no one projecting nor anyone visualizing. There is no one. Only oneness. Absolute oneness. Trillions and trillions of matter and beings supported by the life energy. Fathomless creations. Relativity in its absolute brilliance, just for the father to be aware of himself as separate from his creations. Just for his experimentation on duality. Creations that are visible and those that are invisible to human eyes. Sounds audible and inaudible. A living cell and galaxies. Macrocosms and microcosms. Humans, gods, demi-gods, the good, the bad and the mysterious. The mask and the real one. Maya and the divine. Mind and its power over matter, almost the same effect of the duality between maya and the creator. The creator hides behind it all, watching the show in relative darkness of blinding magnificence. (Relative darkness is our interpretation of blinding brilliance, as brilliance shuts our eyes. The only way to understand that is to become the same brilliance.) The divine play in its magnificence displayed at every point. If only we had the eyes to see the divine magnificence of our father!!! Then would we realize that what we are now, chasing on the terrestrial plane is not even comparable, let alone worthwhile.

Every day, we wake up, wear a mask and present ourselves in the world and to the world. People look at us, we look at people and we judge or conclude about each other: "This is the man.", "This is all that he is." We create frames for each person. In our mind we do not allow him any more walking space. We are often dictatorial in our outlook. We make men in our own image or we destroy them. This is also the philosophy of cults. We also like to destroy what we do not understand, including men whom we cannot understand. We destroy them through our thoughts, words or action. As a general rule, we do not like opposition. We do not like to be questioned. This is also why we love the dead. They never talk back or dispute. We can also make statues of them and put them in the streets so that birds can use them as toilets. The dead do not complain, they have left the earth and they don't care what you do with their physical image. While living we ridicule the great thinkers. After death we glorify them and make associations in their name. We have heavy limitations and we can never admit it. This is one of the fundamental reasons why unconditional love cannot grow and flourish on earth. We see it only randomly, often in unexpected corners of the world and the dwellings of the poor as well as with non-human beings such as animals and birds.

The real man is actually something else. There is always a third dimension. There is an ego-less, time-less entity that we miss amidst the pretensions, comparable to what we are during our deep sleep state. The state where all identities, time and space dissolve into nothingness. He is existing, but not quite, till he wakes up. This lack of understanding of the third dimension of oneself also sometimes leads one to gross disillusionment.

Ego is inevitable. There is no escape. Ego creeps into everything, irrespective of whether you are a karma yogi, bhakti yogi or jnana yogi. It lies in our ability to segregate true thought, word and action from ego that makes us spiritually evolve further. It is our objectivity and awareness that helps the progress. Subjective approach almost always breeds more karmic binding, irrespective of who we are and what we do.

All gross has specific duration. All that is born must die, including the soul. Soul is born from the infinite father and must return back to him at some point of time. Distance and duration could vary, but journey and merger are most certain. In the realms of Parabrahma, the father, who is the subtlest possible, even a soul can be considered gross, especially if it has karmic baggage. When the soul attains the same subtlety as the father, it does not exist as a separate entity. It becomes absolutely one with the father. Until then it experiences duality. Karma is gross even though it is intangible from our realms. It's more tangible in astral realms, especially in comparison to its carrier, the soul. Hence it is gross. Matter is the grossest. The difference in elevation of beings is the difference of the levels of subtlety. So it is not necessarily what one does, but how one does it that matters. Indulgence with emotion is equal to karmic slavery. Indulgence minus emotion is equal to liberation attitude. This means whether a thing exists or not, it does not affect the relative doer. Since it exists, it is being used. When it stops to exist, the relative doer will be the same. It's the same with time and space. Any given time and space are the same, provided the level in which the relative doer operates is objective. There is ownership of action, word and thought in grosser plane. The essence of the more subtle plane is the lack of ownership and doership. Action takes place because it must. Not because karma propelled it. Thence, action is out of necessity and action is not a need.

An incident snowballs into an event in our mind over time. The mind is the culprit. A thought, word or action by someone leaves its impression in our mind. Mind blows it up. Sometimes it provokes a series of thoughts, words and actions within us or by us. Often we become emotional and actions of emotional nature lead to catastrophic ends.

Example: Grapes are sweet and good for health. When they are kept and bottled, they ferment and become wine. Controlled consumption of wine rejuvenates the system. Emotional consumption leads to intoxication and unconscious action as it affects the brain of the consumer. Likewise, any incident leaves a mark in our substratum. We are bombarded with hundreds of incidents each day. If the incident happens and gets archived or trashed without any attachments to it, we will stay liberated. If emotions, the glue, stick it to the subconscious, actions are provoked, karma is created. Emotions breed in the mind. They multiply in the mind. It is temporary, but significant because they breed karmic bindings.

Present

Thinking about the past is the nature of the conscious mind. It keeps oscillating between past and the future, refusing to stay in the present. This can be minimised only through awareness or witness consciousness. Being a witness to your own thought process will help in keeping the mind in the present. The usual reason for energy loss and resulting tiredness is the same thing. Mind uses much more energy than the body uses. It tires the man.

There is no absolute right or wrong. Mind constantly takes references from the past to handle the present. For example, a boy who slipped and fell in the rain, could always have that memory and related fear. Sometimes a newspaper report about an air crash could give an impact to the reader which could develop into the fear of flying. Impressions that we store in our subconscious mind will cause such realities. Taking reference from the past is being done whether we like it or not. The only problem is carrying the garbage from the past and refusing to throw it away. Garbage needs to be trashed. If not trashed, it affects us. Guilt that we carry from the past is the problem. It is not a sin. Sins do not exist. If at all they exist, according to me, the biggest sin is not understanding your true nature, because one lifetime gets wasted for nothing. Or one lifetime was spent in ignorance.

Past is dead. You cannot go back and change anything in the past. So leave the dead. Future is still unborn. You have only the NOW to perform. This is the present, the gift from relativity. When you sleep at night there is no past, present or future. It's all one. Past, present and future exist only during waking hours or in conscious mind. Be aware of that. When you exist in the present, when your mind stays with your current activity, there is just a minimal energy loss. It helps to save energy. Save energy, save life. This keeps you fresh. This is why people say that if you love your profession and always feel inclined to go to work without any other consideration or pressure you will never be tired.

Understand that nothing is a sin. Mind does oscillate between past and future. It also nurtures guilt from the past and fear of the unknown or future, which saps away energy. It also creates tremendous anxiety. The remedy is in being in the present. Mind should be present in all activities. You need to practice this only during waking hours, because, while sleeping, time does not exist or you. You have to wake up to be aware of the time.

ENLIGHTENMENT

Misuse of the word

ENLIGHTENMENT HAS BECOME a cliche. Every acharya claims to take people to enlightenment. Most acharyas are only acharyas, not gurus. They themselves are not enlightened. Like bottled water, enlightenment is sold in the streets nowadays. Many seekers also claim to be enlightened and start behaving in strange ways. When they become too intolerable, neighbors catch them and put them in asylums. We saw that happening in India recently! Ha! ha! People pretend to have siddhis and harm themselves and others. All these are dangerous games and traps. Beware.

My friends, please beware of fraud. Not all that glitters is gold. The Upanishad say: "Faculties have been given to man to recognise harmful from harmless. Not knowing the laws of nature is not an excuse." It is unfortunate that we have started taking enlightenment also as another feather in the cap, while enlightenment actually removes all caps. Caps are needed only for terrestrial recognition. When you are beyond any terrestrial bindings, what are the caps for? Enlightened Masters will look ordinary, and be epitomes of simplicity. They will express extraordinary simplicity and we will wonder if they are enlightened at all. They need nothing from you. They are beyond needs and will perform with perfect equanimity. They even mislead people to avoid self glory and unwanted fanfare. Those who crave for terrestrial glory will pretend and claim many things. Enlightenment will take away the need to even express. You will automatically feel who he is, when he is next to you. Feeling is more superior than talking. Moreover, unless you are eligible, enlightenment cannot happen to you. Enlightenment has to happen. The awareness has to set in by itself. Whatever you try to do, doing can take you only to a certain level. When you are established in being level, enlightenment takes place. It is like cementing your existence in the being level. Then, doing also will become spontaneous, with perfect awareness. The word enlightenment has been misused in today's world.

What is Enlightenment?

Enlightenment cannot be easily explained in words. Enlightenment happens, when the ground is set for its landing. It happens, when doing-ness stops and being-ness takes place. It happens in the absolute level of equanimity, where the ego element remains completely nullified. It is a shift in awareness. Enlightenment is a big leap. This means a leap from limited awareness to unlimited awareness. From the state of limited body consciousness, its attached mind consciousness and its intellect and ego, to unlimitedly expanded awareness state. The awareness is in 360 degrees. You are aware of everything around you and the bodily boundaries are blurred. This happens when the same mind that goes for a stroll with the senses merges and dissolves with the soul instead. Deeper unity and total awareness take place. States of Samadhi are unexplainable. Words fall helpless.

Q: Is the actual experience of enlightenment describable?

M: It is not. Words are far too shallow to explain an experience such as the explosion of silence or cosmic consciousness. Many people have attempted it. Paramahamsa Yogananda does it in the 'Autobiography of a Yogi'. Usually, silence slides in after the experience and the need for expression gets erased. For many people, the need for communication itself gets erased. There is nothing to do, nothing to prove, nothing to say. Everything just is. Everything is a part of our existence and we are part of everything too. In such condition, there is perfect stillness and supreme perfection. How can anyone explain such a state? Even if someone does, it will only become a theory in the reader's mind. Moreover, enlightenment experience is never the same, it differs from person to person. It differs with each person's individual constitution. It differs according to the sattva, rajas, tamas combination of the individual that undergoes the shift. So even though a general idea can be given about the experience, like Paramhamsa did, it is not really describable.

Q: Is enlightenment the final? Then what?

M: Enlightenment is like a graduation. You have arrived at a different level of existence. Then, before complete liberation, there are still miles to travel. However, the push of the mind for results will not be bothering you and hence the journey will be more pleasant. So, once the shift of higher awareness happens within, the path ahead becomes fully illumined. Two main parallel things happen quite simultaneously. One is the self-purification and dissolution, and the second is the repayment of debts to the Mother Earth. This is the most treacherous time. First of all, the grossness and street-smartness of terrestrial existence is less. And secondly, the enlightened one has to live with the gross society while existing in his/her more subtle state. People get tossed around a lot, in this state.

The Real Truth

Q: How do we find it?

M: By looking within. All problems and confusions in the world are due to people trying to find answers outside of themselves, while all answers lie within oneself.

Q: How long does spiritual sadhana or spiritual practices help?

M: Till you cross the river. Sadhana is the ferry. River is the samsara. Once you cross the river, you do not need any sadhana.

Q: Is there any guarantee that certain spiritual practices can ensure enlightenment?

M: Is there any guarantee that you and I will be still in this body to discuss these matters tomorrow? Kill your expectations. Be objective. Do your sadhana. Accept any result that comes your way. Attachment on a result is binding. It kills the enjoyment of the present and breeds anxieties about the future and results. You will rotate in the same circle forever.

The Challenge on the Path

Just take things as they come. Handling expectation would be the biggest challenge that anyone faces in spiritual progression. Expectations always create anxieties and agonies. So just float on, Supreme energy is enveloping you day and night.

Q: According to you, what is the right attitude?

M: Absolute objectivity. And compassion based on absolute objectivity.

Q: You had mentioned that all people are eligible for salvation in this life. What is the minimum qualification?

M: The state of equanimity. One who is established in equanimity is ready for moksha. One who is not affected by the dualities of life like happiness and sorrow, success and failure, good and bad, darkness and light, health and illness, is ready for salvation. One who is not affected by duality is ready for unity. Being united or one with the father is salvation or moksha.

Q: What is against moksha?

M: Attachments. Especially emotional attachments bring you back again and again to the world.

Enlightenment Effects

Q: Does enlightenment mean giving up everything?

M: No. Enlightenment means giving in to everything in perfect equanimity. Nothing affects you anymore. Giving up is renunciation. If you give up consciously while the desire still exists in your subconscious, it will not work. You have to exhaust your desires and evolve further. Then it will stay. No desire can be suppressed and moved forward. Circumstantial suppression is not elimination. The seeds are still there. The desire is still there. It will sprout when the right environment is created.

Enlightenment means complete giving in to the rhythm of the universe. A total tuning in. Individual gratifications get converted into existence in a bliss state which means self-sufficiency. Externalization of the senses and mind will shift to internalization. Man achieves self-sufficiency within himself. Then it's not giving up, but dropping off. Automatically, all that is unwanted in his subconscious gets burnt away or dropped off and that space becomes filled with the bliss of cosmic consciousness. You can also call it blissful emptiness or supreme awareness.

In short, we cannot give up anything, unless that space gets filled with something higher in nature. Karma cannot be deleted unless fully exhausted. It must wear off. Enlightened Masters can definitely dilute one's karmic trash. But usually they let the disciple walk the path, experience and exhaust. Otherwise, as long as desires exist, the need for gratification never leaves the subconscious.

Desires should be replaced with higher awareness. This means, when you got a bicycle, you lost the interest in your toy. When you got a motorcycle, you lost interest in your bicycle. Therefore, something higher replaces the seeming lower. In the case of spirituality, EXPERIENCE SHOULD REPLACE KNOWLEDGE. Then evolution happens. The higher the experiences the more the lower will drop off. The need for doing anything ritualistically will drop off and existence in bliss will provide tremendous strength and equanimity. You will not be affected by any storms of life. You will stay afloat in all conditions and turbulence.

Interaction Or Reclusion

Q: After enlightenment, what provokes Masters to interact with society? Many choose reclusion, if I am not mistaken.

M: You are right. When his silence becomes more eloquent, the enlightened Master chooses isolation. It is compassion or kindness that provokes a Master to interact with society. The enlightened Master is in touch with the Supreme Reality. Some feel obliged to guide the receptive to the same plane of awareness too. There are no karmic agendas here, only extreme compassion and love. Then, his existence is based on love and duty—Dharma.

Existing in Knowledge

Enlightenment means a complete shift in consciousness. It is a shift from the limited to the unlimited. All knowledge is within you. Once enlightened you don't need to read anything. You will always be existing in the present and what you need at that moment, you will be able to access.

Swami Vivekananda used to leaf through big books in a few

seconds and would then answer any question pertaining to that book or its content. He was obviously not reading it.

Reading is also doing, in a way. In enlightenment, doing-ness will give away to beingness and universal consciousness. All data is available in that realm. Enlightenment gives the key to access it. You do not need terrestrial materials to satisfy your need for knowledge when you exist in knowledge and bliss itself.

Acharyas use knowledge from books because they need it to train their students. Once they achieve the bliss state, the "Mastership", they also drop the accumulation of book knowledge and dissolve into beingness. Often we can see drastic shifts in attitudes post enlightenment. We can see many Masters resorting to silence and non-doing. Many become hyperactive, in the non-karmic selfless plane. Many behave like mad men. Many leave society and go into reclusion. It depends on the innate nature of the seeker how they will express themselves after enlightenment. Usually only an enlightened person can recognize another. Others can only guess. Some pretend to be enlightened, but understand that it is for their survival or their emotional need for recognition. With enlightenment all the terrestrial needs will vanish and the enlightened Master will operate from a universal love aspect. There will be nothing conditional in his approach. He will not need anything from anybody. He will become self-sufficient in his supreme beingness, where everything is within his command. This is one visible sign of enlightenment.

Masters' Morality

Q: I always believed that Masters should set standards in morality. Sri Krishna is said to have had 16008 wives. Jesus is accused of having had an affair with Mary Magdalene. If he did this, can we blame regular human beings like us for having more than one wife?

M: Ha! Ha! I liked this question very much. What an idea!!! What an excuse!!! Let me explain.

Fundamental mistake: trying to understand a higher Master and his actions using our limited capabilities of understanding is like a 5th class student trying to explain the books or syllabus of graduation classes. Enlightenment = Unlimitedness. Non-Enlightenment = Limitedness.

Every thought, word and action has a time, space, intellect, environment and effect. If you do not understand that aspect, you will not understand the depth of that action or any action.

An enlightened Master may do many things for the higher good, as he is not operating from the plane of mundane karma. He is operating from the plane of universal awareness where he can see the past, present and future in one platform. He will know the action as well as the consequences, just like we see the flowers blooming outside the window. His actions will always be for the general well being of the masses. He has no selfish interest.

On many occasions, an enlightened Master may use intoxication to dull his perpetual cosmic consciousness and bring himself to terrestrial awareness or body consciousness. If a disciple, who is only in the formation stage resorts to the same technique of using intoxication, he will never achieve enlightenment and will definitely become a drug addict. He may look like a Master with his beard and saffron robes but he will be far from the stature of his Master. So imitating a Master before becoming a Master is extremely dangerous, if your purpose is higher evolution. If the purpose is just to make a living and fool the relatively ignorant public, good enough, the attire will benefit to a great extent.

You can follow the guidance of the Master, but never imitate him, if you have not reached his stature.

Now, regarding your question about Lord Krishna, please understand that it's not humanly possible to entertain 16008 wives! Ha! Ha! Many people cannot even live with one wife. So, how can someone live with 16008 wives? Isn't it a bit too bizarre? Coming to Krishna. How do you know that Krishna had 16008 wives and that this is true in its true sense? My understanding is as follows:

Krishna defeated a king and freed all the prisoners. There were several women too. If you want the exact head count, we can say—

16000 plus women. Some of them were very old, and had spent many years in prison.

When Krishna released the prisoners, he told them: "You are free now. Go to your homes and live in peace. If you encounter any problems or difficulties in the future, come to me and let me know."

They were happy and went back to their homes. Society did not welcome them. Their families were reluctant to accept them, as they believed that an ex-convict at home could give the effect of ex-communication by the society. Their children may not get a good spouse etc. The ex-prisoners were excommunicated by their own society.

In short, the ladies who were prisoners once were back in the streets begging for a living. They went back to Krishna requested his audience and said: "We were prisoners once. It was not an ideal situation to be in. Yet, we were getting three meals every day. We had shelter from sun and rain. Now we are even more miserable.

We have no place to sleep and no food. None of our family members want us back. Please put us back into the prison and save our lives."

Krishna ordered them to be considered as royal wives and ordered a pension for all of them. Royal wives have privileges, eligibilities and respectability. He sent everyone back with these privileges and they started living happily.

Society loves successful people, even if they are ex-convicts. Money matters and reputation can be re-created. Thus, these "16008 wives of Krishna" lived a majestic life as "royal wives". This earned them respect in the society and the younger ones among them got marriage proposals from eligible bachelors!!! All their relatives who were relatively inferior to them, as per their current position, started respecting them and considering them as an integral part of their family. Thus Lord Krishna bestowed them their respect and self-esteem, by giving them the status.

How is this? What do you think now? Krishna is being portrayed as a womanizer because every man is a womanizer, at least in their mind, one way or another. If the Lord represents that quality, it's easy license for the devotees. The truth is different. So, let us not judge an avatar with our limited understanding.

I'm not judging moralities here, nor am I stating whether something is good or bad. This is up to the individual. There are no general rules in the larger perspective. Please do ponder on this and see how you feel.

Do not worry about Jesus and Mary Magdalene. Jesus was mission bound and in a very short span of time, he did his deed. Mary was his most preferred disciple or devotee (nursing and healing karmic wounds) and Jesus empowered her with abilities of healing and Grace. Limited minds cannot comprehend the higher love. We can only visualise carnal love, because our minds are in that peripheral.

This is fine. Let us be what we are. Then we will be based on reality and not on pretension. Being real is very important for higher evolution.

Silence

Q: In the Father's silence, are there any words? What are they? And whom does He talk to?

M: In the Father's silence, there are words. Many words. Yet they all come together and sound like a deep hum or 'OM'. When all colours merge, we experience the colorlessness or white colour. I would call white colourlessness because it's the mother of all colours. Like that, when all sounds merge, it becomes a hum.

The Father talks to Himself. There is nothing apart from Himself, even though maya makes it feel that all these numerous beings in the universe are all separate entities. They are separate entities in the physical plane. They are all one in the plane of the Father. Ego makes us feel separate. In egoless states man realizes that he and his Father are one. So the Father keeps talking to his disillusioned children, which are all the entities of the universe, all the atoms, all the molecules, all the electrons, protons and neutrons. He talks relentlessly. But to hear His words, we must be silent. Our mind must be silent. Deep silence. Perfect silence. Thoughtless silence. When we reach there, the whole external and internal silence will stop and we hear only the words of the Father. To hear the words of the Father we have to tune into His frequency. When we tune into His frequency we will know that there is no difference between us and the Father. I am Him. Then we will also understand that the Father talks to Himself, in perfect being ness, while aiding all the doing-ness of the universe in perfect equanimity. There is nothing apart from him to speak to. In perfect oneness there is no relativity. Man will search a lot before he achieves this silence. Once the silence is achieved there is no more searching. There is only deep peace. Deepest peace.

Eternal Peace and Supreme Strength

I am indebted by your questions. The thought that the words happening through me are guiding some of you is quite a pleasant feeling. This makes me more grateful to the Almighty. Makes me happier about this existence. When I receive more queries, it tells me that the answers are appreciated.

Everything is happening. Questions are happening. Answers are happening. Birth happens. Death happens. Love happens. Hate happens. Thoughts happen. Everything happens. Where is the one who provokes these questions, answers, births, deaths and thoughts? Where is the one who knows everything? Where is the Guru, the teacher? When did the first question arise in any mind? Where did the answer appear from? When did the questions melt into answers? When did we free ourselves from questions and answers? When can we free ourselves from births and deaths?

Brimming with questions, men walk their life. Step by step. There is nothing he can do to change his past. The past has already happened. The present is happening. The future depends on how he uses his present. So, future is uncertain. Past is dead. Future is yet to be. All we have is the present. Many people have entertained similar thoughts. Many such thoughts have conglomerated into events. Many thinkers were blamed for leading the thought process of generations. Yet, we could do nothing about it. Thinkers happened. Thoughts happened. Thoughts gathered words and sound. People listened. Some thoughts were selfish, well camouflaged in beautiful words. This led to greed, enemies and wars. This led to sufferings. But only history could tell that those thoughts and words were grossly selfish. History got the last laugh at the foolishness of mankind. Some thoughts were benevolent. Sometimes they did not find the right words, voice or mouth to travel. So, none heard the words of wisdom. They got dispersed in the crowded world of bizarre sounds. Yet, some were able to hear those subtle voices, through the narrow gate, and transformed themselves to attain the Highest in one lifetime, while their cousins pursued 'likeable and lovable' words and continued with their pursuit of elusive happiness and peace. None bothered. Trial and error were considered as the law of life, which we are supposed to follow. Thus the ignorant preached and gave solace to the ignorant. All were happy. In our prescribed world, what else could we do?

Then came the loud-mouthed wise men. They uttered alien truths. Truths alien to the ignorant. Intangible truths. Truths that cannot be counted in terms of money. Their loudness and seeming madness were intolerable to the great mass of 'sleeping populations' in every era. When their sound increased day by day. When changes became inevitable, they destroyed the source and went back to their sleep. A peaceful sleep after a job well done!!! This is the nature of our world, the world that we live in. We destroy what we cannot gather!!! We ridicule and make fun of those who choose to walk alone or those who carve their own paths.

Thoughts evolved through time and people. Words evolved through time and people. Imagination and greed evolved too. We became funny people. We learned to sell everything that we have. Even our integrity. We learned and accepted that it is fine to sell our spirituality too. The aim was, as always, materialism. So, the usual crossover from materialism to spirituality was well compromised as greed for sales took root. The buyers are the insecure people. The sellers are also insecure.

Fear binds people together. Fear blinds people from the immediate, the obvious. Fear takes people to the extremes. Using fear as the tool for conquering ignorant people, the new age gurus created programs. Some created tantric objects, claiming to ward off evil and earn wealth. The world became a transactional-spiritual mad house. Everything is business. Everything is transactional. Self proclaimed gurus churned out programmes one after the other to keep ignorant people busy and maintain the artificial comfort of escapism from the scorching heat of everyday life. Mental imageries of enlightenment and liberation kept the masses well established in a fool's paradise. Number of courses attended became the criteria of spiritual elevation, just like the usual academic supremacy. Unwanted knowledge strengthened ego. It took man further from God, yet it extended their vocabulary and social status. So for some it was worth it. It also gave them the community effect or feeling. It was worth it to be in a cult because of the comfort. Thus, people jumped from frying pan to fire or vice versa. Same wine, different bottles. All well packed. All displayed in the right light. Very attractive!!! Some teachers read all sorts of books and created a variety of concoctions, suitable for everyone, for a newborn and one on his deathbed!!! Ancient wisdom made to order!!! Good for all!!! Everyone gets their shot!!! Results guaranteed!!! Enlightenment guaranteed!!! Pay more for faster enlightenment!!!

We are indeed existing in a tragic era. This is the naked picture of today's spirituality. Unless we see through the masks of these teachers, we will be rotating around the wrong guide our whole life. Nobody can own wisdom. It existed well before we existed. We are only using our antennae to decipher the meaning of the ever existing wisdom. We are only interpreting the age-old wisdom in the current environment. We never invented words; we never invented the knowledge either. Our role is limited. So, beware. Be aware of words, thoughts and action.

Right from Adi Guru—Lord Shiva—all the saints have spoken

one great and golden truth. It is through beingness that we attain God. It is not by doing. So if you are a veteran who has completed hundreds of various programs, it means nothing. It perhaps only displays your insecurity. Being in yourself and doing relentless selfless service will definitely take you to the Highest. Doing a lot of sadhana and preaching about it or boasting about it will only keep you well established in your ego, as well as in the karmic cycle of birth and death. It is not going to get you liberation. Liberation is in non-doing. This is the feeling when we have it, but do not need it. We stay liberated from it. That mindset has to happen.

Karma gets exhausted by being in the present all the time. By being with every thought, word and deed, all the time. Karma needs to be exhausted through time and corresponding action, thought or word. The same way we created karma, we need to exhaust karma too. There is no short cut. Be well aware of that. Mantras and increased awareness check the creation of more karma. Conscious awareness also destroys the emotions attached to action which aids liberation. Tying a rope is easy. Untying is difficult. The same way, unconscious living fills our hard drive with wanted and unwanted data that really clogs our life. The whole system slows down as data becomes jumbled up or indecipherable. Unclogging becomes essential. Cleaning up the hard drive from unwanted data is essential. We should be very careful as to what we input into our hard drive.

We have the freedom of choice. Using that freedom in the most careless way and later complaining about a confused existence should not happen. Because you created your own destiny!!! You attracted those realities into yourself. Be aware of that.

One more thing. Do not keep complaining that you 'missed the bus'. I ensure you that if you were supposed to catch that bus you would have caught it. Guaranteed. We cannot change the master symmetry. We as individuals are not changing anything from the masterplan. The 'master' plans! We are only expressions of the masterplan. So if we take ownership about anything—even 'missing the bus', it is only our wrong understanding. Likewise, if someone else is blaming you: "Because of you we could not catch the bus", that is also utter foolishness. It was not part of the masterplan that all of you would have caught the bus. Do not buy any such blames. You are not at fault. This is one fundamental principle that we must always remember.

I wish you great wisdom to see through the masks of the world. Consider it all as expressions of ignorance. The one who knows needs nothing, even words or appreciation from others. He will be beyond all such pretensions. Be well aware of that. Also understand that all of us are passing through this existence called life. Do not give over-importance to our small steps or seemingly large terrestrial or spiritual achievements. Just be grateful. Just love all. And please take care of the helpless beings of the world. You will have eternal peace and supreme strength.

When The Blind Leads

Wake up, you are in heaven. There are hundreds of rivers. There is one ocean. Even if there are different names for the same ocean, the ocean is one. Names do not matter. The essence matters. The substance matters.

There was a sea captain. He sailed all his life in search of the Pacific Ocean. He could not find this ocean until a wise seafarer told him: "My friend, where you are now, is the Pacific Ocean. It is not some place away from you. This very ocean that you sail on is the Pacific".

We are all sailors in search of an exotic shore. Our search is so intense that we fail to recognize or appreciate how exotic the place below our feet really is!!! The dream merchants sell stories of fanciful lands far, far away. We believe in their dreams and take up the sail. Until we exhaust ourselves, we seldom find out that the journey itself was unnecessary. The dreams that we sailed for were within us, always. All we needed to do was just open our eyes within and look inside. The treasure chest is not outside of us. It always exists within us. Period. All you need is an inner awakening. So, do wake up. Rise and shine!!!

There was a great dreamer. He thrived on selling his dreams.

Lazy pedestrians stopped by and listened to the narration of his enchanting dreams and many even bought these dreams from him. There was one man who came everyday to listen to his dreams. He used to buy and accumulate dreams. His wife got suspicious. Where was he going every day, spending all the money that he earned? She followed him and reached the dream-seller. After every story, her husband paid him some money. That same evening she cautioned her husband. She made him understand that the money that he was spending was emptying their very coffers. She and their children had no more means for further life. He did not change a bit. He was so used to his comfortable routine. So he continued his regular ways. One day, he knew that his house was not his anymore and he and his family were actually thrown out onto the street. He was homeless and had no money to feed himself and his family. He was shaken by reality. He went out to see the dream-seller and told him his real story expecting him to return some of the money that he had paid earlier. The dream-seller said: "I like your story. But I cannot buy it. This is your reality. Not my dream. You yourself must handle your own reality.

Do we buy dreams about the future? Is someone constantly selling us dreams? Beware. Stick to your waking reality. Life does not happen in the future. Life happens NOW. ACT NOW, wisely.

There was one learned man. Every evening this learned man called the villagers and explained many complicated philosophical materials at length. People were awed at his knowledge. They went back home saying: "What a learned man! We are lucky to have him here with us." He was very intelligent and was quite shrewd as well. He knew very well how to manipulate the seekers who came to him, thirsting for guidance. He was a good businessman. He used his power of speech to capture the hearts of the villagers and soon became their chieftain. His ego and arrogance grew along with his possessions and power. He also added a big title to his name and behaved like a spiritual master, as well as a renunciate. He started calling himself an enlightened master. Instead of humility, his ego and arrogance increased.

There was a poor old saint living close to his house. The villagers respected him. He lived on the food that the villagers gave him as alms. In return, he gave them his blessings and free advice. His very presence purified the people and premises. He wore torn clothes and lived in one room.

During the rainy season, water flowed inside drenching the whole room. Even though he was in a pathetic condition, he had no complaints about anything. He accepted his life as it was. The learned man thought that it was time he proved his worth in front of this saint too. He thought that it would add to his respectability and acceptance in society, if the saint was on his side. The learned man arranged for the saint to live in a house close to him—the saint reluctantly agreed—and he behaved as if this was the saint's approval of his knowledge and stature. The poor guy did not understand that the saint's purpose was to put some real wisdom into him and make him benevolent towards the villagers, rather than increasing his arrogance. The saint, with his divine presence, wanted to lighten the darkness of the terrestrial vasanas of the learned man, and make him truly useful for the society. Society never actually needed the dull intellectual heaviness that the learned man poured into them profusely, everyday. It only added to their confusion and never did anyone get enlightened with it. He himself was a pretender who never got enlightened.

Once during his regular, evening session, a boy asked the learned man: "Sir, whom can we call truly healthy?" The saint was also listening to this question. The learned man started explaining health and the status of being healthy, which he had read and remembered from various books. He had only book knowledge to convey. The whole crowd was dissatisfied. Finally, the boy took permission and asked the same question to the saint who had always been a silent spectator of the drama. The saint slowly muttered: "One who eats in limit, one who sleeps in limit, one who acts in limit, one who is not prone to violent emotions, one whose needs are limited, one who never stands to prove anything, one who maintains equanimity, and one who is beyond duality—is the healthiest man in this whole world." Everyone understood clearly. They realized true wisdom in simple terms. True spirituality is simplicity. It has nothing to do with craving for fame, acceptance and fortune. The whole group of listeners applauded the saint's wisdom. The learned man was also humbled in the most natural way.

Our world is full of learned men who pretend to be saints. They have only book knowledge. They have no real experience. They themselves are blinded and they are leading the rest to the ocean of karmic quagmire. It is not in the looks. It is not in the words, but it's in the ability to deliver experiences that makes a teacher become a real guru. Transferable knowledge is aplenty. All one needs is a good memory. Transferring experience needs calibre and real mettle. This is the difference between an acharya and a guru. We call anybody with a white beard a guru. We even give them fancy titles. These acharyas need titles because they are insecure without it. But, where is the real mettle? Titles cannot guarantee stature. Stature has got to be earned only through generations of rigorous spiritual practice. So is enlightenment. Enlightenment has to happen. It will happen only at the appointed time and space. Even if one does all the right spiritual practices, one cannot achieve enlightenment, until he is ripe and ready; until he is established in the beingness. Book knowledge is a big barrier. Ego is another barrier. Samskaras are all barriers. When the vessel is completely empty, divinity fills in. Otherwise, this is another dream like all other dreams. Masters can deliver, but Masters deliver only when the pot is empty. When the pot is empty, a Master will appear to deliver. We need not go searching for one.

The world is full of pretenders, who obscure the real gurus. They are like clouds obscuring the sun. They cannot take away the sun's glory. Sun does not do anything about the clouds. It allows the clouds to stay as long as they want to. Likewise, the real ones seldom come out into the open. Those ones who pretend, do everything possible to make their voice heard. They say one thing and mean another thing, because they are insecure. They are worried about the erosion of their source of income—disciples. They tell you what you like to hear, so that you stick to them. If that's not working, they put fear and guilt into you, so that you will not run away from them. They cannot take you to enlightenment because they themselves are not enlightened. Beware of the pretenders in the path of spirituality, because they are aplenty and they will look more real than the real ones. In the above story, the old saint was real, but, never pretended and he was ignored by the villagers. The empty pot which made the maximum noise was considered as real and revered. This is the truth of life. This is the way our world is. We vote for colour and glamour, which catches our senses and mind. We ignore the often colourless and unpretentious reality which appeals to our spirit. Who cares about the spirit? Shankaracharya said: "Parame Brahmani Kopina sakta" (who cares about our soul, which is eternal)—Alas!!! No one, not even for a moment, considers the soul, the Brahman which resides in oneself, ever in life until one's death . . . , when one has to leave everything and go. But then, unfortunately, it's too late.

I wish you eyes to see and recognize the real truth. If you choose glamour instead of the life transforming Grace and miracle, it is purely at your discretion. No need to regret anything. Just go ahead. The decision is always yours.

DISSOLUTION

Rebirth and Second Coming

THERE IS SO much confusion about rebirth and second coming. Rebirth and reincarnation of one soul will never have the same physical image. Space, time, parents, body and situations are different and hence there will not be any physical resemblance. There will be resemblance in character.

So, do not look for the image that Michelangelo created. There was no photography during Jesus' time. And he was so busy during his short life on earth. He never had enough time to pose for a personal portrait nor would he have cared. Michelangelo is supposed to have created Jesus and Judas from the same model at different times. So, what was Jesus' actual form? Does it matter, as long as we can feel his energy form, even centuries after his exit?

The rebirth or second coming is the same energy or soul taking a body and not the same image. Please do not be misled by thinking that a man in the same costume that people in Jerusalem wore more than 2000 years ago, would come back in the same fashion. It would look like some kind of fancy dress or costume for some carnival. Same energies have reincarnated in the past. Sri Rama came back as Sri Krishna. He did not come back again as Sri Rama II. The one who writes this and all those who read this have also come back many times in the past. We were all in different places, at different times, with different parents, different genders and for different purposes. Nothing was ever the same.

For a true Master the mission in its grandest sense is the same: to lead the blind to the light. From the darkness of ignorance to the light of awareness. That's the purpose. Masters keep appearing time and time again to talk to the then new people. To discuss contemporary issues and to suggest solutions. To lead from the quagmire of mundane existence to the lightness of higher living.

So second coming is sure and is happening always. As Krishna consciousness happens again and again with each generation. Just as Dattatreya keeps coming back in different forms and bodies, as Jesus consciousness continues to perform with as much efficiency as he displayed when in his physical body or even more, as Shirdi Sai makes himself present at more places than Shirdi after he shed his body, great souls keep coming back through various bodies to lead from darkness to light. Their methods, style and pattern of action often betray their true stature. Otherwise, they will never reveal their true selves. They behave and live their life in extraordinary simplicity. It is very difficult to know a true Master, unless he chooses to reveal himself. Some even exist in wilderness and work silently. Some work amidst the market place. Knowing them and recognising them is difficult. Once you recognise them and feel them, to leave them is also difficult. We get attracted to the fire of wisdom like flies getting attracted to fire. We burn our ego in their presence. Since they are here to liberate, they shake the trees often to shed the dry leaves. Some fruits get thrown around too.

Some have chosen blindness. None can lead them anywhere. They have to shed their spiritual blindness on their own. There is no hurry. There are numerous life times ahead to perform in detail and to work out the samskaras. So let us not push people. Let them walk their strides.

Dissolution and Enlightenment

Q: Can you talk about dissolution in comparison to enlightenment?

M: Enlightenment takes the awareness to the level of the

soul. One who is enlightened understands the symmetry of the larger life behind his regular existence. Enlightenment does not automatically take one to dissolution. Dissolution is still an ongoing process. Dissolution is a sheath by sheath process. Impressions of numerous lifetimes have got stuck in the web of existence and sheaths. In the place of action, impressions of thoughts, words and actions of generations lay preparing the rope for further action. Just like the external world, our internal world also has similar patterns lying deeply embedded to bring forth life to thought, word or action. True liberation happens only once deep and complete cleansing happens on various levels. Enlightenment helps this process, because the awareness is much higher at that state and it gives clarity, understanding and, essentially, objectivity from emotions. Aside from the embedded impressions from the sheaths, detachment from elements is also essential. This happens by itself. When awareness improves, the elements—which are gross in nature—release their grip slowly and steadily. Remember, the lure of the terrestrial world is always waiting outside the doors of your senses. You have to constantly fight them with higher awareness and not by suppression. Suppression is not eradication. Existence without temptations—not needing any of it, even if it is available—is what helps this process.

Higher awareness is the key to detachment. When the grip of elements is less, man's dependency on food, water, and a prescribed space for existence also gives way. He can then survive on universal energy. Ancient Masters have mastered the art of surviving without food or water and thought process. This is possible and indeed real. So, path of dissolution is long and winding. But eventually, everyone must walk this path.

Q: Can complete dissolution happen in one lifetime?

M: Yes. But it does not happen because emotions and attachments creep in with each new life, even if we are very careful and controlled. How could Menaka lure Vishwamitra into having a physical relationship with her? So, the path is very, very narrow and risky. It usually takes life times to eradicate all impressions, desires and dreams to liberate the man from the need to be on earth. If the desires are earthly, man keeps coming back. The final is the debt that he must repay for using the facilities of the earth. That can be achieved only through selfless service for mother earth and her children, which means all beings. The tool for accomplishing that is unconditional love. Complete liberation is a process. The deeper the silence in the Master, the deeper is His detachment. Desire to prove or talk is only on the surface, and that too, just towards the shore, like waves of the ocean.

If a man talks too much, usually, he is surface-oriented and does not have much depth. He will come back again and again till silence deepens and takes over. Silence does not mean physical silence. Silence means the silence within or lack of any mental activity. Switching over to dharmic life precedes complete liberation. He will need nothing from earth. He will give all what he has to the earth and its children. His existence will not hurt the earth. It will only soothe the earth. His walking on earth will make the trees, plants and animals of the earth rejoice. Big cleansing happens to everyone and everything, just by His sheer presence and existence.

What do Masters Want?

Nothing. They are just road signs. Their purpose is to guide you to your destination. If you chose to use the road sign or chose to ignore it and walk your path yourself, it is the same for any real Master. It does not make any difference to the true Master. Only one caution. Do not confuse an acharya with a Guru. An acharya is only an exponent of knowledge. A Guru or Master is the manifested representation of the invisible Almighty. Acharyas who have only book knowledge or theoretical knowledge pose as enlightened Masters and lure people for money. Have you seen any great Master of the past calling himself enlightened? Take the case of Ramana Maharshi, Shirdi Sai Baba, Akkalkot Maharaj, Manik Prabhu, Bhagawan Nithyananda of Ganeshpuri, Sathya Sai Baba and all those truly powerful Masters—they never called themselves enlightened. They never promised enlightenment to anyone because everyone has to go through life times of cleansing to attain liberation, and they positioned themselves on earth to guide us unconditionally. Now, the tragedy is, acharyas or teachers who have no originality, call themselves enlightened, promise enlightenment and hang victims on pretensions. They keep articulating theoretical knowledge and pretend it to be their own experience. Their method of holding on to people is through fear and control. These acharyas will scan the market, identify what sells and package that in their own syllabus. They do not care about the consumer. They change their stance according to market demand. If giving Shaktipat sells, they will start giving Shaktipat and initiate disciples into it. If Pranayam sells, they make modules of it. If Hatha Yoga sells, they will teach it. Thus, they remain very flexible and observant. This is the tragedy of our times. Every acharya pretends to be an enlightened guru. Dresses up accordingly, speaks accordingly and misleads masses. Everything has become commerce—spirituality too.

Spirituality is dharma.

It is sacred. It is individualistic. It is not for sale.

I wish all of you LIBERATION in this lifetime.

Stay liberated, operate in unconditional love, be love.

The Path of Pathlessness

We are following the path of Siddhas which is 'The Path of Pathlessness'. This path is the path of annihilation, of shedding. In this path, there are no routines. Rituals are of no importance. Methods are important, just like a particular combination makes a good curry. If the combination is different, the curry is different too. To understand this path, please read the stories of Shirdi Sai

Baba or Bhagawan Nithyananda of Ganeshpuri (Bade Baba). Our dedication is to the Guru Tattva—the principle that is the Guru.

Guru Tattva

The Guru principle is like the ever flowing Ganges. It keeps flowing, through various cities, nourishing various regions and beings. The Guru principle began when life began. Guru Tattva operates through any being, any mouth and any words that matter to us, time to time. Just like different teachers guided you in different classes, aiding you to reach the higher levels, the Guru Principle works through various beings and helps us climb steps to higher awareness. Guru Tattva flows eternally. Nobody can deny this. All external teachers are only representing this principle. Our soul also represents this principle. God represents this principle. That is why we say Guru is God. Guru is transitory. Guru changes from class to class, or time to time. The principle never changes.

The Guru principle travels through eternity and takes any mouth to convey the wisdom. The mouth is not important as it is transitory. The message it conveys is important for you. Trust the message. Cherish the message. Experience the messages. They are the eternal truths. This will help liberation. Marry the wisdom, not the Guru.

Guru is a tattva—a principle. Guru is not a man or a woman. Guru Tattva flows through time. Terrestrial communication needs tangibility, a body. So Guru happens in human form too, so that people can identify and understand. Everybody is a Guru to somebody. The eternal principle of Guru flows through everybody. Everybody has at least one Guru. Every Guru had a Guru, the one who helped destroy the darkness and ignorance of the limited conscious mind. Soul itself is a Guru. The true Guru, personal Guru of every being is its Soul. Guru could be an object, a message or a thought. Since Guru is a principle it could also be a telepathic communication or a communion. Guru appears when the disciple is eligible. Guru happens when the disciple is ready for that knowledge. When questions arise in mind, sooner or later, the answers appear. When questions block our natural evolution, information or advice happens through some one. Guru principle is beyond body. The supreme Guru is Parabrahma, the eternal Father or Allah. Starting from Him, there are many many mouths that convey the eternal principles of existence or the laws of the universe. The Guru principle will eternally flow. In order to accept and accent the Guru principle, all we need are egoless-ness and surrender. No judgment—just an open mind. That's enough.

Guru tattva will flow through us, washing away all our mental confusions and will always guide us. The moment we feel we know a lot or even worse, we know everything, the principle that is Guru can deliver nothing to us. So the childlike wonder in us will work wonders, as the eternal Guru principle will take us to the highest possible, in one lifetime. Guru principle is based on unconditional love. It is based on zero expectations and complete benevolence. Pranaams to the great Guru principle that eternally flows like Ganga.

Equanimity

Our tradition teaches us the path of equanimity as the best path. A perfect balance through happiness and sorrow. If a seeker approaches spirituality with extreme equanimity, he will be well balanced in Guru Tattva, with supreme gratitude to existence and all the mouths that expound the tattva. If emotion is driving the seeker, and especially if doer-ship is predominant in him, he will tend to get attached to the image of the Guru. They miss the tattva and fall for the Guru. They build expectations and mental images. When the images fail to hold, they fall flat too. Many get disillusioned. Many get out of disillusionment and finally leave their need for the stick and start to walk on their own, thereafter.

The Path of Liberation

Our tradition has always accented liberation from the birth and death cycle. Our tradition never bound anyone to any system. It allowed free choices to everyone. This is the true path. In this path, the Guru, our Soul and the God are one and the same. Our soul is our primary Guru. The external Guru is only an exponent of the eternal principle called Guru Tattva. In the path of liberation, sooner or later, the image, name and form must get nullified and the tattva should shine bright. So whatever image that we hold on to for our immediate progress, like our class teacher, will vanish and will be replaced by another and another until the completion of our journey.

The Path of liberation is always the path of annihilation. Everything, including our body, mind and intellect must perish and dissolve, sooner or later.

MOHANJI

Q & A

Q: You are expressing the qualities of Baba, which we have observed consistently, with the exception of materialization or some miracles. Why can't you just say that you are part of Baba? Why are you not declaring that?

M: Why can't you say that you are part of Baba? I have not seen one soul on earth who is not part of Baba. Then, how can I say that only I am part of Baba? When I look around, I see only His expressions. It's all Baba. If Baba is Parabrahma or the Father, you and I are all part of the same Parabrahma. The moment I start alienating myself from others, how can I ever work through you? How can I work on you? Understand that all beings are expression of one supreme Almighty. You can call it Baba or Allah or Krishna or Jesus. You are that. Another important aspect is that there is nothing to prove for me or you. There is none neither superior nor inferior. Everyone is a bundle of gunas (operational principle), except those who are self-realized.

I should be worried only if I have to keep a certain reputation. In this path of evolution, it's all about changes. Movements lead to the stage of beingness, where external movements do not affect internal stillness. Mind does not drag the being. Being stays put while mind wanders, if at all. Then the mind gets tired and surrenders to the being. Then, senses and mind are in tune with the being, which we call self-realization. Sensory objects do not affect you anymore. The presence or absence of an entity or material is the same for you. You are in bliss state always. You will not be worried about what others think of you nor will you speculate about other souls who are only acting out their own karma. You are in peace with all beings.

Q: What is your relevance in our lives?

M: Same as your relevance in my life. Nobody is inferior or superior, if that is what you meant by this question. Every life has the same value, because essentially, it's all part of one life and maya (illusion) is making it seem dual. All have the same importance. Each does their part in this huge show called life. Importance is a need of the ego. When you keep your ego under constant watch, you will not crave for importance. Tomorrow, if nobody cares for me, I will still remain the same.

My Philosophy

I have only one philosophy, one message, one religion—Universal Love. I am by birth a Brahmin, by nature a Kshatriya, and used to be by profession a Vaishya. Thus, I transcend all natures. Gunas form characters and characters form religions. There are good and bad in all communities. In absolute sense, there is no good or bad. In relative sense, there is good and bad. There is duality. We attract the realities close to our innate nature. Our innate nature is not fully visible to outsiders and ourselves. Only about 20% is visible even to us. 80% lies hidden. We meet the people whom we deserve to meet. We arrive at situations according to our innate nature. There is duality in all. Only goodness and only 'badness' does not exist. They only exist in relative terms, in degrees. What is more predominant becomes visible to oneself and the society.

All of us believe what we are doing is right, always right even though we do not realize it is relative right. We also believe that what others are doing is wrong against your right. This often creates stress and conflicts.

Nature has punished wrongdoings categorically. If you look at history, you will see that. Mongolian tribes attacked and massacred many in 1400-1600s. I am sure you have heard about Ghengis Khan etc. The Japanese army did most of their experiments on live human beings (unit 731) in Mongolia and China. They wreaked havoc in Nanking, where they massacred women and children. America used the atomic bomb on Japan. America suffered in Vietnam, Iraq, Afghanistan and elsewhere. Aggression always gets punished. It may take some time because the offenders often have to die and come back in another body to suffer what they inflicted on others. Nature waits patiently. This is also applicable to cruelty against animals and other beings. We suffer what we inflict on others, in this life or the next. No doubt. In the absolute sense, there is no difference between men, animals or birds. It's only different equipment, one soul. So, the more we consider ourselves superior, the more we will have problems. If we consider ourselves as fellow beings and truly a part of the macrostructure and approach everything with kindness and love, life will be smooth and more peaceful.

Love is the only balm. Love is the only remedy. Unconditionality is the only method that will work in the long term.

I do not believe in castes, creeds, colors, communities and country barriers. I believe in the universality of the soul and its expression through various forms. I see them all as one. One soul, different equipment. Same feelings, same emotions, same ego. When we cut across all seeming dualities, it's one entity smiling through all. No difference. One Almighty in all its wonderful diversities!

The Journey

My aim and purpose of existence is to serve the universe, through all my diverse expressions. My thoughts, words and actions are only meant to help you understand different realms of existence. Some of you do not need them, because you already know all that. This is quite understandable as each person is at his or her own level of evolution. We cannot and must not compare people's statures. Never will the same words work on two different individuals in exactly the same way. I do not want to and will never recommend anybody to stay and listen out of compulsion or some kind of fear. We are a fearless community. Let's stay fearless—and in absolute unconditional love.

I do not want to give you any promises. I do not want to make you dependent on me either. My mission is to liberate you from all kinds of fears and bindings, to show you realms that I have experienced and to guide you the way I can, so that you also experience the same.

Some of you are constantly asking me to explain my relationship with Baba (meaning the supreme Almighty = all the Masters). Let me tell you, it's the same relationship that you have with Baba. There is no difference between you and me. If you believe that I am connected to Baba, understand that it will only satisfy your mind which needs definite explanations. If you feel that I am not connected at all to Baba, it's the same. For me, whatever you think of me, whether it is positive or negative, is the same. I am not bound by opinions. I am mission-driven, not opinion-driven. Why should I deliberately create an image? Why do we put people in certain compartments? Why can't we just let them be? Each individual is God Himself. Man minus ego/mind = GOD. We must remember this always.

Images only bind us and restrict us. I am not interested in claiming anything. Why should I? If an image has to happen, let it happen automatically. I have nothing to prove or disprove here. What do I gain by pretending?

Understand that status can be bought, if you have the money. Stature can never be bought with money. One needs to attain spiritual stature, through sadhana and divine grace. Status is like your qualification. Stature is like your experiences. You gain experience only through hard work and time. You cannot buy it. Nor can experience be taken away from you, whereas you could be stripped of your certificates and status, if things go wrong. So, status should automatically happen due to one's stature. Then it's permanent. On the other hand, if status is created, it's temporary, because without stature, it will crumble and fall, sooner or later.

If you had experiences through the practices that we do, I am more than blessed. If you blocked the energy flow because the physical frame in front of you did not suit your mental frame of a Master, I have no complaints either. That's the experience that you wanted and you got it.

I appreciate your questions which show your thinking mind and I hope my answers are useful too. Some people are shy to share their thoughts and they are calling me to explain things or sending me mails. It is impossible to attend to all the mails. I would recommend sharing your true spiritual experiences with others because it will clarify the thoughts of others who have had similar experiences, or at least write a daily spiritual diary. Mind creates doubts usually. It's the mind's job to create doubts. It's your intellect's job to get out of it through proper reasoning. So, shift to your intellect when fears and doubts plague you initially, and to your 360 degrees awareness to eradicate all negativities. Fears are formed out of emotions. Intellect always stays above emotions and fears. True awareness is beyond that too.

I have received many mails after some of our meditators shared their reports. I know that their messages have helped people to see higher realms. These messages have cleared many doubts and increased clarity. So, why not share? It also means seva (selfless service). We must appreciate that. Nobody is looking for any personal gains here. Writing reaffirms your experience. Usually we deny our own experience because others tell us that it cannot be true. This is equal to self-denial. Others' words are others' words, including mine. Your experience is the only thing real to you. So, never let your books or your friends influence your thoughts and make you disown your own experiences. This would affect your evolution. Also, always live with gratitude for all these blessings—all these experiences. It will take you higher. Thank the Masters who came and guided you. Gratitude is one quality which guarantees spiritual progress.

I wish you great evolution and bliss.

APPENDICES

About Mohanji

(Compilation of descriptions by those who have and are experiencing his Grace.)

It is very difficult to define who Mohanji is. He cannot be framed easily because he walks a path that he terms as the Pathless Path—of non-conformity, with neither bounds nor rituals, and with the sole aim of liberation by lifting the seeker's consciousness. Mohanji is multidimensional.

His existence is completely purpose bound. He is a Siddha in an ordinary human form.

Mohanji is a Master who constantly makes us aware that 'The Spiritual Master is a principle, not the body'. One may never understand him fully if one only looks at or gets attached to Mohanji's form or physical frame. To understand him and feel his presence, one has to tap into his consciousness through his eyes. How true it is when Mohanji says: "Marry the consciousness, which is permanent and unshakeable. Never marry any Guru". Just reading his words is not enough. One has to live his teachings with constant awareness, on daily basis.

Mohanji is completely selfless. He operates from a very high, expanded consciousness, while at the same time balancing that with all the rules and limitations of the body's physical form, the business world he works in and other societal constraints. Due to his simple, accessible, humble, unassuming, down-to-earth and modest nature, the higher qualities of his existence can be recognized only by those who have the subtlety to perceive them.

The plane in which Mohanji operates and the magnanimity of his operations are difficult to explain. What he has to offer can only be experienced according to one's connectivity and receptivity with him.

Mohanji expresses many Masters, and many Masters express through him. He always says that in terms of consciousness they are all One.

Mohanji's eyes are the gateway to his consciousness. All required is that one connects with his eyes (download photo from www. mohanji.org) with full faith and deep surrender for a few minutes daily and just be receptive.

Mohanji's Grace flows and one can experience it. It does not matter where a person is on this Earth. Miracles follow. Answers happen. Calamities dissolve. Cures happen.

Being in the physical form at present, Mohanji is performing his duties as a son, husband, brother and spiritual guide. However, despite all these duties, he manages to deliver life-transforming, authentic experiences to all those who connect with him.

His Grace is to be experienced.

Mohanji Foundation

The mission of Mohanji Foundation is based on the timeless tradition of unconditional love. With Faith and Purity as its pillars, this group aims at creating a movement of unconditionality-going beyond all man-made barriers of caste, creed, color, culture, community, country and religion.

Mohanji Foundation thus aims at lifting people's consciousness, inspiring all members of society to operate from the level of unconditional love and to surrender to Existence with utmost faith and purity. Experiential Spirituality is therefore at the very heart of this movement.

Mohanji Foundation expresses its mission in two main ways:

- "By conducting meditations and satsangs (spiritual gatherings) free of cost in order to develop a deeper understanding of one's existence and cleanse the blockages that prevent our full blossoming. Our meditations are growing in popularity and at present being conducted in satsangs in Oman, UAE, India, Germany, Serbia, South Africa, UK and USA and also individually across the globe with sizeable followers mainly in Qatar, UK, Croatia, Greece, Latvia, USA, and South Africa besides many other countries. There are many who practice the meditations individually. When practicing individually, all one has to do is to connect to Mohanji through his eyes as explained above and receive Shaktipat from him astrally as Mohanji continuously exists and operates in an expanded consciousness state.

- The Power of Purity Meditation (POP), the 360 Degrees meditation and the Blossoms of Love meditation are freely downloadable at www.mohanji.org The POP meditation is presently available in English, French, Spanish, Russian, Serbian and in a few of the Indian languages like Hindi, Malayalam, Tamil and Marathi. Power of Purity is much more than a meditation—it is more of a deep communion with yourself.

- In our meditation sessions during satsangs, all meditators receive Shaktipat (transfer of consciousness from the higher realms of the divine existence to the gross level of human existence). Shaktipat is a completely safe and totally effective and ancient Indian method of cleansing past life baggages or karmas. Shaktipat is delivered by Mohanji personally or by the people (the initiates) whom Mohanji initiated into performing Shaktipat. In terms of higher consciousness, these initiates can be considered as Mohanji having created himself. This is because during Shaktipat delivery, these initiates shift to and operate in Mohanji's consciousness. There are no rules or regulations which meditators should follow. Just as we take a bath everyday to keep ourselves clean, similarly, we meditate to keep our inner space clean and rejuvenated.

- By encouraging and conducting selfless service (Seva) initiatives. These activities are expressions of love and purity and are done without expectation in return or any attachment to the results. With utmost purity and transparency, everyone is encouraged not only to just offer thoughts or words but ACT to focus on providing food, shelter, clothing, medical/nursing care, empowerment through education, and other ways of serving and uplifting the helpless and needy.

GLOSSARY

2012 shift Shift of consciousness.

Aagamya Accumulated or acquired in the current life in the context of karma.

Acharya One who imparts knowledge.

Adi Guru Refers to Lord Shiva as Dakshinamoorty. It also refers to Lord Dattatraya.

Adi Shankaracharya An Indian philosopher who also is believed to be an incarnation of Lord Shiva. He consolidated the doctrine of Advaita (non-dual) Vedanta philosophy. He simplified Upanishad, Bhagavat Geeta and set up monasteries in various locations in India. He also set up temples and codified the worship systems.

Agni Fire.

Agnihotra It is an offering to fire. It is a Vedic ritual or fire sacrifice performed in orthodox Hindu communities. This is a sacred tradition started by the 'Rishis' of ancient India. It is an aggregation of meditation, remembering the name of the Lord, act of devotion, surrender and Yoga. The tradition is handed down the generations by Agnihotries and fire is kept burning alive in their house through generations. Fire is a purifying element that keeps us alive.

Ahimsa Nonviolence.

Ajna chakra It is chakra (*see chakra*) positioned between eyebrows and also called the 'third eye'.

Akash Ether.

Akkalkot Maharaj Believed to be an incarnation of Lord Datta-treya (*see Dattatreya tradition*) the name of this spiritual master, popularly called Swami Samarth.

Anahata Heart chakra.

Apsaras Celestial beauties/dancers in the court of Lord Indra.

Arjuna Third in the order of five Pandavas. Close friend of Lord Krishna.

Ashram A hermitage.

AUM or OM. Hindus believe that as creation began, the divine, all-encompassing consciousness took the form of the first and original vibration manifesting as sound "AUM". Before creation began it was Shunyakasha the emptiness or the void. Shunyaka-sha, meaning literally "no sky", is more than nothingness, because everything then existed in a latent state of potentiality. The vibra-tion of "AUM" symbolizes the manifestation of God in form ("*saguna brahman*"). "AUM" is the reflection of the absolute real-ity, it is said to be "Adi Anadi", without beginning or the end and embracing all that exists. The mantra "AUM" is the name of God, the vibration of the Supreme. When taken letter by letter, A-U-M represents the divine energy (*Shakti*) united in its three elemen-tary aspects: Bhrahma Shakti (*creation*), Vishnu Shakti (*preserva-tion*) and Shiva Shakti (*liberation, and/or destruction*).

Aura An aura is a field of subtle, luminous radiation surrounding a person or object like the halo

Avadhoot A complete and total renunciate. A traditional Indian term for one who has "shaken off" or "passed beyond" all worldly attachments and cares, including all motives of detachment (*or conventional and other-worldly renunciation*), all conventional notions of life and religion, and all seeking for "answers" or "solutions" in the form of conditional experience or conditional knowledge.

Baba Father as the omnipresent almighty and its finite forms such as Shirdi Sai Baba, and other nameless Masters.

Babaji The immortal yogi of the Kriya Yoga tradition referred as Mahaavatar in the Autobiography of Yogi.

Bhagavad Gita The Bhagavad Gita (*Song of God*), also more simply known as Gita, is a Hindu scripture produced from the colloquy given by Sri Krishna to Arjuna during the Kurukshetra War. Its philosophies and insights are intended to reach beyond the scope of religion and to humanity as a whole. It is at times referred to as the "manual for mankind".

Bhagawan The Supreme Being or Absolute Truth, but with specific reference to that Supreme Being as possessing a personality

Bhagawan Nithyananda A great Siddha Avadhoota who lived in Ganeshpuri, India until 1961 in his Physical body, an Indian Sadguru (*see sadguru*).

Bhagawan Ramana Maharshi Of Arunachala hills. A great Rishi of the celestial order.

Bhakta Devotee.

Bhakti Devotion.

Bhakti yoga Devotion as the path of spirituality.

Bhishma Son of Mother Ganga, and is one of the strongest characters of the Mahabharata. He was the grandfather of both the Pandavas and the Kauravas.

Bhoganathar Siddha Bhoganathar is considered to be the Guru of Babaji. His Samadhi is in Palani, Tamil Nadu. He is immortal, just like His famous disciple. Bhoganathar and His disciples are still supposed to be meditating inside the caves of the hills of Palani. It is also considered that Bhoganathar created the idol of Lord Muruga, the presiding deity of Palani Hill. The idol is made out of nine types of herbs or 9 poisons (*Nava Paashaan*), which individually have the capacity to kill, but if combined in a particular proportion, becomes the medicine for any type of disease. This is called Siddha-Oushadh (*Siddha Medicine*). It is also said that Siddha Bhoganathar created the idol of Muruga in the form of the youthful Babaji, His favorite disciple.

Brahma Is one of the three predominant deities representing creation, maintenance and destruction. Brahma creator of the trinity.

Brahma Muhurtha Approximately 3 am to 6 am.

Brahman Individual Soul, the soul inside the man, the Supreme Universal Spirit that is the origin and support of the phenomenal universe; Universal soul or Para Brahman.

Brahmin Priestly class considered to be the upper class in the Indian society.

Buddhi Intellect

Causal body The Causal body—originally *Karana-Sarira*—is a Yogic and Vedantic concept. This is the space where seeds of all traits of human character exist.

Chakra Transformers through which *pranic* energy flows and which channels energy and nourishes various parts of our system. They form part of a subtle energy body, along with the energy channels, or naadis, and the subtle winds, or pranas. They are located along a central nadi, Sushumna, which runs either alongside or inside the spine. Two other nadis, Ida and Pingala, also run through the chakras, and alongside Sushumna. They occasionally cross Sushumna at the location of the chakras. They possess a number of 'petals' or 'spokes'. In some traditions, such as the Tibetan, these spokes branch off into the thousands of nadis that run throughout the human body. They are generally associated with a mantra seed-syllable, and often with a variety of colours and deities. Seven primary chakras are commonly described (*see Mantras and Chakras under Why Meditation in Chapter 8 Meditation and Satsang in the text*).

Chillum Is a kind of narrow funnel, which is used for smoking.

Communion/s Telepathic conversation with higher entities.

Crore 10 million.

Daan Giving without expectation or recognition.

Dakshinaayan A period of six months when the Sun's direction is towards South.

Dattatreya Avatar Dattatreya is the Adi Guru who incarnated through times to serve the world. Some of the incarnations are Shripad Shri Vallabh, Sri Narasimha Saraswati, Shree Swami Samartha and Sri Sai Baba of Shirdi.

Dattatreya tradition The tradition which begins with Lord Dattatreya. Lord Dattatreya is a very ancient incarnation, highly venerated through the ages. Dattatreya—a Universal Guru manifested in the time of Kaliyug, when humanity had fallen far from its pristine state and all kinds of vices had already taken root. With dharma in decay, the pious souls made fervent appeals for the salvation of mankind. He descended on this earth to establish Satya *(the Universal Truth)* and Dharma *(the perennial principles)*, in all its entirety.

Dharma Eternal principles of existence, the basic ground rules of creation.

Dharmic mode Shift towards the mode of Dharma, extreme selflessness.

Dhyana Meditation. In Dhyan yoga, the main accent is on meditation or self.

Dwarakamayi The abode of Shirdi Sai Baba.

Ennui Tedium or tiredness due to repetitive actions.

Etheric One of the 7 bodies/layers in the human energy field or aura.

Fr. Anthony de Mello Author of "1 minute wisdom".

FYI For your information.

Gandhiji Mahatma Gandhi—Father of the Indian Nation.

Ganges Mother Ganga the most sacred river worshipped in the Hindu tradition.

Guna/s Our primary qualities and operating tendencies or nature. The primary gunas are Sattva, Rajas and Tamas.

Guru One who exists in altered consciousness state and delivers as per the requirement of the disciple. He raises the consciousness of the disciple by his presence. Guru is not an acharya or an exponent of an acquired knowledge.

Guru Poornima Is a full moon festival dedicated to Guru of one's tradition. It falls on the day of full moon, *Poornima,* in the Hindu month of *Ashadha (June-July).*

Guru Tattva The guru principle.

God Generate, Operate and Destroy, Parabrahma, Allah or Father.

Hanumanji Hindu deity, who is an ardent devotee of Rama, a central character in the Indian epic *Ramayana.*

Hatha Yoga Is the yoga of physical purification.

Higher Masters *see Sadguru*

Homa/s Offering materials into fire with specific chanting of mantras for specific purposes.

Jagadguru World guru.

Jai Hail, to cheer, salute, or greet.

Jal Water.

Jivatma Individual soul; Unit of Brahman

Jnana Knowledge.

Jnana yoga Knowledge as Path of Spirituality.

Jnanendriyas Five sense organs viz: ear, skin, eye, tongue and nose.

Jnyana or gnyana Knowledge.

Karka Sankranti Is the day when Sun embarks its journey to the southern hemisphere which is known as Dakshinaayan (*see*) in Hindu parlance.

Karma/s Engrams, baggage.

Karma yoga Selfless action as Path of Spirituality.

Karma yogi One who practices karma yoga.

Karmendriyas Five organs of action, viz., speech, hands, legs, genitals and anus.

Karmic being Is an average individual whose existence is controlled karma.

Kathopanishad Is the conversation between Nachiketa and Yamraj (*God of death*). Nachiketa was a seeker, and Yamraj was a Guru (*knower of secrets*).

Koshas Layers of our being.

Krishna or Sri Krishna Avatar of Lord Vishnu, the key character of epic Mahabharata, exponent of Bhagvad Gita.

Kriya Any action.

Kriya yoga Ancient Yoga system revived in modern times by Mahavatar Babaji through his disciple Lahiri Mahasaya, c. 1861, and brought into popular awareness through Paramhamsa Yogananda's book *Autobiography of a Yogi*. The system consists of a number of levels of Pranayama based on techniques that are intended to rapidly accelerate spiritual development and engender a profound state of tranquility and God-communion.

Kshatriya Meaning warrior, is one of the four varnas (*social orders*) in Hinduism.

Kshethra Temple or the body.

Kshethrajna Deity or tenant or in dweller or the soul.

Kundalini A sleeping, dormant potential force in the human system. It is described as 3 ½ coiled serpent usually existing below the Mooladhara chakra.

Laya Complete merger in consciousness.

Lord Dakshinamoorthy Shiva as the supreme Guru. Shiva as the supreme and all encompassing knowledge. An aspect of supreme consciousness of wisdom of creation.

Lord Shiva The dissolver aspect of trinity of the Hindu tradition.

Maha Guru Guru of Gurus.

Mahaavtar Babaji see Babaji.

Makar-Sankranti The transition of the Sun from *Dhanu rashi* (Sagittarius) to *Makara rashi* (Capricorn). Traditionally, this has been one of many harvest days in India.

Manana Contemplation.

Manik Prabhu One of the Dattatreya avatars.

Mantra A mantra is a sound, syllable, word, or group of words that are considered capable of "creating spiritual transformation".

Master/s Guru. *Also see Sadguru.*

Mata Mother.

Mata Amrithanandamayi An enlightened spiritual Guru in her own right. She is also called as "Amma" or "Ammachi".

Maya Illusion.

Menaka One of the apsaras (*see Apsara*).

Moksha Is complete liberation from *Samsara (see)* and the concomitant suffering involved in being subject to the cycle of repeated death and reincarnation.

Mother Ganga Refers to Ganges which is the second largest river on the Indian subcontinent by discharge. The 2,510 km (1,560 miles) river rises in the western Himalayas in the Indian state of Uttarakhand. It has long been considered holy by Hindus and worshiped as the goddess *Ganga* in Hinduism.

Mukti Liberation *same as* Moksha (see).

Naadi/s Meridians. Energy channels which are a part of the subtle energy body.

Nachiketas Nachiketa was a seeker. Kathopanishad deals with the conversation between Nachiketa and Yamraj (*God of death*) where Yamraj was a Guru (*knower of secrets*).

Nagas Higher celestial entities operating in the form of snakes.

Navnath Lord Krishna instructed nine higher entities to carry forward His mission of Dharma on the Earth. They are called the Navanath Sadhus. The tradition began from Lord Dattatreya. Navanath tradition consists of Machhindranath, Gorakshanath, Jalandharnath, Kanifnath, Gahininath, Bhartrinathor Bhartarinath or Raja Bhartari, Revananath, Charpatinath and Naganathor Nageshnath and numerous known and unknown Saints also fall into this tradition.

Nirvana Moksha (*see*).

Nisargadatta Maharaj An Indian spiritual teacher and philosopher of Advaita (Non-dualism), and a Guru, belonging to the Inchgiri branch of the Navnath (see) Sampradaya.

Om see AUM

Panchagni Panchagni literally means five fires. People used to do repentance (Prayaschitta) or cleansing through five fires; four fires lit by us and the Sun as the fifth used for cleaning five internal negative fires such as passion, anger, greed, attachment and jealousy. This means endurance and cleansing the conscience. The panchagni during Uttaraayan triggers light and liberation for the soul. Dakshinaayan denotes rebirth and return to life on earth.

Parabrahma The Father, The Supreme God.

Paramhamsa Supreme swan who cannot or will not touch the earth. It is a high and lofty state of existence. In the Hindu mythology, swan flies very high in the sky, lays egg in the sky while flying, when egg falls down, before it touches the earth it hatches and baby flies away. It can never accept gross. It is also a title conferred to great saints who exists at that high level.

Paramahamsa Yogananda Author of *Autobiography of a Yogi*. A great exponent of Kriya Yoga.

Paramatma The Supreme Father.

Parthi Sai Baba Satya Sai Baba.

Pashupati vratha Worship using panchagni (*see*) dedicated to the Supreme saint Shiva.

Patanjali Compiler of Yog Sutras, one of the 18 Siddhas in the Kriya Yoga tradition.

PETA People for Ethical Treatment of Animals www.peta.org

Praayaschittha Repentance.

Prana Soul element.

Pranayam Is a Sanskrit word meaning "extension of the prana or breath" or more accurately, "extension of the life force". The word is composed of two Sanskrit words, Prana, life force, or vital energy, particularly, the breath, and "ayama", to extend or draw out.

Pranic Of prana (*vital life*).

Prarabdha Responsibility.

Prarabdha karma The karma that provoked the birth. It provided us with this constitution, including the mind, intellect and character. Destiny is prarabdha karma, the karma that created this birth.

Prithvi The earth.

Puja Worship.

Raavan/Ravana The king of Sri Lanka and the primary antagonist in the Ramayana. Ravana is described as a devout follower of Shiva, a great scholar, a capable ruler and a maestro of the Veena. He has his apologists and staunch devotees within the Hindu traditions, some of whom believe that his description as a *ten-headed person* is a reference to him possessing a very thorough knowledge over the 4 Vedas and 6 Upanishads, which made him as powerful as 10 scholars.

Rahim Refers to attributes of the One. Often translated simply as compassionate. Describes that aspect of the source which is issued forth only in response to the actions and behavior of the recipient.

It is in this manner that God takes ten steps toward us when we take even a single step toward God. Rahim conveys the idea of constant renewal and giving liberal reward in response to the quality of our deeds and thoughts. According to Ibn Qayyum (1350 AD), Rahim expresses the continuous manifestation of the Grace in our lives and its effect upon us as a result of our own activities.

Rajas One of the three *gunas (see)* in the Samkhya school of Hindu philosophy which is responsible for motion, energy and preservation and thereby upholds and maintains the activity of the other two gunas, known as Sattva and tamas.

Rajasic One who manifests qualities of Rajas (*see*).

Rama/Ram The sought, the guna-less. Lord Rama was the seventh incarnation of Lord Vishnu and a central figure in the Ramayana epic.

Rama Krishna Paramahamsa An enlightened Indian Sadguru (*see*). He was the guru of Swami Vivekananda.

Ramana Maharshi *see* Bhagawan Ramana Maharshi.

Renunciate Having everything but not needing or be dependent on anything.

Saakshi Bhaav State of witness-hood.

Sadguru A complete Guru, highest of Gurus. He is selfless and compassionate. He is the one who perpetually exists on guna less state (*beyond Tamas, Rajas and Sattvic guna [see]*) or being state and completely detached from the being state. He elevates consciousness of disciples through his thought, words and action at all times. He has no expectation and is objective and purpose bound at all times. Sadgurus or Perfect Masters or Higher Masters are in reality, the seers who have realized the Absolute or have reached the highest realm of spiritual attainment, are present for ever in the whole universe whether in an embodied or in an unembodied state. They can operate in gross, subtle, or mental world. They have been actually chosen to execute the Divine Mission and for that, free from individual ego, work together for the execution of the Divine Mission. A Sadguru is the one who leads the created to the creator. Their actions are universal in nature cutting across religions, nations and all divisions of society. In fact the descent of the Divine in human form is to create conditions for the human to ascend to his Divine essence. Everything that happens is but the expression of the Divine Will and the descent of the Divine energy and the ascent of the human aspiration are mutually complementary.

Sadhak/s or Saadhak/s Aspirant/s.

Sadhana Practice.

Sadhus Wandering monks.

Sahasrara The spiritual centre at the crown of the head, 1000 petalled lotus.

Samadhi The body, mind and intellect as one, concentrating on one point, completely united, ego eliminated, merging with your own soul.

Samsara Continuous flow or wheel of the cycle of birth, life, death, rebirth or reincarnation.

Samskara/s Inherent impressions or basic traits, impressions from the past lives.

Sannyas Renunciation.

Sannyasi/s Renunciate/s.

Sat-Chit-Ananda Eternal Bliss State.

Satsang Spiritual gathering or get together.

Sattva Existing in subtle state or pure consciousness.

Sattvic Pure, the who predominantly expresses Sattva guna.

Sathya Sai Baba Parthi Sai Baba.

Seva Selfless service without any expectation or recognition in return.

Shaivic Expressing the nature of Shiva. Shiva has two natures; Kshiprakopy and kshipraprasadi meaning instant anger and instant blessings respectively.

Shakti Power. A vital force. The great feminine energy, sacred force or empowerment, is the primordial cosmic energy and represents the dynamic forces that are thought to move through the entire universe in Hinduism. Shakti is the concept, or personification, of divine feminine creative power, sometimes referred to as "The Great Divine Mother' in Hinduism. On the earthly plane, Shakti most actively manifests through female embodiment and fertility, though it is also present in males in its potential, unmanifest form.

Shaktipat Conferring of spiritual "energy" upon one person by another. It can be transmitted with a sacred word or mantra, or by a look, thought or touch—the last usually to the ajna chakra or third eye of the recipient. It is considered an act of Grace (*anugraha*) on the part of the guru or the divine. Absolute faith opens the receiver during Shaktipat. It shifts consciousness of the receiver.

Shankaracharya *see* Adi Shankaracharya.

Shanti Peace.

Shirdi Sai Baba/Sai Baba A great Sadguru who is respected and worshipped by all religions. Incarnation of Dattatreya and part of Navanath tradition. He is also considered as an incarnation of Lord Shiva.

Shiva *see* Lord Shiva.

Siddha/s In Sanskrit means "one who is accomplished". Siddhas are great saints who constantly defy the gross element and possess great supernatural powers such as ashtha siddhis or nava siddhis.

Siddhis Spiritual powers.

Sita The seeker, the Shakti element. Wife of Rama (*see*).

Surya Namaskar Sun salutation.

Sushumna/Sushumna naadi The central canal in the subtle body.

Sutratma "Thread-self," the abiding self or soul which survives death, the spiritual essence (*atman*), stream of self-consciousness, individuality, or thread of radiance upon which the personalities of its various incarnations are strung.

Swami A saint. Usually proffered as an expression of reverence towards a saint.

Swami Ram Tirth A great Indian saint.

Swami Sivananda A great Indian saint.

Swamiji In Indian language respect is addressed with suffix 'ji'.

Tamas Traits based on Inertia.

Tamasic vasanas Vasanas (*see*) full of tamas (*see*).

Tantra Principle or system or doctrine. Also applies to any of the scriptures (*called* "*Tantras*") commonly identified with the worship of Shakti (*see*). Tantra deals primarily with spiritual practices and ritual. forms of worship, which aim at liberation from ignorance and rebirth, the universe being regarded as the divine play of Shakti and Shiva (*see*).

Tantric ritual Rituals pertaining to tantra (*see*).

Tapas Austerity.

Tapovan A place for doing penance.

Tattva *here* Principle.

Tejus Halo.

Turiya state 4th state or state of perpetual awareness. The four states of existence are wakefulness, deep sleep, dream state and Turiya.

Upanishad Ultimate knowledge codified by great Masters; sitting at Gurus feet.

Uttaraayan A period of six months when the Sun's direction is towards North (*from June to December*).

Vaishya One of the four *varnas* (social order) of Hinduism. According to Vedic tradition, this order primarily comprises merchants, cattle-herders and artisans.

Vasanas Natural traits of the character. Natural inclinations, inherent traits, basic inherent desire, inherent traits with emotions attached, inherent traits and terrestrial bindings.

Vasishta cave It is near Rishikesh, in Gullar, Himalayas where the many great yogis from sage Vasishta onwards did penance for thousand years.

Vayu Air

Ved Vyas Ansha of Lord Vishnu and author of Epic Mahabharata and a great sage.

Vedanta Thesis work of great saints towards path of enlightenment. It also means beyond the Vedas or beyond the state of doing.

Vedas Codified structure of rituals handed over time to tradition. A large body of texts originating in ancient India. Composed in Vedic Sanskrit, the texts constitute the oldest layer of Sanskrit literature and the oldest scriptures of Hinduism.

Vedic times Since the ancient times of vedas (*see*).

Vishnu Mahavishnu, The 'Maintainer or 'Preserver' from among the Trimurti, the Hindu Trinity of the primary aspects of the divine.

Vishwamitra One of the most venerated rishis or sages of ancient times in India.

Vivek Wisdom.

Vivekananda Same as Swami Vivekananda, an Indian Sadguru (*see sadguru*) *who* was the foremost disciple of Rama Krishna Paramahamsa (*see*).

Yaga, Yagnya or Yajna Ancient Vedic ritual of sacrifice.

Yama *here* God of death who is also a Guru (knower of secrets).

Yogi A practitioner of yoga.